KETO DIET BOOK
FOR BEGINNERS
2022

....

"All-in-One", Keto Diet Cookbook with the Complete Guide
to understand Ketogenic Lifestyle
with Quick and Healthy....

450
EFFORTLESS
RECIPES

MURIEL DAVIES

CONTENTS

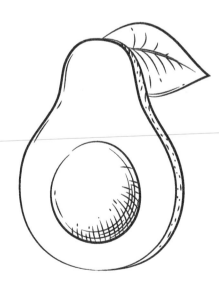

Introduction

Welcome to the Club!

You have chosen to get fit and embark on a healthy lifestyle, so many could be the reasons, and whatever yours is, congratulations! You are making the right choice.

I know something about it. I spent 20 years of my life overweight, all aggravated after giving birth to my son Manuel. I never gave importance to food and how it made my life heavy and slow. I went through periods of depression and loneliness without going out anymore.
Like everyone else, I tried the band-aid solutions, never focusing on long-term goals. All I wanted was to lose weight quickly without effort, and nothing worked. Then I got interested in the Ketogenic Diet, but in the beginning, this also did not give me satisfactory results. I found out the reason later. **Confusion.**

I was looking for information from everywhere, so I was mixing everything up and wasting time. My motivation dropped, and I lost focus. The biggest mistake is not having the direction, the One Thing. But then everything changed. The strength came from my son's sweet face, the desire to stay close to him as long as possible with power and energy. I didn't want to be heavy anymore and be out of breath when I went shopping. I had said enough is enough.

That's why I created this manual to be easy to get started and never fail again to achieve your goals. To do this, I realized that there was a need to create a resource where people could find **everything they needed: instructions, tips, meal plans, and recipes,** without doing unnecessary and stressful research.

The recipes in this book are designed to defeat carbohydrate cravings. After years of eating full of carbs switching to Keto will not be easy the craving for carbs will be normal. But in this book, you'll find simple, tasty recipes that have been tested over the years and shared with thousands of people.

The Ketogenic Diet will improve your lifestyle. It has helped me lose weight, but the benefits are many.

Over the years, I've become fascinated and talked to people who have used the Ketogenic Diet recommended by their nutritionist for anxiety and depression problems, restore brain function for people who have Alzheimer's and Dementia, fix Diabetes, and lower cholesterol to treat chronic inflammation.

Many are the benefits.

Whatever your reason, starting a Keto lifestyle is the right choice, and this manual is your starting point.

CHAPTER 1

What is Keto Diet?

As you'd probably already know, the ketogenic diet is a low-carb diet where you eliminate or minimise carbohydrate consumption. Proteins and fats replace the extra carbs while cutting back on pastries and sugar.

How Does It Work?

When you consume less than 50 grams of carbs per day, your body starts to run out of blood sugar (which is used as fuel to provide your body quick energy). Once there are no sugar reserves left, your body will start to utilise fat and protein for energy. This entire process is known as ketosis, and this is precisely what helps you lose weight.

Compared to other diets, keto has a better chance of helping you lose weight more quickly. The diet is trendy as you're not encouraged to starve yourself. It would help if you worked towards a more high-fat and protein diet, which isn't as difficult as counting calories.

Is Keto Going all right for People With Diabetes?

Now you're probably wondering, what do I do if I have diabetes? For starters, visit your physician. Talking to your physician is essential regardless of what kind of diet you choose. However, note that keto diets generally work well to improve insulin sensitivity.

For better results, seek a doctor's help if you have diabetes. Keto diets can drastically impact your body and overall lifestyle; hence, it's always better to seek professional guidance.

Macronutrients and Keto

Macronutrients

The food you consume provides nutrition to the body. Various types of nutrients are present in the food. They are broadly classified into macronutrients and micronutrients. Macronutrients are those nutrients required in significant quantities in the food to provide the necessary energy and raw material to build different body parts. These are:

· Carbohydrates
· Proteins
· Fats

Carbohydrates

Carbohydrates are essential energy sources for the body. In a Keto diet plan, you have to cut on your carbs to eliminate this energy source and compel your body to spend the already present food stores in your body. These food stores are as current as fat in your body. Once your body turns to these fat deposits in the body for energy, you start to lose weight. Carbohydrates should not constitute more than 5–10% of your daily caloric intake.

Carbohydrates are present in a variety of foods. You should make sure that the small quota of carbohydrates you can consume comes from healthy carbohydrate sources like low-carb vegetables and fruits, e.g., broccoli, lemon, and tomatoes.

Proteins

Proteins are essential because they provide subunits, which are building blocks of the body. They produce various hormones, muscles, enzymes, and other working machinery of the body. They provide energy to the body as well. No more than 20–25% of your daily caloric intake should come from proteins. As a rule of thumb, a healthy person should consume about 0.5–0.7 grams of proteins per pound of total body weight.

Many people make a mistake in a keto diet consuming much more protein than they should. This not only puts additional strain on their kidneys but is also very unhealthy for the digestive system.

Eat a good variety of proteins from various sources like tofu, fish, chicken, and other white meat sources, including seeds, nuts, eggs, and dairy (though you shouldn't fill your diet with cheese). Red meat like beef can be enjoyed less frequently. We also suggest you avoid processed meats, which are typically laden with artificial preservatives. Processed meat refers to meat that's modified through a series of processes, which might include salting, smoking, canning, and, most importantly, treated with preservatives. Such variants typically include sausages, jerky, and salami. As these meats are not even considered healthy for normal diets, we suggest limiting your portions to only once or twice a week.

Fats

In keto, fats serve as the mainstay of your diet. It seems counterintuitive to consume what you want to eliminate from your body, but that is exactly how this strategy works.

But before you go about loading your body with all types of fats, keep the following things in your mind:

1. You have to cut on carbs before this high-fat diet can be of any benefit to the body.
2. Fats should take up about 70–75% of your daily caloric intake.
3. Fats are of various types, and you have to be aware of the kind of fats you should consume.

Dietary fats can be divided into two kinds: healthy and harmful. Unsaturated fats belong to the more beneficial group, whereas saturated and trans-unsaturated fats belong to the unhealthier category. Aside from their health effects, these fats essentially differ in chemical structure and bonding.

Saturated Fats

A diet high in saturated fat has an increased chance of reducing the risks of heart diseases. Saturated fats drive up cholesterol levels and contain harmful LDL cholesterol that can clog arteries anywhere in the body, especially the heart, and increase the risk of cardiovascular diseases. These fats are mainly of animal origin (except fish, which includes a small part). They are also present in plant-based foods, such as coconut oil. However, coconut oil contains medium-chain fatty acids and saturated fats different from animal origin and is considered a healthy food.

Saturated fats are primarily contained in:

· Whole milk dairy products, including milk and cheese
· butter
· Skin-on chicken
· Red meat such as pork, lamb, and beef

While there's no doubt that these foods are keto-friendly, they should not be consumed in large quantities, regardless of what diet you follow. It's also worth noting that some saturated fats are rated better in the health department than others. For instance, milk is healthier than consuming red meat. We suggest limiting butter and pork derived from animal fat as they tend to be unhealthy.

Unsaturated Fats

These 'good fats' contain healthy cholesterol. Unsaturated fats can most commonly be found in nuts, veggies, and fish. These fats keep your heart healthy and are a good substitution for saturated fats.

Unsaturated fats can be divided into:

Trans Fats: Trans fats, or trans-fatty acids, are a particular form of unsaturated fat. These unhealthy fats are manufactured through a partial hydrogenation food process. Moreover, some studies differentiate the health risks of those obtained industrially or transformed by cooking from those naturally present in food (for example, vaccenic acid); the latter would be harmless or even beneficial to health.

The industrial foods that contain these hydrogenated fats are mainly: fried foods (especially French fries), margarine, microwave popcorn, brioche, sweet snacks, and pretzels.

While these foods may taste good, they're an unhealthy kind of fat and should be avoided.

Trans fats are known to increase unhealthy cholesterol levels in the blood, thus increasing the risks of cardiovascular disease. The WHO (World Health Organization) aims to global eliminate industrially-produced trans fats from food supplies by 2023.

Calculating Your Daily Caloric Intake

Many people think that calculating your calories while on a keto diet is not very important, but watching how many calories you consume a day is always good. It would help if you calculated how many calories you get to consume every day by the idea of how much weight you want to lose.

If your body needs 2,000 calories a day, but you consume only 1,400, your body is in a caloric deficit, so it will have to tap into its fat reserves, resulting in a loss of weight. Various calculators available online can calculate your daily caloric intake, taking into account your objectives, age, height, activity level, and other factors.

If you want to lose weight, you need to subtract around 600 calories from your daily caloric needs. So less than 1,000–1,200 calories if you are a woman and less than 1,400–1,600 calories if you are a man.

Having a Meal Plan

When you have a complete meal plan laid out in front of you, you are better positioned to have an idea of what your diet will look like in the days to come. If you have to spontaneously decide what you will prepare to eat every time you are in the kitchen, your chances of getting off the rails become pretty high.

You can start by first calculating how many calories you will consume a day.

The next step would be to decide which macro-nutrients will have to be incorporated and what proportion your body will reach that goal. Remember that the rule of thumb is 75, 20, and 5: for fats, proteins, and carbs, respectively.

CHAPTER 2

The Science Behind the Keto Diet

To bring the body into a Ketogenic condition, you need to follow a high-fat diet and small carbohydrates without grains. The composition will be roughly 80% fat and 20% protein. That will be the rule for the very first two days.

Common sense assures us that if we eliminate carbs, the insulin does not hold excess calories as the perfect fat. When the body absorbs carbs, it induces an insulin surge with the insulin emitted by the pancreas. Now your body has no carbs as an energy source, so your body should look for a new source.

If you decide to remove extra weight, this works well. The body must break down the extra fat and function with it, rather than carbs, as energy.

That particular condition is known as 'Ketosis.' This state, in which you want the body to be, can make great sense if you're going to lose excess fat while keeping muscle.

Let's move on now to the portion of the diet and how to prepare it. With every pound of lean mass, you would need to ingest no less than one gram of protein. That means 65% protein and 30% fat. It will aid with strengthening and restoring muscle tissue during exercises.

Effectively, if you weigh 150 pounds, that means 150 g of protein a day. If you multiply it four times (number of calories equivalent to 600 calories in a gram of protein), any calories will come from fat. If the caloric maintenance is 3,000, you need to consume about 500, less that might imply that one day if you require 2,500 calories, about 1,900 calories should come from the fats!

To fuel the body, you have to consume fats, which will also burn up excess fat! That is the diet plan rule; you've got to consume fats! The downside of taking healthy fats and the keto diet is that you're not going to be thirsty. Fat food processing is slow, operating to the benefit and making you feel satisfied.

You're going to be working on Monday–Friday, and then on the other days, you're going to have a 'carb-up.' When this process begins when the last exercise is on Friday, post-training, you need to take a liquid carbohydrate with your whey shake. This will help produce an insulin surge, allowing us to provide the carbohydrates that the body urgently requires to restore muscle mass and for glycogen stores to expand and refill.

Consume whatever you like during this specific process (carb-up): pizzas, crisps, spaghetti, and ice cream. Somehow, this will be beneficial for you because it can refresh the body for the week ahead and provide your body's food.

Switch your focus to the no-carb and high-fat average protein diet program as Sunday starts. Holding the body in Ketosis and losing fat is the optimal remedy, for muscle.

An additional benefit of Ketosis is when you enter the ketosis state and burn the fat, the body will deplete carbohydrates. Packing up with carbs can make you appear as full as before (but with even less body fat!), perfect for holiday activities if you visit the seaside or parties!

Let us recap on the diet schedule now.

Get in a ketosis state by removing carbs and taking moderate/low protein and high fat.

Take some fibre to keep the pipes as clear as ever; you should realize what I mean.

If the ketosis protein consumption has been collected, the lean mass per pound will be no less than that of one gram of protein.

So it is! It does require determination not to eat carbs during the week because certain products contain carbs; however, note that you would be greatly rewarded for the devotion.

You must not live on end days in Ketosis condition because it is dangerous and will wind up with yourself turning to make use of protein as a source of food which is a no-no.

Ketogenic diet systems are structured primarily to trigger a ketosis condition within the body. If the volume of glucose in the body is low, the whole body turns to fat as a source of energy replacement.

The body has main sources of fuel, one of which is:

Glucose

Free fatty acids (FFA) and, to a lesser degree, ketones from FFA Fat by-products are kept in the triglyceride type. Typically, they are split into long-chain fatty acids and glycerol.

The removal of glycerol from the triglyceride molecule enables the three free fatty acid (FFA) molecules to be used as energy to introduce the bloodstream.

The glycerol molecule goes into the liver, where three molecules combine to create one molecule of sugar. Additionally, when the body consumes fat, it creates glucose as a by-product. Its glucose may be used to power different regions of the brain and body parts that can't operate on FFA molecules.

However, though glucose on its triglycerides will travel through the blood, cholesterol takes a carrier to go through the bloodstream. In a carrier known as LDL or low-density lipoprotein, cholesterol and triglycerides are packed. Thus, the larger the LDL particles, the greater the number of triglycerides it has.

The general process of energy-burning of fat deposits produces CO_2, oxygen, and ketone-known components. The liver produces ketones out of the free essential fatty acids. Right now, they consist of two classes of atoms joined by a purposeful carbonyl unit.

The body cannot store ketones, and therefore they should be used or excreted at times. The body often passes them as acetone through the breath and as acetoacetate through the urine.

The ketones may be used as a source of energy for body cells. The subconscious will use ketones to generate between 70- and 75 per cent of the energy requirement.

As for alcoholic drinks, ketones take priority over carbohydrates as food resources. That means that they should be consumed first when filled with the bloodstream before glucose can be used as a fuel.

CHAPTER 3

The Main Features of the Ketogenic Diet
Losing Weight

For most people, this is the foremost benefit of switching to keto! Their previous diet method may have stalled for them, or they noticed weight creeping back on. With keto, studies have shown that people have been able to follow this diet and relay fewer hunger pangs and suppressed appetite while losing weight at the same time! You minimise your carbohydrate intake, which means more occasional blood sugar spikes.

Studies show that low-carb diets effectively reduce visceral fat (the fat you commonly see around the abdomen increases as you become obese). Those fluctuations in blood sugar levels often make you feel more hungry and prone to snacking in between meals. Instead, by guiding the body towards ketosis, you eat a more fulfilling diet of fat and protein and harness energy from ketone molecules instead of glucose. This reduces your risk of obesity and improves your health in the long term.

Reduce the Risk of Type 2 Diabetes

The problem with carbohydrates is how unstable they make blood sugar levels. This can be very dangerous for people who have diabetes or are pre-diabetic because of unstable blood sugar levels or family history. Keto is a great option because of its minimal carbohydrate intake. Instead, you harness most of your calories from fat or protein, which will not cause blood sugar spikes and, ultimately, pressure the pancreas to secrete insulin. Many studies have found that diabetes patients who followed the keto diet lost more weight and eventually reduced their fasting glucose levels.

This is monumental news for patients who have unstable blood sugar levels or hope to avoid or reduce their diabetes medication intake.

Improve Cardiovascular Risk Symptoms to Overall Lower Your Chances of Having Heart Disease

Most people assume that following a keto diet that is so high in fat content has to increase your risk of coronary heart disease or heart attack, but the research proves otherwise! Research shows that switching to keto can lower your blood pressure, increase your HDL good cholesterol, and reduce your triglyceride fatty acid levels.

The fats you are consuming on keto are healthy and high-quality fats, so they reverse many unhealthy symptoms of heart disease. They boost your "good" HDL cholesterol levels and decrease your "bad" LDL cholesterol levels. It also reduces the level of triglyceride fatty acids in the bloodstream. A high level of these can lead to stroke, heart attack, or premature death. And what are the high levels of fatty acids linked to?

Low Consumption of Carbohydrates

You drastically cut your carbohydrate intake with the keto diet to improve fatty acid levels and other risk factors. A 2018 study on the keto diet found that it can improve 22 out of 26 risk factors for cardiovascular heart disease! These factors can be critical to some people, especially those who have a history of heart disease in their family.

Increases the Body's Energy Levels

Let's briefly compare the difference between the glucose molecules synthesised from a high carbohydrate intake versus ketones produced on the keto diet. The liver makes ketones and uses fat molecules you already stored. This makes them much more energy-rich and a lasting fuel source than glucose, a simple sugar molecule. These ketones can physically and mentally give you a burst of energy, allowing greater focus, clarity, and attention to detail.

Decreases Inflammation in the Body

Inflammation on its own is a natural response by the body's immune system, but when it becomes uncontrollable, it can lead to an array of health problems, some severe and some minor.

The health concerns include acne, autoimmune conditions, arthritis, psoriasis, irritable bowel syndrome, and even acne and eczema. Removing sugars and carbohydrates from your diet can often help patients of these diseases avoid flare-ups—and the delightful news is that keto does just that!

A 2008 research study found that keto decreased a blood marker linked to high inflammation in the body by nearly 40%. This is glorious news for people who may suffer from inflammatory disease and want to change their diet to see improvement.

Increases Your Mental Functioning Level

As we mentioned earlier, energy-rich ketones can boost the body's physical and mental alertness levels. Research has shown that keto is a much better energy source for the brain than simple sugar glucose molecules are. With nearly 75% of your diet coming from healthy fats, the brain's neural cells and mitochondria have a better energy source to function at the highest level.

Some studies have tested patients on the keto diet and found they had higher cognitive functioning, better memory recall, and less memory loss. The keto diet can even decrease the occurrence of migraines, which can be very detrimental to patients.

Heart Diseases

Keto diets help women over 50 to shed those extra pounds. Reducing any weight greatly reduces the chances of a heart attack or any other heart complications. Through the carefully selected diet routine, you are not only losing weight and enjoying delicious meals, but you are significantly boosting your heart's health and reviving yourself from the otherwise dull state that you may have been in before.

Diabetes Control

Needless to say, the careful selection of ingredients, when cooked together, provides rich nutrients, free from any processed or harmful contents such as sugar. Add to that the fact that keto automatically controls your insulin levels. The result is a glucose level that is always under control, and continued control would lead to a day where you will say goodbye to the medications you might be taking for diabetes.

CHAPTER 4

What to Eat and Avoid

I've had people complain about the difficulty of switching their grocery list to one that's Ketogenic-friendly. The fact is that food is expensive, and most of the food you have in your fridge is probably packed full of carbohydrates. It is why if you're committing to a Ketogenic Diet, you need to do a clean sweep. That's right, everything that's packed with carbohydrates should be identified and set aside to make sure that you are not overeating.

What to Eat on the Keto Diet
Fats and Oils

Because fats will be included in all your meals, we recommend choosing the highest quality ingredients you can afford. Some of your best choices for fat are:

- Ghee or Clarified butter
- Avocado
- Coconut Oil
- Red Palm Oil
- Butter
- Coconut Butter
- Fish rich in Omega-3 Fatty
  Acids like salmon, mackerel, trout, tuna, and shellfish
- Peanut Butter
- Chicken Fat
- Beef Tallow
- Non-hydrogenated Lard
- Macadamias and other nuts
- Egg Yolks

Protein

Those on a keto diet will generally keep fat intake high, carbohydrate intake low, and protein intake at a moderate level. Some on the keto diet for weight loss have better success with higher protein and lower fat intake.

· **Fresh meat:** beef, veal, lamb, chicken, duck, pheasant, pork, etc.
· **Deli meats:** bacon, sausage, ham (make sure to watch out for added sugar and other fillers)
· **Eggs:** preferably free-range or organic eggs
· **Fish:** wild-caught salmon, catfish, halibut, trout, tuna, etc.
· **Other seafood:** lobster, crab, oyster, clams, mussels, etc.
· **Peanut Butter:** this is an excellent source of protein, but make sure to choose a brand that contains no added sugar

Dairy

Compared to other weight-loss diets, the keto diet encourages you to choose dairy products that are total fat. Some of the best dairy products that you can choose are:

· **Hard and soft cheese:** cream cheese, mozzarella, cheddar, etc.
· Cottage cheese
· Heavy whipping cream
· Sour cream
· Full-fat yoghurt

Vegetables

Overall, vegetables are rich in vitamins and minerals that contribute to a healthy body. However, if you're aiming to avoid carbs, it's best that you limit starchy vegetables such as potatoes, yams, peas, corn, beans, and most legumes. Other vegetables high in carbohydrates, such as parsnips and squash, should also be limited. Instead, stick with green leafy vegetables and other low-carb veggies. Choose local or organic varieties if it fits with your budget.

· Spinach
· Lettuce
· Collard greens
· Mustard greens
· Bok choy
· Kale
· Alfalfa sprouts
· Celery
· Tomato
· Broccoli
· Cauliflower

Fruits

Your choice of fruit on the keto diet is typically restricted to avocado and berries because fruits are high in carbohydrates and sugar.

Drinks

· Water
· Black coffee
· Herbal tea
· **Wine: White and dry red wines** are OK if only consumed occasionally.

Others

· **Homemade mayo:** if you want to buy mayo from the store, make sure that you watch out for added sugar
· Homemade mustard
· Any spices or herbs
· Stevia and other non-nutritive sweeteners such as Swerve
· Ketchup (Sugar-free)
· Dark chocolate/cocoa

Foods to Avoid

1. Bread and Grains

Bread is a staple food in many countries. You have loaves, bagels, tortillas, and the list goes on. However, no matter what form bread takes, they still contain many carbs. The same applies to whole-grain because they are made from refined flour. Eating a sandwich or bagel can put your way over your daily limit depending on your daily carb limit. So if you want to eat bread, it is best to make keto variants at home instead. Grains such as rice, wheat, and oats contain a lot of carbs too. So limit or avoid that as well.

2. Fruits

Fruits are healthy for you. They are found to make you have a lower risk of heart disease and cancer. However, there are a few that you need to avoid in your keto diet. The problem is that some of those foods contain quite a lot of carbs, such as bananas, raisins, dates, mango, and pear. As a general rule, avoid sweet and dried fruits. Berries are an exception because they do not contain as much sugar and are rich in fibre. So you can still eat some of them, around 50 grams. Moderation is key.

3. Vegetables

Vegetables are healthy for your body. Most keto diet does not care how many vegetables you eat so long as they are low in starch.

Vegetables that are high in fibre can aid with weight loss. On the one hand, they make you feel full for longer, so they help suppress your appetite. Another benefit is that your body would burn more calories to break and digest them.

Moreover, they help control blood sugar levels and aid your bowel movements. But that also means you need to avoid or limit vegetables high in starch because they have more carbs than fibre. That includes corn, potato, sweet potato, and beets.

4. Pasta

Pasta is also a staple food in many countries. It is versatile and convenient. As with any other suitable food, pasta is rich in carbs. So when you are on your keto diet, spaghetti or many different types of pasta are not recommended.

You can probably eat a small portion, but that is not suggested. Thankfully, that does not mean you need to give up on it. If you are craving pasta, you can try some other alternatives that are low in carbs, such as spiralised veggies or shirataki noodles.

5. Cereal

Cereal is also a massive offender because sugary breakfast cereals contain many carbs. That also applies to "healthy cereals." Just because they use other words to describe their product does not mean you should believe them.

That also applies to oatmeal, whole-grain cereals, etc. So if you get your cereal when you are doing keto, you are already way over your carb limit, and we haven't even added milk! Therefore, avoid whole-grain cereal or cereals that we mention here altogether.

CHAPTER 5

Tips for Who Want to Start

Learn How to Count Your Macros

This is especially important at the beginning of your journey. As time goes on, you will learn how to estimate your meals without using a food scale.

Prepare Your Kitchen for Your Keto-friendly Foods

Once you've chosen, it's time to eliminate all the foods in your kitchen that aren't allowed in the keto diet. To do this, check the nutritional labels of all the food items. Of course, there's no need to throw everything away. You can donate foods you don't need to food kitchens and other institutions that give food to the needy.

Purchase Some Keto Strips for Yourself

These are important to check your ketone levels and track your progress. You can purchase keto strips in pharmacies and online. For instance, some of the best keto strips available on Amazon are Perfect Keto Ketone Test Strips, Smackfat Ketone Strips, and One Earth Ketone Strips.

Find an Activity You Enjoy

When you have done enough exercise, you will know what activities you like. One way to encourage yourself to exercise more regularly is by making it entertaining than a chore. If possible, stick to your favourite activities, and you can get the most out of your exercises. Keep in mind that the activities you enjoy may not be practical or needed, so you need to find other exercises to compensate for what you may not enjoy. For instance, if you like jogging, you can work your leg muscles, but your arms are not involved. So, you need to do pushups or other strength training exercises.

Check with a Healthcare Provider

Your dietitian can tell you whether a keto diet would work. Still, it helps to check in with your healthcare provider to ensure that you do not have any medical condition that prevents you from losing weight, such as hypothyroidism and polycystic ovarian syndrome. It helps to know well in advance whether your body is even capable of losing fat in the first place before you commit and see no result.

Hydrate Properly

Making the transition will be difficult for the first few weeks, but your body will thank you. That means drinking enough water or herbal tea and ditching sweetened beverages or other drinks that contain sugar altogether. There is nothing healthier than good old plain water, and the recommended amount is 2 gallons a day.

Have the Right Mindset

Your mindset is one of the most important things you need to change when you've decided to follow the keto lifestyle. Without the right attitude, you might not stick with the diet long enough to enjoy all its benefits. Also, the proper mindset will keep you motivated to keep going no matter what challenges come your way.

Get Enough Sleep

Getting enough sleep helps your body regulate its hormones, so try to aim for 7 to 9 hours of sleep a day. You can get more restful sleep by creating a nighttime routine that involves not looking at a computer, phone, or TV screen for at least 1 hour before bed. You can drink warm milk or water to help your body relax or even do 10 to 20 minutes of stretching to get a restful sleep.

Keep a Food Log

Add the calories and divide them into three to get an average. Now that you know how many takes, you can figure out how much you need to pay on average per day to reach your goals.

CHAPTER 6

7-Days Plan Detox for Weight Loss

DAY 1
Breakfast: Chorizo Breakfast Bake
Lunch: Sesame Pork Lettuce Wraps
Supper: Avocado Lime Salmon
All out macros: Calories: 1,520 **Protein:** 110g **Fat:** 109g
Net Carbs: 16g

DAY 2
Breakfast: Leftover Chorizo Breakfast Bake with 3 Slices Thick-Cut Bacon
Lunch: Spiced Pumpkin Soup
Supper: Leftover Avocado Lime Salmon
All out macros: Calories: 1,570 **Fat:** 124g **Protein:** 92g
Net Carbs: 16g

DAY 3
Breakfast: Baked Eggs in Avocado
Lunch: Easy Beef Curry
Supper: Veggies and Rosemary Roasted Chicken
All out macros: Calories: 1,700 **Fat:** 128.5g **Protein:** 103g
Net Carbs: 22g

DAY 4
Breakfast: Lemon Poppy Ricotta Pancakes with 3 Slices Thick-Cut Bacon
Lunch: Leftover Spiced Pumpkin Soup with ½ Medium Avocado
Supper: Leftover Rosemary Roasted Chicken and Veggies
All out macros: Calories: 1,665 **Fat:** 130g **Protein:** 95.5g
Net Carbs: 23.5g

DAY 5
Breakfast: Leftover Lemon Poppy Ricotta Pancakes with 3 Slices Thick-Cut Bacon
Lunch: Leftover Spiced Pumpkin Soup
Supper: Cheesy Sausage Mushroom Skillet with 1 Slice Thick-Cut Bacon
All out macros: Calories: 1,650 **Fat:** 126g **Protein:** 100.5g
Net Carbs: 22.5g

DAY 6
Breakfast: Sweet Blueberry Coconut Porridge with 1 Slice Thick-Cut Bacon
Lunch: Leftover Easy Beef Curry
Supper: Leftover Cheesy Sausage Mushroom Skillet
All out macros: Calories: 1,670 **Protein:** 100g **Fat:** 112g
Net Carbs: 33.5g

DAY 7
Breakfast: Leftover Sweet Blueberry Coconut Porridge
Lunch: Leftover Easy Beef Curry
Supper: Rosemary and Garlic with Lamb Chops
All out macros:Calories: 1,625 **Protein:** 110.5g **Fat:** 108g
Net Carbs: 27g

CHAPTER 7

Improve Your Ketogenic Diet With Fitness

Can you remember when the last time you squatted was? During physical education at school? Or maybe you tried to do a workout a few months ago, but then you lost your motivation?

Every diet you respect must be associated with an adequate training regimen; they are two sides of the same coin, both important and necessary sacrifices and motivations.

It only takes a second to decide that it's worth it, 10 minutes for your first workout, and two weeks to feel the difference.

Everyone knows that doing physical activity improves well-being, but many are not familiar with all the benefits.

Here are the main benefits you can get when you start exercising:

· Lower risk of chronic diseases
· Mood and mental health improve
· Balanced energy levels during the day and better sleep quality
· Slowing down of ageing processes
· Better brain health
· Positive effects on the microbiome
· Guaranteed sex life

My general advice is:

· **Cardio** (minimum amount of activity): at least 150 minutes of moderate activity during the week. You can replace them with 75 minutes of intense activity or a combination of both.
· **Train your strength** (highly recommended): exercises involving the main muscle groups two or more days a week.
· **For extra benefits:** all minimal cardio activity can add 300 minutes (moderate level) or 150 minutes (intense level) per week (or a combination of both).

Tips for Who Want to Start Fitness

It may sound challenging, but the good thing is that you can adapt these tips to your schedule. As long as cardio activities are performed for at least 10 minutes, you can divide your active minutes into how many training sessions. Depending on your personal goal, you can choose to start with cardio or strength training.

Types of Physical Activities

What are the most common types of physical activity?

Cardio: any activity that increases your heart rate and makes you breathe faster is considered cardio. Usually refers to activities aimed at improving endurance, such as:

· **Moderate level:** brisk walking, dancing, jumping, jogging, cycling, swimming, push-ups, etc.
· **Intense level:** running, fast cycling, fast walking uphill, fast swimming.

Strength training: any activity that uses endurance to increase muscle strength. Using your body weight as resistance has many benefits!

Flexibility and mobility training: exercises to maintain and improve passive (flexibility) and active (mobility) movement.

What Type of Physical Activity is Best for Losing Weight?

Any exercise that requires high effort (for you) will have similar effects, especially for beginners. So the truth is that... it doesn't matter! Choose activities that you enjoy and that you can imagine continuing to do for more than a month or two. After all, losing weight depends on the calorie deficit. So be sure to adjust your diet to get the results you want.

Tips to Start Working Out

The first step is to reach a level of fitness where you no longer feel you "hate sport." Here's how to do it:

Find the Inspiration and Set a Goal

How many times have you forced yourself to start a training plan to lose 5 kg, and you have not succeeded? Try a different approach and first decide what you want to improve. Think about what you would like to do—whether it's exercising for 30 minutes without stopping or participating in the next marathon, improving your fitness for more energy and being more productive at work, and being able to keep up with your children.

CHAPTER 8

Health Tips

Nobody told you that life was going to be this way! But don't worry. There's still plenty of time to make amendments and take care of your health. Here are a couple of tips that will allow you to lead a healthier life in your fifties:

Start Building on Immunity

Every day, our body is exposed to free radicals and toxins from the environment. The added stress of work and family problems doesn't make it easier. To combat this, you must start consuming healthy veggies that contain plenty of antioxidants and build a more beneficial immune system.

This helps ward off unwanted illnesses and diseases, allowing you to maintain good health.

Adding more healthy veggies to your keto diet will help you obtain various minerals, vitamins, and antioxidants.

Consider Quitting Smoking

It's never too late to quit smoking, even if you are in your fifties. Once a smoker begins to quit, the body quickly starts to heal the previous damages caused by smoking.

Once you start quitting, you'll notice how you'll be able to breathe easier while acquiring a better sense of smell and taste.

Over a period of time, eliminating the habit of smoking can greatly reduce the risks of high blood pressure, strokes, and heart attack. Please note how these diseases are much more common among people in the fifties and above than in younger people.

Not to mention, quitting smoking will help you stay more active and enjoy better health with your friends and family.

Stay Social

We recommend you stay in touch with friends and family or become a part of a local community club or network. Some people find it comforting to get an emotional support animal.

Being surrounded by people you love will give you a sense of belonging and will improve your mood. It'll also keep your mind and memory sharp as you engage in different conversations.

Intermittent Fasting and Keto Diet

What Is Intermittent Fasting?

Intermittent fasting is when you keep away any foodstuff involving calories among ordinary nutritious ingredients. It is not starvation or a way for you to eat junk food with no consequences.

There are various methods used to practice IF; they divide time into hours or divide time into days. Since the regiment's response varies from person to person, no process can be called the best.

Knowing that intermittent fasting cannot make you lose the additional pounds you may have instantaneously is essential, but it can prevent unhealthy addictions to meals. It's a nutritional practice that requires you to be determined to follow to get the maximum gain.

If you already have a minimum duration to eat due to your schedule, this regiment will suit you like a duck to water, but you will always need to be conscious of what you are eating if you are a foodie.

Choose the appropriate regiment after expert guidance. You should see it as a segment of your schedule to get healthy, but not the only component.

Intermittent fasting is for those who want to regulate their hormones and burn surplus body fat.

This diet allows for healthier whole foods and an all-round diet, which is better than living off processed foods and sugars, which are unhealthy.

It can also benefit individuals who are sugar-addicted or those who ate empty calories.

Drinks and sodas with very few nutrients, but full of calories, are included in these products.

Finally, people generally want to do better in life and enjoy a food plan that doesn't require too much planning or maintenance.

Even if intermittent fasting may not be for you reading this book will equip you with the necessary information required to help another person or to use it eventually in life.

Different Methods

IF regiments are numerous to the point that you can choose from any, you like. Always make sure to select a regimen that will fit in your schedule so that it is possible to maintain it.

There are several short methods for fasting, including:

The 12-Hour Fast

The regular living routine is called as you eat three meals a day and fast at night as you sleep. The generally small breakfast would break the fast. It is called the traditional method. Any regiment can help you lose weight only if you follow it correctly.

The higher the insulin levels are as a result of more people adding regular eating and snacking. It can cause resistance to insulin and, ultimately, obesity. This fasting technique sets aside twelve hours in which the body has low insulin levels, reducing the likelihood of insulin resistance. It can't help you lose excess fat, but it can help prevent obesity.

The 16-Hour Fast

This fasting for 16 hours is followed by an 8-hour window where you can eat what you like. Because it requires only small changes like just skipping your lunch, it has an enormous advantage over others, such as the 12 hours fast. Luckily you can sleep through most of it, so it's not difficult to keep doing it.

The 20-Hour Fast

It's called the "warrior diet." It includes fasting all day long and eating a lot of calories at night. It's meant to keep you from having breakfast, lunch, and other meals for most of the day, so you're getting all your nutrients from dinner. It is a division scheme of 20:4 with four hours of food followed by twenty hours of fasting. It's one of the easiest to do as you're allowed to eat a huge meal of calorific value, so you're going to feel fuller for longer. Start your daytime calories and have a big evening dinner to relax on this diet. You will gradually reduce what you're eating during the day and eventually leave dinner as your only meal.

The longer you do these fasting regiments, the more you will be able to maintain a fast. You will come to find out that you will not always feel hungry. The excitement of benefits will make you increase your fasting period by a couple of hours. Unknowingly, therefore, you are plunging into longer stages of fasting. You can adhere to your regiment religiously, but eating an extra hour will not ruin your fasting or fat burning.

The easiest way to track your feeding is to do it once a day is because it doesn't require much thought. It's just eating at that moment every day for one dinner so that you can use your mental energy on the more important stuff. Unfortunately, it can cause a plateau of weight loss, where you are not losing or gaining weight. That's because you're going to consume the same number of calories every day and significantly less on a typical working day than you would eat. That's the best way to maintain your weight. You will have to change your fasting regimen to lose fat. Timing your meals and fasting windows will lead to optimal loss of fat instead of random fasting. Choose one that can be maintained and modified if necessary.

There are longer fasting regiments. These include:

The 24-Hour Fast

It's a scheme of eating breakfast, lunch, or dinner in a day and then eating the following day at the same time. If you decide to eat lunch, then it only involves skipping breakfast and dinner, so nothing is disrupted in your life. It saves time and money because you're not going to eat as much, and piling up dishes will not be a worry of yours. Knowing that you are fasting will be a task for people unless they are very interested in eating methods. Eating unprocessed natural foods should have enough vitamins, minerals, and oxygen to avoid nutrient deficiencies. You can do this weekly, but twice or three times a week, it is suggested.

During such long fasts, you should not knowingly avoid eating calories. What you are taking should be high in fat, low in carbohydrates, and unprocessed; there's nothing you shouldn't eat. It would be best to consume until you are adequately fed as the duration of fasting lets you burn a bunch of fat, and it will be difficult overtime to cut more purposefully.

The 36-Hour Fast

You retain in this fast for one and a half days without eating. For instance, if you eat lunch today, you consume no meal until the day's breakfast after the following day. This fast should be done about three times a week for people with type 2 diabetes. After the person reaches the desired weight and all diabetes medications are successfully removed, they can reduce the number of days of fasting to a level that will make it easier for them to do while maintaining their gains. Blood sugar should usually be checked as small or high.

The 42-Hour Fast

It adds six hours to the 36 hours fast, resulting in a fast of forty-two hours carried out about two times a week.

The 5:2 Fast

This technique is conducted to prevent you from totally abstaining from meals and having cycles of calorie consumption. These calories are reduced to a rate that leads to many hormonal advantages of fasting. It consists of five days of regular feeding with two days of fasting. With some protein and oil-based sauce or green vegetables and half an avocado, you can eat some vegetable salad during these fasting days; do not eat any dinner. These days of fasting can be placed randomly or following each other in a week at specific times. This method is designed to create faster for more people, as many find it challenging to avoid eating altogether. There's no exact time to follow; as soon as you want, you can follow it.

The Alternate-Day Fast

It may seem similar to the 5:2 fasting regimen, but it is not. It's fasting every day. This technique can be followed until you lose as much weight as you want, and then you can reduce days of fasting. It allows weight loss to be maintained.

Moving to different fasting regimens is possible as your schedule can change. Intermittent fasting is not about a time-limiting eating window; it is flexible, so you can move your eating and fasting time to suit you, but don't keep changing them all the time; this reduces the effect of fasting on your body. You can even combine some fasting regiments like the 5:2 technique and the 24-hour fasting by having lunch before your fasting day at a particular moment and adding only lunch at the fasting lunch and doing the same for the following fasting day. With this, for twenty-four hours, you could not eat any calories and set your days of fasting as in the 5:2 method of fasting. Choose the fasting day technique that works well with you and can synchronise with your life.

You can plan, but there's no problem if you can't. Even if you can't plan too fast, you should be open-minded to fasting to opportunities. You can fast every month or every year. A schedule allows you to create a routine after frequent fasting that makes it easier to integrate into your life. Frankly, you won't lose weight on losing annual fasts.

Intermittent and Keto Diet

You know all the different ways to fast, and you know what the ketogenic diet is. The primary purpose of intermittent fasting is to not eat as much during the day. Intermittent fasting can boost your fat burning. When your body is in a fasted state, your body will turn to your fat stores for energy when the body starts forming ketones to fuel you and your brain. Now, the ketogenic diet does the same thing without any fasting. However, many people don't feel as hungry when following a keto diet. It means that they start fasting simply because they don't feel like they need to eat.

You don't have to fast when on keto, and you don't have to follow keto when fasting. You can choose whichever method, but some people find fasting becomes easier on a ketogenic diet.

People who follow a ketogenic diet will have lower insulin levels and blood glucose levels. They have a reduced appetite because of the effects of the ketogenic diet. It means that they won't have any sugar crashes, and they won't feel as hungry.

If you maintain a regular diet high in carbs and fasting, you may experience an increase in hunger hormones, and your blood glucose may drop quickly. It doesn't always happen, however. It could end up causing you to feel irritable, shaky, and weak. It could mean that you feel hungry all of the time.

Using both the ketogenic diet and intermittent fasting for weight loss is a great idea, but remember, you can use them separately.

CHAPTER 9

How to Prepare Your Kitchen

Before I move on to the recipes, I want to list some of the most-used gadgets to cook keto-friendly meals. I'm not proposing that you have to have all of this in your Kitchen to follow the ketogenic diet successfully, so please don't go out and buy anything you won't use.

I'm not listing cutlery and crockery, and other items commonly found in a kitchen. In your 50 years on earth, you've spent enough time in a kitchen to know the basics required to cook food.

Kitchen Scales

Out of all the things on the list, this is one I would highly recommend buying. In the beginning, you won't be able to eyeball your macros as the more experienced keto dieters can. You will have to use a kitchen scale to weigh your food to know how much you are eating. You can then punch these numbers into a Carb and calorie tracker app, and it will let you know if you're on track.

Storage and Food Prep Containers

Essential for meal prepping and storing leftovers.

Slow Cooker

If you plan on prepping your meals in advance, I suggest investing in a slow cooker. Cook a large amount of food right away and then divide it into portions for the week. If meal prepping is not your thing, you can still use the slow cooker to prepare a keto-friendly meal in a fraction of the time.

Spiralizers

It is a nifty little gadget if you want to fool your eyes into thinking you're eating pasta. You can spiral different veggies into forms and sizes that resemble spaghetti, fettuccine, or other shapes.

Egg Cooker

Okay, you'll soon find that you'll be eating more eggs than usual. They're high in fat and protein and low in carbs, making eggs a great snack. Boil a few eggs, pop them in the fridge and enjoy when you're feeling a little hungry.

Immersion Blender

This is a baby food processor that you can hold in your hands to blitz up smoothies, make your Hollandaise sauce, ground nuts, or whip some cream to add to your coffee. Just make sure you buy one with multiple attachments.

Frying Pan/Skillet

You'll be eating many steaks, so why not get a frying pan or skillet to cook it in?

Roasting Pan

A whole chicken or beef roast surrounded by veggies, roasted in the oven, and then covered in a creamy cheese sauce. It doesn't sound like you're on a diet. A roasting pan is a perfect container to make delicious meals.

Safety First

As this guide ends and you get ready to try out some top keto recipes, just a reminder to put your safety first. You can get so carried away in what you're doing that to forget some standard safety rules. It is dangerous when working with open flames, boiling water, steam, and knives.

Many people don't know how to handle knives safely because they try to mimic the cutting techniques they see on TV. I once showed off my non-existent chopping skills and almost lost a finger.

So, allow me to talk about a quick crash course in knife safety:

· Always use a cutting board. Don't cut anything while holding it in your hand.

· Do not leave knives lying around in the sink. Clean them as soon as possible and put them away.

· Don't store knives loose in a drawer. You may be reaching for something else and then get a nasty surprise.

· Dull knives cause more injuries. Always use a sharp knife.

· On the hand holding the item that is being cut, curl your fingers under. If you keep them straight, they'll be in the way.

· Always point the knife away from you; blade facing down. Don't run or fool around with a knife in your hand.

· Keep your focus while you're chopping, dicing, or mincing.

· If you drop a knife, don't try to catch it. Please step back and let it fall.

Okay, for you to look through the recipes, find one you like, and head to the Kitchen! I hope you found the Keto knowledge in this guide helpful and feel that you now know enough to start the ketogenic diet confidently.

I promise you—that this diet will change your life for the better.

Muriel Davies

Blueberry Nutty Oatmeal

Preparation Time: 10 minutes **Cooking Time:** 6 to 8 hours **Servings:** 6

15 ml. of coconut oil (melted)
60 grams chopped pecans
60 grams sliced almonds
1 avocado, chopped
120 grams of coconut milk
120 grams coconut, shredded
250 grams water
56 grams of protein powder
30 grams granulated erythritol
5 ml. cinnamon, ground
1.25 ml. nutmeg, ground
60 grams blueberries

Melt the coconut oil and coat the inside of the slow cooker with it. Put all ingredients except for the blueberries in the slow cooker and stir until thoroughly mixed. Cook covered on low heat for about 6 to 8 hours. Divide the oatmeal among six serving bowls and garnish with the blueberries before serving.
TIP: To add more flavours to this oatmeal, serve topped with a spoonful of plain Greek yoghurt.

Nutrition: Calories: 372 **Fat:** 33.2g **Carbs:** 3.9g **Protein:** 14.3g

Keto Goat Cheese Salmon Fat Bombs

Preparation Time: 10 minutes **Cooking Time:** 0 minutes **Servings:** Makes 12 fat bombs

60 grams butter
60 grams of goat cheese
56 grams of smoked salmon
2 teaspoons lemon juice, squeezed
A pinch of pepper, ground

Line a baking sheet with parchment paper. Set aside. Make the fat bombs: Mix the butter, goat cheese, smoked salmon, pepper, and lemon juice in a bowl. Stir well to incorporate. Scoop mounds of the mixture onto the parchment-lined baking sheet. Transfer the fat bombs to the fridge for 2 to 3 hours until firm but not completely solid. Remove from the refrigerator and let chill at room temperature for 8 minutes before serving.
TIP: Store the fat bombs in a sealed, airtight container in the fridge for up to 1 week.

Nutrition: Calories: 196 **Fat:** 18.2g **Carbs:** 0g **Protein:** 8.1g

Salmon Cakes with Fried Pork Rind

Preparation Time: 10 minutes **Cooking Time:** 12 minutes **Servings:** 4

SALMON CAKES:
170 grams wild salmon, dried
1 egg, lightly beaten
2 tablespoons pork rinds (crushed)
3 tablespoons mayonnaise
Pink Himalayan Salt
Pepper

MAYO DIPPING SAUCE:
1 tablespoon ghee
½ tablespoon Dijon mustard

Mix the salmon, beaten egg, pork rinds, mayo, salt, and pepper in a large bowl until well combined. Make the salmon cakes: scoop out from the salmon mixture on a lightly floured surface and form a patty with your palm. Repeat with the remaining salmon mixture. Melt the ghee in a large skillet over medium-high heat. Fry the patties for about 6 minutes until golden brown on both sides, flipping once. Remove from the heat to a plate lined with paper towels. Set aside. Combine the remaining mayo and mustard in a small bowl. Stir well. Serve the salmon cakes with the mayo dipping sauce on the side.

TIP: If you don't have a large skillet that fits all the patties, you can cook them in batches.

Nutrition (per cake): Calories: 121 calories **Fat:** 6g
Carbohydrates: 0g **Protein:** 15g

Artichoke Caponata with Grilled Salmon Fillets

Preparation Time: 15 minutes **Cooking Time:** 20 minutes **Servings:** 4

CAPONATA:
½ **tablespoon olive oil**
2 **celery stalks (chopped)**
1 **tablespoon garlic**
1 **onion (chopped)**
60 **grams marinated artichoke hearts (chopped)**
2 **tomatoes (chopped)**
2 **tablespoons dry white wine**
30 **grams of apple cider vinegar**
2 **tablespoons chopped pecans**
30 **grams pitted green olives (chopped)**
120 **grams of salmon fillets**
Freshly ground black pepper (to taste)
2 **tablespoons chopped fresh basil (for garnish)**

Make the caponata: heat olive oil in a nonstick skillet over medium heat until shimmering. Add the celery, garlic, and onion to the skillet and sauté for 4 minutes or until the onion becomes translucent. Add the artichoke hearts, tomatoes, dry white wine, vinegar, pecans, and olives to the skillet. Sauté to mix well and bring to a boil. Turn down the heat to low and simmer for 6 minutes or until the liquid is reduced by one-third. Set the skillet aside—Preheat the grill to medium-high heat. Brush the salmon fillets with olive oil on a clean work surface, and sprinkle the salt and pepper over to the season. Arrange the salmon on the preheated grill grates and grill for 8 minutes or until cooked through. Flip the salmon halfway through. Transfer the salmon into four plates and pour the caponata over each.

TIP: To make it a complete meal, you can serve it with roasted green beans and spicy chicken stew.

Nutrition: Calories: 340.9 **Fat:** 25.3g **Carbohydrates:** 4.1g **Protein:** 24.2g

Avocados Stuffed with Crab Salad

Preparation Time: 20 minutes **Cooking Time:** 0 minutes **Servings:** 2

CRAB SALAD:
60 **grams cup of cream cheese**
130 **grams of Dungeness crab meat**
30 **grams chopped (peeled English cucumber)**
30 **grams chopped red bell pepper**
1 **teaspoon chopped cilantro**
60 **grams scallion (chopped)**
Pinch of sea salt and freshly ground black pepper

STUFFED AVOCADOS:
1 **avocado (peeled, halved lengthwise, and pitted)**
½ **teaspoon freshly squeezed lemon juice**

Make the crab salad: place the cream cheese, crab meat, cucumber, red pepper, cilantro, scallion, salt, and pepper in a medium bowl. Mix well until blended. Set aside. Rub the cut parts of the avocado with fresh lemon juice. Using a spoon, stuff each avocado halve with the crab salad. Serve immediately or cover it with plastic wrap and refrigerate until ready to serve.

TIP: The crab salad can be made ahead and refrigerated until you want to stuff the avocado halves.

Nutrition: Calories: 204 Fat: 19g Carbohydrates: 2g Protein: 6g

Bacon & Avocado Omelet

Preparation Time: 5 minutes **Cooking Time:** 5 minutes **Servings:** 1

1 **slice of crispy bacon**
2 **organic eggs**
25 **grams grated parmesan cheese**
30 **grams Ghee**
1 **Avocado**
50 **grams spinach**
100 **grams tomatoes**

Cook bacon in a nonstick pan until crisp, stirring regularly. Remove the grease from the skillet. Add the cherry tomatoes and the spinach. Cook until the spinach is wilted and the cherry tomatoes are soft, approximately 1 minute, over medium heat.

Take out and put aside. Wipe out the skillet. Whisk eggs with kosher salt and black pepper to taste. In a pan over medium-high heat, melt the butter—Cook for approximately 5 seconds after adding the eggs. Lift cooked egg around sides to enable the uncooked egg to flow below, about 2 minutes, until omelette is set, but the top is still wet. Arrange bacon, spinach, tomatoes, and avocado on one side of the omelette and fold over gently. Reduce the heat to low and simmer for another 1 to 2 minutes, or until the chicken is cooked. Serve the omelette immediately on a platter.

Nutrition: Calories: 516 Fat: 18g Carbohydrates: 2g Protein: 34g

Bacon & Cheese Frittata

Preparation Time: 5 minutes **Cooking Time:** 5 minutes **Servings:** 6:

120 grams Heavy cream
6 eggs
5 slices of bacon
2 green onions
115 grams of Cheddar cheese

Preheat oven to 175 degrees C. Lightly grease a 7x11-inch baking dish. Place bacon in a large skillet and cook over medium-high heat, turning occasionally until evenly browned, about 10 minutes. Drain bacon slices on paper towels and crumble.
Beat eggs, milk, butter, salt, and ground pepper in a bowl; pour into prepared baking dish. Sprinkle with onions, bacon, and Cheddar cheese. Bake in preheated oven until a knife inserted near the centre comes out clean, 25 to 30 minutes.

Nutrition: Calories: 249 Fat: 19g Carbohydrates: 3g Protein: 14g

Bacon & Egg Breakfast Muffins

Preparation Time: 15 minutes **Cooking Time:** 30 minutes
Servings: 12

5 large eggs
125 grams crisp-cooked bacon, crumbled
130 grams grated cheddar, or any cheese you like
Salt and fresh cracked pepper, to taste
1/2 teaspoon Italian seasoning and
1/2 teaspoon crushed chilli pepper flakes (optional)

Preheat your oven to 200°Celsius. Grease a 6-count muffin pan with oil or non-stick cooking spray. Set aside. In a large mixing bowl, crack in eggs and whisk together with salt and black pepper. Stir in cooked bacon, cheddar cheese, Italian seasoning, and red chilli pepper flakes (if using). Divide evenly into muffin cups filling each about 2/3 full. Top with more bacon and cheese if you like. Bake the egg muffins in preheated oven for 12-15 minutes, or until set.
Allow to cool a bit and serve your cheesy bacon egg muffins immediately, or enjoy cold, or at room temp.

Nutrition: Calories: 397 Fat: 21g Carbohydrates: 29g Protein: 22g

Bacon Hash

Preparation Time: 5 minutes **Cooking Time:** 10 minutes **Servings:** 2

700 grams potatoes
2 tablespoons olive oil
200 grams diced bacon
2 scallions
4 large eggs
90 grams shredded mozzarella
Pepper
Salt

Preheat oven to 200°Celsius. Arrange the potatoes in a single layer in a cast iron skillet or oven proof pan (or baking sheet). Spray with a light coating of cooking oil spray and bake for about 30 minutes, mixing them around halfway through cook time, until they are crisp and golden. Remove from oven, add the bacon, and place back into the oven for a further 10 minutes or until the bacon is crispy. Make four wells in the hash, crack an egg into each well and arrange the mozzarella around each egg. Place skillet (or pan) back into the oven until the whites are set and the eggs are cooked to your liking.
Serve immediately.

Nutrition: Calories: 230 Fat: 24 grams Carbohydrates: 9 grams Protein: 23 grams

Bagels with Cheese

Preparation Time: 10 minutes **Cooking Time:** 15 minutes **Servings:** 6

210 grams of mozzarella cheese
1 teaspoon baking powder
85 grams of Cream cheese
200 grams of Almond flour
2 eggs

Shred the mozzarella and combine with the flour, baking powder, and cream cheese—microwave for one minute. Mix well. Cool and put the eggs. Break into six parts and shape them into round bagels—Bake for 12 to 15 minutes. Serve.

Nutrition: Calories: 134g Fat: 11g Carbohydrates: 51g Protein: 13g

Baked Apples

Preparation Time: 10 minutes **Cooking Time:** 1 hour **Servings:** 4

4 teaspoons keto-friendly sweetener
1,75 teaspoon cinnamon
130 grams chopped pecans
4 apples

Set the oven temperature to 190° Celsius. Mix the sweetener, cinnamon, and pecans. Core the apple and put the stuffing. Add enough water into the baking dish apple. Bake for 45 minutes to 1 hour. Serve.

Nutrition: Calories: 147 Fat: 0g Carbohydrates: 36g Protein: 1g

Eggs with Leaks

Preparation Time: 10 minutes **Cooking Time:** 20 minutes **Servings:** 2

1½ tablespoon rapeseed oil, plus a splash extra
2 trimmed leeks, sliced
2 garlic cloves, sliced
½ teaspoon coriander seeds
½ teaspoon fennel seeds

pinch of chilli flakes, plus extra to serve
200 grams spinach
2 large eggs
2 tablepoons Greek yoghurt
squeeze of lemon

Heat the oil in a large frying pan. Add the leeks and a pinch of salt, then cook until soft. Add the garlic, coriander, fennel and chilli flakes. Once the seeds begin to crackle, tip in the spinach and turn down the heat. Stir everything together until the spinach has wilted and reduced, then scrape it over to one side of the pan. Pour a little oil into the pan, then crack in the eggs and fry until cooked to your liking. Stir the yoghurt through the spinach mix and season. Pile onto two plates, top with the fried egg, squeeze over a little lemon and season with black pepper and chilli flakes to serve.

Nutrition: Calories: 231g Fat: 16g Carbohydrates: 11g Protein: 10g

Banana Pancakes

Preparation Time: 10 minutes **Cooking Time:** 15 minutes **Servings:** 3

Butter
2 bananas
4 eggs
1 teaspoon cinnamon
½ teaspoon baking soda (optional)

Mix all the ingredients together until well combined. Melt a knob of butter in a pan over a medium heat and cook about 4 pancakes per batch (depending on the size of the pan). Allow the pancakes to cook about 1-2 minutes per side. I like to cover the pan while the pancakes cook on the first side before flipping—this allows the top to steam a little bit, making it fluffier and also easier to flip. Serve immediately as is, or with a dollop of coconut cream and fresh strawberries.

Nutrition: Calories: 124g Fat: 7g Carbohydrates: 13g Protein: 6g

Turkey Scrabmle

Preparation Time: 10 minutes **Cooking Time:** 15 minutes **Servings:** 2

450 grams of organic ground turkey
6 organic eggs
120 grams of Keto-friendly salsa

Grease the skillet, then put the turkey and simmer. Fold in the salsa and simmer for 2 to three minutes. Put the eggs on the top of the turkey base—Cook for seven minutes. Serve.

Nutrition: Calories: 280 Fat: 17g Carbohydrates: 5g Protein: 25g

Brunch BLT Wrap

Preparation Time: 5 minutes **Cooking Time:** 15 minutes **Servings:** 1

4 bacon slices
2 Romaine lettuce leaves
68 grams tomatoes
2 teaspoons Mayo
Pepper

Cook the bacon until crispy in a skillet. Spread mayonnaise on one side of the lettuce. Add the bacon and tomato. Roll it up and serve.

Nutrition: Calories: 409 Fat: 25g Carbohydrates: 31g Protein: 15g

Cheesy Bacon & Egg Cups

Preparation Time: 10 minutes **Cooking Time:** 20 minutes **Servings:** 6

6 bacon slices
6 large eggs
200 grams cheese

1 spinach
Pepper

Set the oven setting to 200° Celsius. Cook the bacon on medium heat—grease muffin tins. Put the slice of bacon. Mix the eggs and combine with the spinach. Add the batter to tins and sprinkle with cheese. Add salt and pepper—Bake for 15 minutes. Serve.

Nutrition: Calories: 156 Fat: 11g Carbohydrates: 0,6g Protein: 11g

Coconut Keto Porridge

Preparation Time: 15 minutes **Cooking Time:** 10 minutes **Servings:** 1

1 egg, beaten
1 tablespoon coconut flour
¼ teaspoon ground psyllium husk powder
¼ teaspoon salt
28 grams butter
4 tablespoons coconut cream

In a small bowl, combine the egg, coconut flour, psyllium husk powder and salt. Over low heat, melt the butter and coconut cream. Slowly whisk in the egg mixture, combining until you achieve a creamy, thick texture. Serve with coconut milk or cream. Top your porridge with a few fresh or frozen berries and enjoy!

Nutrition: Calories: 301 Fat: 17g Carbohydrates: 31g Protein: 6g

Cream Cheese Eggs

Preparation Time: 5 minutes **Cooking Time:** 5 minutes **Servings:** 1

1 tablespoon butter
2 eggs
2 tablespoons soft cream cheese with chives

Warm-up a skillet and melt the butter. Whisk the eggs with the cream cheese. Cook until done. Serve.

Nutrition: Calories: 184 Fat: 13g Carbohydrates: 1,6g Protein: 13g

Creamy Basil Baked Sausage

Preparation Time: 5 minutes **Cooking Time:** 5 minutes **Servings:** 12

1,5 kg Italian sausage
220 grams of cream cheese
50 ml. double cream
100 grams Basil pesto
100 grams Mozzarella

Set the oven to 200° Celsius. Put the sausage in the dish and bake for 30 minutes. Combine the double cream, pesto, and cream cheese. Pour the sauce over the casserole and top it off with the cheese—Bake for 10 minutes. Serve.

Nutrition: Calories: 160 Fat: 12g Carbohydrates: 2g Protein: 12g

Almond Coconut Egg Wraps

Preparation Time: 5 minutes **Cooking Time:** 5 minutes **Servings:** 4

5 organic eggs
1 tablespoon coconut flour
Sea salt
2 tablespoons almond meal

Preheat a skillet on medium-high heat. In a blender, pulse the ingredients together—Cook the mixture for 6 minutes, 3 minutes per side. Serve.

Nutrition: Calories: 120 Fat: 8g Carbohydrates: 3g Protein: 8g

Banana Waffles

Preparation Time: 30 minutes **Cooking Time:** 30 minutes **Servings:** 4

4 eggs
1 banana
100 ml. coconut milk
100 grams of almond flour
Salt
1 tablespoon psyllium husk powder
½ teaspoon vanilla extract
1 teaspoon baking powder
1 teaspoon ground cinnamon
Butter

Mix all of the ingredients together and let sit for a while. Make in a waffle maker or fry in a frying pan with coconut oil or butter. Serve with hazelnut spread or whipped coconut cream and some fresh berries, or just have them as is with melted butter. You can't go wrong!

Nutrition: Calories: 197 Fat: 3g Carbohydrates: 37g Protein: 7g

Keto Coffee

Preparation Time: 5 minutes **Cooking Time:** 5 minutes **Servings:** 1

2 tablespoons ground coffee
45 grams of heavy whipped cream
1 teaspoon ground cinnamon
470 ml. of water

Start by mixing the cinnamon with the ground coffee. Pour in hot water and whip the cream. Serve with cinnamon.

Nutrition: Calories: 155 Fat: 14g Carbohydrates: 1g Protein: 1g

Keto Waffles with Blueberries

Preparation Time: 15 minutes **Cooking Time:** 10 to 15 minutes **Servings:** 8

8 eggs
140 grams of melted butter
1 teaspoon vanilla extract
2 teaspoons baking powder

43 grams of coconut flour
Topping:
40 grams butter
30 grams blueberries

Mix the butter and eggs, and put in the remaining ingredients except those for the topic. On medium-high heat, make the waffles. Leave them aside, and add blueberries and butter on top.

Nutrition: Calories: 188 Fat: 14g Carbohydrates: 4g Protein: 10g

Tomato Eggs

Preparation Time: 30 minutes **Cooking Time:** 60 minutes **Servings:** 4

900g ripe vine tomatoes
3 garlic cloves
3 tbsp olive oil
4 large free range eggs
2 tbsp chopped parsley and/or chives

Preheat the oven to fan 180C/ conventional 200C/gas 6. Cut the tomatoes into quarters or thick wedges, depending on their size, then spread them over a fairly shallow 1.5-litre ovenproof dish. Peel the garlic, slice thinly and sprinkle over the tomatoes. Drizzle with the olive oil, season well with salt and pepper and stir everything together until the tomatoes are glistening. Slide the dish into the oven and bake for 40 minutes until the tomatoes have softened and are tinged with brown. Make four gaps among the tomatoes, break an egg into each gap and cover the dish with a sheet of foil. Return it to the oven for 5-10 minutes until the eggs are set to your liking. Scatter over the herbs and serve piping hot with thick slices of toast or warm ciabatta and a green salad on the side.

Nutrition: Calories: 204 Carbohydrates: 7g Fat: 16g Protein: 13g

Mushroom Omelet

Preparation Time: 15 minutes **Cooking Time:** 5 minutes **Servings:** 1

3 eggs
30 grams cheese
30 grams butter
¼ yellow onion, chopped

4 large mushrooms
Vegetables by choice
Salt
Pepper

Beat the eggs, and put in some salt and pepper—Cook the mushroom and onion. Put the egg mixture into the pan and cook on medium heat. Put the cheese on top of the still-raw portion of the egg. Pry the edges of the omelette and fold it in half. Serve.

Nutrition: Calories: 484 Fat: 23g Carbohydrates: 5g Protein: 20g

Chocolate Sea Salt Smoothie

Preparation Time: 15 minutes **Cooking Time:** 5 minutes **Servings:** 2

1 avocado
470 ml. almond milk
1 tablespoon tahini
30 grams cocoa powder
1 scoop Keto chocolate base

Combine all the ingredients in a high-speed blender. Add ice and serve!

Nutrition: Calories: 386 Fat: 4g Carbohydrates: 53g Protein: 15g

Vegan Keto Scramble

Preparation Time: 15 minutes **Cooking Time:** 10 to 15 minutes **Servings:** 1

400 grams of firm tofu
Avocado oil
1 yellow onion, chopped
1/5 tablespoon nutritional yeast
½ teaspoon turmeric
½ teaspoon garlic powder
130 grams of baby spinach
3 grape tomatoes
85 grams of vegan cheddar cheese
Salt

Sauté the chopped onion until it caramelizes. Crumble the tofu on the skillet—grease avocado oil onto the mixture with the dry seasonings. Stir. Fold the baby spinach, cheese, and chopped tomato—Cook for a few more minutes. Serve.

Nutrition: Calories: 108 Fat: 4g Carbohydrates: 2g Protein: 10g

Bavarian Cream with Vanilla and Hazelnuts

Preparation Time: 15 minutes **Cooking Time:** 0 minutes **Servings:** 3

54 grams mascarpone
7 grams Soy lecithin
2 grams Hazelnuts
8 grams of Fruit mousse

Prepare the mousse by mixing the mascarpone at room temperature, sweetening with one or two drops of liquid saccharin and flavoured with a pinch of vanillin. Add the lecithin, blending the mixture well. Put the Bavarian cream in a dessert bowl and decorate with the fruit puree and chopped hazelnuts. Chill and serve.

Nutrition: Calories: 318 Fat: 25g Carbohydrates: 17g Protein: 6g

Vanilla Mousse

Preparation Time: 15 minutes **Cooking Time:** 0 minutes **Servings:** 5

30 grams Mascarpone
70 grams Cream
4 grams Butter
3 grams Rusk rich in fibre
40 grams Cheese

Prepare the mousse with mascarpone and butter. Sweeten with liquid saccharin and sprinkle with a little decaffeinated coffee in granules. Serve the cheese separately with the buttered rusk and the hot drink prepared with cream and barley coffee sweetened with saccharin.

Nutrition: Calories: 215 Fat: 17g Carbohydrates: 17g Protein: 1g

Blueberry Bavarian Cream

Preparation Time: 15 minutes **Cooking Time:** 0 minutes **Servings:** 3

40 grams Mascarpone
5 grams Soy lecithin
10 grams Hazelnuts
10 grams Blueberries

Prepare the mousse by mixing the mascarpone at room temperature sweetened with one or 2 drops of liquid saccharin and flavoured with a pinch of vanillin. Add the lecithin, blending the mixture well. Put the Bavarian cream in a dessert bowl and decorate it with chopped blueberries and hazelnuts. Chill and serve.

Nutrition: Calories: 180 Fat: 1g Carbohydrates: 40g Protein: 4g

Strawberry Bavarian

Preparation Time: 15 minutes **Cooking Time:** 0 minutes **Servings:** 5

260 grams fresh strawberries
30 grams powdered sugar
2 eggs
60 g granulated sugar
200 ml. whole milk
13 grams gelatin
200 ml. whipping cream

Separate egg yolks from whites. Combine the yolks with the granulated sugar and beat for a couple of minutes with an electric mixer. Stir in the milk and set on medium heat. Stir the mixture until it reaches boiling temeprature. It will thicken slightly— Remove from the heat when done. Soak the gelatin and prepare it according to package instructions. Stir gelatin into egg custard. Let cool to room temperature making sure not to leave it too long or the gelatin will harden this mixture before the other ingredients are added. Clean and cut the strawberries, combine with powdered sugar. Blend until smooth. Stir into custard mixture when it has reached room temperature. Whip the cream to soft peaks and fold into Bavarian cream mixture—divide strawberry Bavarian cream into four moulds and refrigerate for a minimum of 2 hours before serving.

Nutrition: Calories: 153 Fat: 6g Carbohydrates: 24g Protein: 2g

Almond Mousse

Preparation Time: 15 minutes **Cooking Time:** 0 minutes **Servings:** 2

3 sheets gelatin vanilla bean
2 eggs
250 milliliters
100 grams of ground almonds
2 tablespoons almond liqueur
80 grams sugar
80 milliliters whipped cream
4 tablespoons almonds

Soak gelatine in plenty of cold water. Slit vanilla pod lengthwise and scrape out seeds. Separate eggs. Slowly heat milk in a pot. Add ground almonds and vanilla seeds, bring to a boil and set aside. Whisk egg yolks with almond liqueur and 30 grams (approximately one ounce) of sugar until foamy over hot water bath. Gradually add milk to egg yolk mixture, constantly whisking, until mixture thickens. Add gelatine and dissolve, stirring—cool cream, whisking, in ice water bath. Add 60 ml. of cream. Beat egg whites until stiff and fold into mixture. Pour cream into six glasses and refrigerate for 2 hours. Add remaining cream and remaining sugar into the pan and caramelize slightly. Add whole almonds and coat with caramel, stirring. Place on waxed paper and cool. Place caramelized almonds on top of mousse and serve.

Nutrition: Calories: 251 Fat: 19g Carbohydrates: 12 Protein: 6g

Nougat

Preparation Time: 15 minutes **Cooking Time:** 0 minutes **Servings:** 4

100 grams whole blanched almonds
100 grams peeled pistachios
100g peeled hazelnuts
2 sheets edible rice paper
icing sugar for dusting
150 grams clear honey
300 grams white caster sugar
100 grams liquid glucose
2 medium egg whites

Heat oven to 180 degrees Celsius. Scatter the nuts over a baking tray and toast in the oven for 10 mins, then set aside (they don't need to cool). Cut the two pieces of rice paper to fit a 20 x 20cm square tin. Line the tin with one sheet of rice paper, brush the sides of the tin with oil, then dust the tin with icing sugar. Put the honey into a saucepan, then in another saucepan tip in the sugar, glucose and 100ml of water. Put the egg whites in the very clean bowl of a tabletop mixer with a whisk attachment and whisk on a low speed. Heat and boil the honey until it reaches 121 degrees Celsius on a digital cooking thermometer, then straightaway pour the honey over the egg whites and set the speed to medium. While the whites and honey are whisking, bring the sugar and water to the boil and keep boiling until the syrup reaches 145 degrees Celsius exactly on a digital cooking thermometer. Pour the hot syrup in a slow, steady stream into the beating egg white mixture. Continue beating for about 10 mins until you have a thick, glossy, firm meringue. It's hard to over-whisk at this stage but easy to under-whisk, so keep going until the meringue looks like sticky chewing gum. Use a spatula to stir though the nuts (which should still be warm), the vanilla extract and a small pinch of salt.

Scrape the mixture into the lined tin, then smooth over to spread the mixture out evenly (if you have an offset spatula, now is the time to use it). Finally, top with the remaining sheet of rice paper and press down. Leave the nougat to set for at least 2 hours or overnight. To turn out and portion, use a spatula to loosen the edges of the nougat away from the tin, then invert the tin on to a clean board and use a sharp serated, hot knife to portion into bars or squares. The nougat will keep, stored in an airtight container, for up to a month.

Nutrition: Calories: 55 (per serving) Carbohydrates: 12g Fat: 0g Protein: 0g

Chocolate Crepes

Preparation Time: 15 minutes **Cooking Time:** 10 minutes **Servings:** 4

36 grams Whole egg
5 grams Dark chocolate
34 grams Mascarpone
17 grams Butter

Beat the egg. Cook the crepes in a non-stick pan. Prepare the filling by mixing mascarpone and butter at room temperature, sweetening with one or 2 drops of liquid saccharin. Melt the dark chocolate in a bain-marie and mix it with the mascarpone cream. Stuff the crepes and serve with a cup of decaffeinated tea without sugar.

Nutrition: Calories: 150 Fat: 8g Carbohydrates: 19g Protein: 2g

Rusk with Walnut Cream

Preparation Time: 15 minutes **Cooking Time:** 10 minutes **Servings:** 1

8 rusks
5 teaspoon condensed milk
60 grams sugar
1-litre milk
4 drops vanilla essence

In a saucepan, add milk. Heat it over high flame. Once the milk starts to boil, add sugar and mix well. Boil till it reduces to 3/4th and pour 1/4 of the boiled milk over two rusks and blend together in a mixer for 5 minutes. Add condensed milk and vanilla essence. Blend again for two more minutes. Add this to the remaining milk and transfer to freezer safe ice cream bowls. Put it in the freezer for one hour. Place one scoop on each rusk, garnish with mint leaves and serve.

Nutrition: Calories: 97 Fat: 4g Carbohydrates: 12g Protein: 1g

Bavarian Coffee with Hazelnuts

Preparation Time: 15 minutes **Cooking Time:** 10 minutes **Servings:** 1

67 grams Mascarpone
11 grams Hazelnuts

Prepare the hot drink by heating the water. Weigh the hazelnuts and pass them to the mixer, then add them by mixing with the mascarpone held for a few moments at room temperature. Add the remaining part of soluble decaffeinated coffee.
Sweeten with saccharin.

Nutrition: Calories: 20 Fat: 1g Carbohydrates: 3g Protein: 0g

Bavarian Strawberry Butter

Preparation Time: 15 minutes **Cooking Time:** 0 minutes **Servings:** 1

50 grams of Fresh cream
30 grams Butter
15 grams Hazelnuts
13 grams Strawberries
Fish glue
Saccharin
37 grams Cheese

Soak a piece of gelatin in hot water. Please put it in the Bavarian container and add the exact amount of cream. Add the softened butter to room temperature. Sweeten with liquid saccharin and add the vanilla flavour. Chill and serve with strawberries, a small leaf of mint, and the coarsely chopped hazelnuts. Serve the cheese separately with a cup of jasmine tea sweetened with saccharin.

Nutrition: Calories: 100 Fat: 7g Carbohydrates: 5g Protein: 1g

Cheese Platters

Preparation Time: 15 minutes **Cooking Time:** 0 minutes **Servings:** 1

45 grams of Ricotta cheese
35 grams Cheese
22 grams Hazelnuts
30 grams Mascarpone cheese
26 grams Butter
Saccharin and orange flavour

Weigh the cheeses' exact quantity and serve them on a small wooden cutting board with hazelnuts. Prepare the mascarpone pastry by weighing the precise amount of mascarpone and softened butter at room temperature.

Nutrition: Calories: 220 Carbohydrates: 6g Fat: 4g Protein: 12g

Hazelnut Bavarian with Hot Coffee Drink

Preparation Time: 15 minutes **Cooking Time:** 0 minutes **Servings:** 1

85 grams Mascarpone cheese
21grams Hazelnuts
3 grams Butter
15 grams of Wild strawberries
150 ml. water

Prepare the Bavarian by mixing mascarpone, butter, and hazelnuts passed in the mixer at room temperature, sweetening. Prepare the drink by heating 150 ml of water. Add a teaspoon of decaffeinated coffee and saccharin.
Garnish with wild strawberries and chill. Serve.

Nutrition: Calories: 263 Carbohydrates: 10g Fat: 5g Protein: 4g

Muffins and Coffee

Preparation Time: 5 minutes **Cooking Time:** 0 minutes **Servings:** 1

50 grams Sugar-free muffins
12 grams Butter
47 grams of White flour
45 grams Cream with 35% fat

Prepare the hot coffee drink by mixing the white flour, cream, and American coffee in a mug. Sweeten to taste. Butter the sugar-free muffin. Serve

Nutrition: Calories: 284 Fat: 24g Carbohydrates: 4g Protein: 9g

French Toast with Coffee Drink

Preparation Time: 15 minutes **Cooking Time:** 10 minutes **Servings:** 1

24 grams cream with 35% fat
14 grams egg
15 grams of sweet cheese
12 grams low carb bread without crust
11 grams butter
For the hot drink:
10 grams White flour
80 grams Cream with 35% fat

Scramble the egg, cream, and finely grated cheese in the mixer in a small bowl. Toast the bread in butter, turn it several times and pour the mixture over it. Prepare the hot drink by shaking the white flour with the cream. Add the soluble decaffeinated coffee and saccharin. Garnish with chopped fresh parsley.

Nutrition: Calories: 229 Carbohydrates: 12g Fat: 5g Protein: 1g

Cheese Crepes

Preparation Time: 15 minutes **Cooking Time:** 20 minutes **Servings:** 5

170 grams of cream cheese
43 grams Parmesan cheese
6 large organic eggs
1 teaspoon granulated erythritol
1 ½ tablespoon coconut flour
1/8 teaspoon xanthan gum
2 tablespoons unsalted butter

Using a blender, pulse the cream cheese, Parmesan cheese, eggs, and erythritol Place the coconut flour and xanthan gum and pulse again. Now, vibration at medium speed Transfer and put aside for 5 minutes. Melt butter over medium-low heat Place 1 portion of the mixture and tilt the pan to spread into a thin layer—Cook for 160 grams. Flip the crepe and cook for 15-20 seconds more Serve.

Nutrition: Calories 297 Fat 25g Carbohydrates: 3.5g Protein 13.7g

Ricotta Pancakes

Preparation Time: 10 minutes **Cooking Time:** 20 minutes **Servings:** 4

4 organic eggs
65 grams of ricotta cheese
65 grams of vanilla whey protein powder
½ teSalt
½ teaspoon liquid stevia
2 tablespoons unsalted butter
teaspoon organic baking powder

Pulse all the fixing in the blender—warm-up butter over medium heat. Put the batter and spread it evenly—Cook for 2 minutes. Flip and cook again for 1–2 minutes. Serve.

Nutrition: Calories 195 Fat 11g Carbohydrates: 20g Protein 13g

Yoghurt Waffles

Preparation Time: 15 minutes **Cooking Time:** 25 minutes **Servings:** 5

65 grams golden flax seeds meal
65 grams of almond flour
1 ½ tablespoon granulated erythritol
1 teaspoon of vanilla whey protein powder
¼ teaspoon baking soda
½ teaspoon organic baking powder
¼ teaspoon xanthan gum
Salt
1 organic egg
1 ½ teaspoon unsalted butter
2 tablespoons unsweetened almond milk
85 grams of plain Greek yoghurt

Preheat the waffle iron and then grease it. Mix and add the flour, erythritol, protein powder, baking soda, xanthan gum, and salt. Beat the egg white until stiff peaks. Add two egg yolks, whole egg, almond milk, butter, and yoghurt, and beat in a third bowl. Put the egg mixture into the bowl of the flour mixture and mix. Gently fold in the beaten egg whites. Place 30 grams of the mixture into preheated waffle iron and cook for about 4–5 minutes. Serve.

Nutrition: Calories 236 Fat 18g Carbohydrates: 14g Protein 9g

Broccoli Muffins

Preparation Time: 15 minutes **Cooking Time:** 20 minutes **Servings:** 6

2 tablespoons unsalted butter
6 large organic eggs
60 grams of heavy whipping cream
60 grams Parmesan cheese
Salt
Pepper
160 grams broccoli
2 tablespoons parsley
60 grams of Swiss cheese

Warm up the oven to 190° Celsius, then grease a 12-cup muffin tin. Mix the eggs, cream, Parmesan cheese, salt, and black pepper. Divide the broccoli and parsley into the muffin cup. Top with the egg mixture with Swiss cheese.
Bake for 20 minutes. Cool for about 5 minutes. Serve.

Nutrition: Calories 230 Fat 14g Carbohydrates: 5g Protein 14g

Pumpkin Bread

Preparation Time: 15 minutes **Cooking Time:** 1-hour **Servings:** 16

210 grams almond flour
1 ½ teaspoon organic baking powder
60 grams pumpkin pie spice
½ teaspoon pumpkin pie spice
½ teaspoon cinnamon
½ teaspoon cloves
½ teaspoon salt
230 grams of cream cheese
6 organic eggs
1 teaspoon coconut flour
130 grams powdered erythritol
1 teaspoon stevia powder
1 teaspoon organic lemon extract
130 grams of pumpkin puree
60 ml. coconut oil

Warm-up oven to 190° Celsius. Grease 2 bread loaf pans. Mix almond flour, baking powder, spices, and salt in a small bowl.

In a second bowl, add the cream cheese, one egg, coconut flour, 30 grams of erythritol, and 1.21 teaspoon of stevia, and beat. In a third bowl, add the pumpkin puree, oil, five eggs, erythritol, and a spoon of the stevia and mix. Mix the pumpkin mixture into the bowl of the flour mixture. Place about 60 grams of the pumpkin mixture into each loaf pan. Top each pan with the cream cheese mixture, plus the rest pumpkin mixture. Bake for 50–60 minutes. Cold for 10 minutes. Slice and serve.

Nutrition: Calories 179 Fat 4g Carbohydrates: 33g Protein 3g

Eggs in Avocado Cups

Preparation Time: 10 minutes **Cooking Time:** 20 minutes **Servings:** 4

2 avocados
4 organic eggs
Salt
Ground black pepper
4 tablespoons cheddar cheese
2 slices of cooked bacon
1 tablespoon scallion greens

Preheat the oven to 200° Celsius. Remove the flesh from the avocado. Place avocado halves into a small baking dish. Crack an egg in each avocado half and sprinkle with salt plus black pepper. Top each egg with cheddar cheese evenly—Bake for 20 minutes. Serve with bacon and chives.

Nutrition: Calories 343 Fat 30g Carbohydrates: 20g Protein 12g

Cheddar Scramble

Preparation Time: 10 minutes **Cooking Time:** 8 minutes **Servings:** 6

2 eggs
80 grams cheddar cheese, grated (or Monterey Jack)
½ teaspoon olive oil (or butter)
salt and pepper to taste
1 slice wholegrain bread (toasted)

Put a frying pan onto a medium heat and put in the butter or oil. Break the eggs into a bowl and beat quickly with a fork.
Grate the cheese and have it ready. Tip the beaten eggs into the frying pan. Layer the cheese on top. The eggs will start to solidify almost straight away – as soon as they do use a spatula and 'pull' the eggs in from the side to the middle. Repeat the pulling several times. It does not take long. The idea behind this is you'll have soft, lightly cooked fresh eggs. It's hard to undercook an egg really but very easy to overcook. 2 – 3 minutes cooking time is all you'll need.
When the egg has no 'watery' bits left, you're done! Done! Quickly remove from heat and transfer to plate – preferably on top of some lovely, hot, unbuttered bread. Add some salt and pepper to taste.

Nutrition: Calories 250 Fat: 22 Carbohydrates: 20g Protein 18g

Keto Pizza Wraps

Preparation Time: 10 minutes **Cooking Time:** 15 minutes **Servings:** 2

2 large eggs
½ tablespoon butter
½ tablespoon tomato sauce
14 grams mozzarella cheese, shredded
45 grams salami, sliced

Heat a large, non-stick frying pan to medium heat. Crack the eggs into a bowl, and whisk until smooth in color. Add the butter.

Slowly pour the eggs into the pan, allowing the mixture to go right to the edges. Cook until the edges begin to lift off the side of the frying pan. Using a spatula all around the edge, lift the egg from the pan. Flip and cook on the other side for 30 seconds.

Remove from the pan. Layer tomato sauce, mozzarella cheese, and salami in the middle. Roll it together into a wrap.

Nutrition: Calories 348 Fat 18g Carbohydrates: 22g Protein: 6g

Green Veggies Quiche

Preparation Time: 20 minutes **Cooking Time:** 20 minutes **Servings:** 4

6 organic eggs
60 ml. unsweetened almond milk
Salt
Pepper
250 grams of baby spinach
60 grams green bell pepper
1 scallion
30 grams cilantro
1 tablespoon chives
3 tablespoons mozzarella cheese

Warm-up oven to 200° Celsius. Grease a pie dish. Beat eggs, almond milk, salt, and black pepper. Set aside. In another bowl, add the vegetables and herbs, then mix. Place the veggie mixture and top with the egg mixture in the pie dish—Bake for 20 minutes. Remove, then sprinkle with the Parmesan cheese. Slice and serve.

Nutrition: Calories 176 Fat: 12g Carbohydrates 24g Protein: 9g

Chicken & Asparagus Frittata

Preparation Time: 15 minutes **Cooking Time:** 12 minutes **Servings:** 4

60 grams grass-fed chicken breast
40 grams Parmesan cheese
6 organic eggs
Salt
Ground black pepper
40 grams boiled asparagus
30 grams cherry tomatoes
30 grams of mozzarella cheese

Warm up the oven's broiler, then mix Parmesan cheese, eggs, salt, and black pepper in a bowl. Melt butter, and cook the chicken and asparagus for 2–3 minutes. Add the egg mixture and tomatoes and mix. Cook for 4–5 minutes. Remove, then sprinkle with the Parmesan cheese. Transfer the wok under the broiler and broil for 3–4 minutes. Slice and serve.

Nutrition: Calories 158 Fat 9g Carbohydrates 22g Protein: 10g

Scrambled Egg Bites

Preparation Time: 10 minutes **Cooking Time:** 23 minutes **Servings:** 4

5 eggs
1/2 teaspoon hot pepper sauce
43 grams tomatoes
3 tablespoons green chillies
1 teaspoon black pepper
Salt
2 tablespoons non-dairy milk

Mix both the eggs and milk in a large cup. Add the hot sauce, pepper, and salt. Put small, chopped chillies and chopped tomatoes in. Fill each with 3/4 full with the egg mixture. Put the trivet in the pot and pour 120 ml. of water. Put the mold on the trivet. Set on high for 8 minutes. Let it cool before serving.

Nutrition: Calories: 124 Fat: 7g Carbohydrates: 2g Protein: 6g

Bacon Egg Bites

Preparation Time: 10 minutes **Cooking Time:** 22 minutes **Servings:** 9

130 grams cheese
1/2 green pepper
60 grams cottage cheese
4 slices bacon
Pepper
Salt
130 grams of red onion
130 ml. water
30 grams whip cream
30 grams egg whites
4 eggs

Blend egg whites, eggs, cream, cheese (cottage), shredded cheese, pepper, and salt for 30 to 45 seconds in a blender. Put the egg mixture into mini muffin cups. Top each with bacon, peppers, and onion. Cover the muffin cups tightly with foil. Put the cups on the trivet. Place the trivet in the pot and pour 120 ml. water. Set to steam for 12 minutes. Cooldown before serving.

Nutrition: Calories: 155 Fat: 8g Carbohydrates: 16g Protein: 9g

Cheese and Egg Bites

Preparation Time: 5 minutes **Cooking Time:** 8 minutes **Servings:** 3

1 handful mushrooms
1 Green onion
3 Green peppers
1/8 teaspoon hot sauce
 pepper, salt, mustard, garlic powder
60 grams cheese cheddar
60 grams cheese cottage
2 deli ham slices
4 eggs

Whisk eggs, then the cheddar and cottage цхеесе. Put the ham, veggies, and seasonings, and mix. Pour the mixture into greased silicone moulds. Put the trivet with the moulds in the pot, then fill with 250 ml. water—steam for about 8 minutes. Transfer, cool down before serving.

Nutrition: Calories: 177 Fat: 4g Carbohydrates: 14g Protein: 7g

Cheddar & Bacon Egg Bites

Preparation Time: 10 minutes **Cooking Time:** 8 minutes **Servings:** 7

120 grams of sharp cheddar cheese
1 teaspoon parsley flakes
4 eggs
4 tablespoons cream
Hot sauce
120 ml. water
60 grams cheese
4 slices bacon

Blend the cream, cheddar, cottage, and egg in the blender; for 30 seconds. Stir in the parsley—grease moulds silicone with egg. Divide the crumbled bacon between them. Put the egg batter into each cup. With a piece of foil, cover each mould. Place the trivet with the moulds in the pot, then fill with 120 ml. water—steam for 8 minutes. Remove, let rest for 5 minutes. Serve, sprinkled with black pepper and optional hot sauce.

Nutrition: Calories: 170 Fat: 14g Carbohydrates: 3g Protein: 12g

Avocado Pico Egg Bites

Preparation Time: 15 minutes **Cooking Time:** 10 minutes **Servings:** 7

Egg bites:
200 grams cheese cottage
60 grams cheese Mexican blend
1/4 teaspoon chilli powder
1/4 teaspoon cumin
1/4 teaspoon garlic powder
4 eggs
Pepper
Salt
Pico de Gallo:
1 avocado

1 jalapeno
Salt
Half an onion, chopped
5 grams cilantro
2 tablespoons lime juice
4 Roma tomatoes

Mix all of the Pico de Gallo fixing except for the avocado. Gently fold in the avocado. Blend all the egg bites ingredients in a blender. Take one teaspoon of Pico de Gallo into each egg and bite the silicone mould. Place the trivet in the pot, then fill with 120 ml. water. Put the moulds in the trivet. Set to high for 10 minutes. Remove. Serve topped with cheese and Pico de Gallo.

Nutrition: Calories: 118 Fat: 23g Carbohydrates: 13g Protein: 10g

Salmon Scramble

Preparation Time: 10 minutes **Cooking Time:** 5 minutes **Servings:** 1

2 teaspoon vegetable oil
8 eggs
115 grams crumbled smoked salmon
2 tablespoons cream cheese, softened
75 grams chopped green onions, divided

Heat the oil in a large frying pan over a medium heat. Combine the eggs and salmon and mix lightly with a fork. Cook until just beginning to scramble. Add the cream cheese and mix until everything is a smooth texture. Add 1/2 the spring onions and stir into the scrambled eggs. Cook long enough to heat through. Serve the salmon scrambled eggs on a plate and garnish with the remaining spring onions.

Nutrition: Calories: 352 Fat: 14g Carbohydrates: 12g Protein: 8g

Mexican Scrambled Eggs

Preparation Time: 5 minutes **Cooking Time:** 10 minutes **Servings:** 6

6 eggs
2 jalapeños
1 tomato
90 grams cheese
2 tablespoons butter

Warm up the butter over medium heat in a large pan. Add tomatoes, jalapeños, and green onions, then cook for 3 minutes. Add eggs and continue for 2 minutes. Add cheese and season to taste. Serve.

Nutrition: Calories: 230 Fat: 17g Carbohydrates: 18g Protein: 12g

Caprese Omelet

Preparation Time: 10 minutes **Cooking Time:** 10 minutes **Servings:** 2

6 eggs
2 tablespoons olive oil
460 grams cherry tomatoes, halved
1 tablespoon dried basil
160 grams of mozzarella cheese
Hot sauce
120 ml. water
60 grams cheese
4 slices bacon

Mix the basil, eggs, salt, and black pepper in a bowl. Place a large skillet with oil over medium heat. Once hot, add tomatoes and cook. Top with egg and cook. Add cheese, adjust heat to low, and allow to set before serving fully.

Nutrition: Calories: 533 Fat: 43g Carbohydrates: 4g Protein: 30g

Sausage Omelet

Preparation Time: 10 minutes **Cooking Time:** 15 minutes **Servings:** 2

230 grams gluten-free sausage links
60 grams of heavy whipping cream
Salt
Black pepper
8 large organic eggs
130 grams of cheddar cheese
¼ teaspoon red pepper flakes

Warm-up oven to 190° Celsius. Grease a baking dish. Cook the sausage for 8–10 minutes.
Put the rest of the fixing in a bowl and beat. Remove sausage from the heat. Place cooked sausage in the baking dish, then top with the egg mixture—Bake for 30 minutes. Slice and serve.

Nutrition: Calories: 320 Fat: 14g Carbohydrates: 20g Protein: 14g

Brown Hash with avocado

Preparation Time: 10 minutes **Cooking Time:** 20 minutes **Servings:** 2

1 small onion
6 to 8 mushrooms
250 grams of grass-fed ground beef
1 pinch salt
1 pinch of ground black pepper
1 teaspoon smoked paprika
2 eggs
1 avocado
10 black olives

Warm-up air fryer to 175° Celsius. Grease a pan with coconut oil. Add the onions, mushrooms, salt, and pepper to the pan.
Add the ground beef and the smoked paprika, and eggs. Mix, then place the pan in Air Fryer. Set to cook for 18 to 20 minutes with a temperature of 190° Celsius. Serve with chopped parsley and chopped avocado!

Nutrition: Calories: 300 Fat: 12g Carbohydrates: 20g Protein: 11g

Crunchy Radish & Courgettes

Preparation Time: 10 minutes **Cooking Time:** 10 minutes **Servings:** 6

1 teaspoon onion powder
60 grams Courgettes
130 grams of cheddar cheese
60 grams radishes
3 egg whites
Pepper
Salt

Mix the egg whites in a bowl. Stir in the radishes, zucchini, seasonings, and cheese. Shape into six patties. Warm-up skillet over the medium-high setting. Grease. Cook the patties. Adjust to medium-low; cook for 3 to 5 minutes more. Serve.

Nutrition: Calories: 125 Fat: 5g Carbohydrates: 12g Protein: 6g

Fennel Quiche

Preparation Time: 15 minutes **Cooking Time:** 18 minutes **Servings:** 4

300 grams fennel
120 grams spinach
5 eggs
60 grams almond flour
1 teaspoon olive oil
1 teaspoon butter
1 teaspoon salt
30 grams of double cream
1 teaspoon ground black pepper

Combine the chopped spinach and chopped fennel in the big bowl. Whisk the egg in a separate bowl. Combine the whisked eggs with the almond flour, butter, salt, heavy cream, and ground black pepper. Warm-up air fryer to 190° Celsius. Grease.
Then add the spinach-fennel mixture and pour the whisked egg mixture —Cook for 18 minutes. Remove, then chill. Slice and serve.

Nutrition: Calories: 249 Carbohydrates: 9.4g Protein: 11.3g Fat: 19.1g

Turkey Hash

Preparation Time: 10 minutes **Cooking Time:** 25 minutes **Servings:** 5

380 grams cauliflower florets
1 small yellow onion
Salt
Ground black pepper
30 grams of double cream
2 tablespoons unsalted butter
1 teaspoon dried thyme
450 grams of cooked turkey meat

Put the cauliflower in salt boiling water and cook for 4 minutes. Then chop the cauliflower and set it id. Dissolve the butter over medium heat in a large skillet and sauté onion for 4-5 mi te. Add thyme, salt, and black pepper and sauté again for 1 m nut. Stir in cauliflower and cook for 2 minutes. Stir in turkey and cook for 5-6 minutes. Stir in the cream and cook for 2 minutes more. Serve.

Nutrition: Calories: 169 Fat: 14g Carbohydrates: 6g Protein: 18g

Crustless Veggie Quiche

Preparation Time: 10 minutes **Cooking Time:** 30 minutes **Servings:** 6

250 grams Colby Jack cheese
1 red pepper
60 ml. coconut milk
Salt
Vegetables
120 grams tomatoes
60 grams of arrowroot flour
Black pepper
2 green onions
8 eggs

Whisk the milk, egg, flour, pepper, and salt in a large bowl. Mix in the veggies and 120 grams of cheese. Pour the mixture into a heatproof container. Cover it with foil. Place the trivet in the pot, then fill with 120 ml. water—Cook high for 30 minutes. Remove and uncover. Top with the rest of the cheese. Cover then let sit for 2 minutes. Serve!

Nutrition: Calories: 212 Fat: 14g Carbohydrates: 7g Protein: 12g

Crustless Broccoli & Cheddar Quiche

Preparation Time: 10 minutes **Cooking Time:** 25 minutes **Servings:** 4

120 grams of cheddar cheese
60 grams of non-dairy milk
Black pepper
Kosher salt
6 eggs
1 broccoli head
3 green onions
Salt

Grease a soufflé dish. Whisk the milk, eggs, pepper, and salt in a bowl. Stir in the cheese, broccoli, and green onions. Pour the mixture into the greased dish. Place the trivet in the pot, then fill with 190 ml. water. Set to medium-high for 25 minutes. Slice and serve.

Nutrition: Calories: 296 Fat: 20g Carbohydrates: 5g Protein: 15g

Keto Courgettes Bread

Preparation Time: 10 minutes **Cooking Time:** 50 minutes **Servings:** 4

220 grams almond flour
½ teaspoon Kosher salt
½ teaspoon Ground Cinnamon
60 grams Granular Sweetener
1 teaspoon Baking soda
2 large Eggs, Beaten
30 grams Melted butter
220 grams Grated Courgettes with peel

Preheat oven to 220 degrees Celsius. Grease an 9x5 loaf pan with butter or cooking spray. In a large bowl, combine the almond flour, salt, cinnamon, swerve, and baking soda. Wrap the grated courgettes in a kitchen towel and squeeze out as much liquid as you can. Discard liquid and add zucchini to the dry ingredients followed by the eggs and melted butter. Stir batter until combined. See notes for instructions on adding walnuts, chocolate chips, or blueberries. Pour batter into greased loaf pan and bake in the 220 degrees Celsius oven for 60 minutes or until a toothpick comes out clean. Let cool before serving. Slice into 12 slices. See notes for freezing, making muffins, and for a savory bread.

Nutrition: Calories: 267 Fat: 23g Carbohydrates: 11g Protein: 4g

Quick Keto Toast

Preparation Time: 10 minutes **Cooking Time:** 5 minutes **Servings:** 4

45 grams of almond flour
1/2 teaspoon baking powder
1/8 teaspoon salt
1 egg
1 tablespoon ghee

Warm up the oven to 200 degrees Celsius. Put all the bread components in a container and mix well. Microwave the mixture for 90 seconds. Cooldown and cut it into four slices—Bake for 4 minutes. Serve with additional ghee.

Nutrition: Calories: 270 Fat: 27g Carbohydrates: 3g Protein: 6g

Keto Loaf of Bread

Preparation Time: 10 minutes **Cooking Time:** 60 minutes **Servings:** 6

140 grams Wholesome Yum Blanched Almond Flour
60 grams Wholesome Yum Coconut Flour
2 teaspoon baking powder
1/4 teaspoon Sea salt
5 tablespoons Butter
12 large Egg whites

Preheat the oven to 163 degrees Celsius. Line an 8 1/2 x 4 1/2 in (22×11 cm) loaf pan with parchment paper, with extra hanging over the sides for easy removal later. Combine the almond flour, coconut flour, baking powder, erythritol, xanthan gum, and sea salt in a large food processor. Pulse until combined. Add the melted butter. Pulse, scraping down the sides as needed, until crumbly. In a very large bowl, use a hand mixer to beat the egg whites and cream of tartar (if using), until stiff peaks form. Make sure the bowl is large enough because the whites will expand a lot. Add 1/2 of the stiff egg whites to the food processor. Pulse a few times until just combined. Do not over-mix! Carefully transfer the mixture from the food processor into the bowl with the egg whites, and gently fold until no streaks remain. Do not stir. Fold gently to keep the mixture as fluffy as possible. Transfer the batter to the lined loaf pan and smooth the top. Push the batter toward the center a bit to round the top. Bake for about 40 minutes, until the top is golden brown. Tent the top with aluminum foil and bake for another 30-45 minutes, until the top is firm and does not make a squishy sound when pressed. Internal temperature should be 200 degrees. Cool completely before removing from the pan and slicing.

Nutrition: Calories: 117 Fat: 15g Carbohydrates: 5g Protein: 4g

Blueberry Loaf

Preparation Time: 10 minutes **Cooking Time:** 50 minutes **Servings:** 4

220 grams almond flour
½ teaspoon Kosher salt
½ teaspoon Ground Cinnamon
60 grams Granular Sweetener
1 teaspoon Baking soda
2 large Eggs, Beaten
30 grams Melted butter
220 grams Grated Courgettes with peel

Preheat oven to 220 degrees Celsius. Grease an 9x5 loaf pan with butter or cooking spray. In a large bowl, combine the almond flour, salt, cinnamon, swerve, and baking soda.
Wrap the grated courgettes in a kitchen towel and squeeze out as much liquid as you can. Discard liquid and add zucchini to the dry ingredients followed by the eggs and melted butter. Stir batter until combined. See notes for instructions on adding walnuts, chocolate chips, or blueberries. Pour batter into greased loaf pan and bake in the 220 degrees Celsius oven for 60 minutes or until a toothpick comes out clean. Let cool before serving. Slice into 12 slices. See notes for freezing, making muffins, and for a savory bread.

Nutrition: Calories: 267 Fat: 23g Carbohydrates: 11g Protein: 4g

Quick Keto Toast

Preparation Time: 10 minutes **Cooking Time:** 5 minutes **Servings:** 4

45 grams of almond flour
1/2 teaspoon baking powder
1/8 teaspoon salt
1 egg
1 tablespoon ghee

Warm up the oven to 200 degrees Celsius. Put all the bread components in a container and mix well. Microwave the mixture for 90 seconds. Cooldown and cut it into four slices—Bake for 4 minutes. Serve with additional ghee.

Nutrition: Calories: 270 Fat: 27g Carbohydrates: 3g Protein: 6g

Simple Loaf of Bread

Preparation Time: 10 minutes **Cooking Time:** 60 minutes **Servings:** 6

350 grams almond flour
Olive oil
50 ml. almond milk
3 eggs
2 tablespoons baking powder.
1 teaspoon baking soda.
Salt

Warm-up oven to 140°Celsius. Grease the bread. Mix all the ingredients—Bake for 60 minutes. Leave to cool. Serve.

Nutrition: Calories: 266 Fat: 2g Carbohydrates: 32g Protein: 7g

Keto Chocolate Bread

Preparation Time: 10 minutes **Cooking Time:** 45 minutes **Servings:** 5

300 grams finely milled almond flour measured and sifted
100 grams sugar substitute
30 grams cocoa powder
1 1/2 teaspoons of baking powder
1/4 teaspoon of sea salt
120 grams cream cheese, room temperature
4 eggs, room temperature
4 tablespoons of unsalted butter, room temperature
100 grams baking chocolate (melted)
1 teaspoon of instant coffee (optional for enhancing chocolate)

Preheat oven to 220 degrees Celsius. Grease an 8-inch loaf pan and line with parchment paper for easier release. In a medium-size bowl, combine all the dry ingredients (except sugar substitute) and set them aside. In a large mixing bowl beat on high the softened butter and sugar substitute until light and fluffy. Add the cream cheese and combine well until fully incorporated. Add the eggs one at a time making sure to mix well after each addition. Add all the dry ingredients mixing well until fully combined. Lastly, add the melted baking chocolate in a stream and beat the mixture until thoroughly mixed. Bake the bread for 50-60 minutes or until an inserted toothpick comes out clean. Allow cooling for 10 minutes before taking it out of the mold. Then place on a baking rack to fully cool before slicing. Store leftovers in the refrigerator for up to five days or freeze for up to three weeks.

Nutrition: Calories: 198 Carbohydrates: 9g Fat: 16g Protein: 7g

Sunflower Bread

Preparation Time: 120 minutes **Cooking Time:** 15 minutes **Servings:** 15

1 ¾ teaspoon fresh yeast
30 ml. water
380 grams of ground rye flour
250 grams of wheat flour
200 grams rye sourdough starter
Salt
3 tablespoons honey
85 grams of sunflower seeds
1 tablespoon cumin

Melt the yeast in a bit of water. Add all ingredients, and mix well. Let the dough rise for 1 to 2 hrs. Shape the dough right into fifteen small rolls. Please put it on the cooking sheet and let them surge until doubled in dimension. Knead the dough after it has increased and shaped it into a long roll. Cut the dough into fifteen parts. Form right into rounded loaves—Bake at 190° Celsius for 10 minutes. Slice and serve.

Nutrition: Calories: 140 Fat: 4g Carbohydrates: 12g Protein: 3g

Collagen Keto Bread Keto Collagen Bread

Preparation Time: 20 minutes **Cooking Time:** 40 minutes **Servings:** 15

60 grams of Unflavored Grass-Fed Collagen Protein
6 tablespoons almond flour
5 pastured eggs
1 tablespoon unflavored fluid coconut oil
1 teaspoon aluminum-free baking powder
1 teaspoon xanthan gum
Pinch of Himalayan pink salt
A squeeze of stevia

Warm-up stove to 220° Celsius. Grease the glass loaf pan with coconut oil. In a large bowl, break the egg whites, and set them aside. In a little bowl, blend the dry components and set them aside. In a bit dish, whisk together the wet ingredients, egg yolks, and liquid coconut oil. Include the dry and the damp components to the egg whites and blend till well integrated.
Bake for 40 minutes. Slice before serving.

Nutrition: Calories: 177 Fat: 7g Carbohydrates: 14g Protein: 15g

Keto Breakfast Pizza

Preparation Time: 20 minutes **Cooking Time:** 15 minutes **Servings:** 2

250 grams grated cauliflower
2 tablespoons coconut flour
Salt
4 eggs
1 tablespoon psyllium husk powder
Toppings: smoked salmon, avocado, natural herbs, spinach, olive oil

Warm-up stove to 220° Celsius. Line a pizza tray with parchment. In a mixing dish, add all ingredients except toppings and mix up. Leave for 5 minutes. Thoroughly put the breakfast pizza base onto the pan— Cook for 15 minutes. Garnish with toppings. Serve.

Nutrition: Calories: 454 Fat: 31g Carbohydrates: 26g Protein: 22g

Cauliflower Bread

Preparation Time: 20 minutes **Cooking Time:** 35 minutes **Servings:** 2

250 grams grated cauliflower
1-2 tablespoons coconut flour
Salt
4 eggs
1/2 teaspoon garlic powder
1/2 tablespoon psyllium husk
3-4 pieces' of bacon
¼ springtime onion, chopped.
1 avocado

Warm up the oven to 220° Celsius. Mix the 200° Celsius grams of grated cauliflower, salt, two eggs, 15 grams of coconut flour, psyllium, garlic powder, and flour. Divide the cauliflower and mix well to combine. Place each cauliflower ball onto one of the lined cooking trays, and shape the blend into even rectangular shapes. Cook on the stove for 15 minutes. Bake with the bacon for an additional 10 minutes. Boil water in a bit of pan, including the dash of apple cider vinegar plus salt. Split two eggs into the boiling water to poach. Cook. Transfer the cauliflower bread, then serve with the poached eggs, crispy bacon, spring onion, and avocado.

Nutrition: Calories: 412g Fat: 38g Carbohydrates: 14g Protein: 27g

Coconut Flour Donuts

Preparation Time: 15 minutes **Cooking Time:** 18 minutes **Servings:** 8

43 grams of coconut flour
43 grams Swerve Sweetener
3 tablespoons cocoa powder
1 teaspoon baking powder
Salt
4 eggs
30 grams butter thawed
½ teaspoon vanilla essence
6 tablespoons brewed coffee
Glaze:
30 grams powdered Swerve Sweetener
11 teaspoon cocoa powder
15 grams of double cream
4 grams of vanilla essence
30ml. water

Warm up the oven to 220° Celsius and grease the doughnut frying pan. Mix the coconut flour, sweetener, cacao powder, baking powder, and salt. Then the eggs, melted butter, and vanilla essence. Stir in the cold coffee. Separate the batter amongst the wells of the doughnut pan. Bake 16 to 20 minutes. Cooldown.
Glaze: In a medium shallow bowl, mix the powdered sugar and cocoa powder. Add the hefty cream and vanilla and whisk. Put water up until the glaze thins out. Serve.

Nutrition: Calories: 150 Fat: 9g Carbohydrates: 18g Protein: 5g

Tofu Mushrooms

Preparation Time: 5 minutes **Cooking Time:** 10 minutes **Servings:** 3

1 block tofu
120 grams mushrooms
4 tablespoons butter
4 tablespoons Parmesan cheese
Salt
Ground black pepper

Toss tofu cubes with melted butter, salt, and black pepper in a mixing bowl. In a skillet, over medium-high heat, sauté tofu for 5 minutes. Stir in cheese and mushrooms. Sauté for another 5 minutes. Serve.

Nutrition: Calories 215 Fat: 19g Carbohydrates: 3g Protein 12g

Onion Tofu

Preparation Time: 8 minutes **Cooking Time:** 5 minutes **Servings:** 3

2 blocks tofu
2 onions
2 tablespoons butter
120 grams of cheddar cheese
Salt
Ground black pepper

Rub the tofu with salt and pepper in a bowl. Add melted butter and onions to a skillet to sauté for 3 minutes. Toss in tofu and stir cook for 2 minutes. Stir in cheese and cover the skillet for 5 minutes on low heat. Serve.

Nutrition: Calories 198 Fat: 13g Carbohydrates: 6g Protein 11g

Spinach Rich Ballet

Preparation Time: 5 minutes **Cooking Time:** 30 minutes **Servings:** 4

680 grams of baby spinach
40 grams coconut cream
400 grams cauliflower
Two tablespoons of unsalted butter
Salt
Ground black pepper

Warm up the oven at 220° Cels. Melt butter, then toss in spinach to sauté for three minutes. Divide the spinach into four ramekins. Divide cream, cauliflower, salt, and black pepper in the ramekin—Bake for 25 minutes. Serve.

Nutrition: Calories 190 Fat: 13g Carbohydrates: 5g Protein 15g

Pepperoni Egg Omelet

Preparation Time: 5 minutes **Cooking Time:** 20 minutes **Servings:** 4

15 pepperonis
6 eggs
2 tablespoons butter
4 tablespoons coconut cream
Salt and ground black pepper

Whisk eggs with pepperoni, cream, salt, and black pepper in a bowl. Add 60 grams of the butter to a warm-up pan.
Now pour 60 grams of the batter into this melted butter and cook for 2 minutes on each side. Serve.

Nutrition: Calories 145 Fat: 11g Carbohydrates: 15g Protein 8.9 g

Nut Porridge

Preparation Time: 10 minutes **Cooking Time:** 15 minutes **Servings:** 4

120 grams of cashew nuts
120 grams pecan
30 grams stevia
4 teaspoons coconut oil
260 ml. water

Grind the cashews and peanuts in a processor. Stir in stevia, oil, and water. Add the mixture to a saucepan and cook for 5 minutes on high. Adjust on low for 10 minutes. Serve.

Nutrition: Calories 260 Fat: 23g Carbohydrates: 13g Protein 7g

Parsley Soufflé

Preparation Time: 5 minutes **Cooking Time:** 6 minutes **Servings:** 1

2 eggs
1 red chilli pepper
2 tablespoons coconut cream
One tablespoon parsley
Salt

Blend all the soufflé ingredients into a food processor. Please put it in the soufflé dishes, then bake for 6 minutes at 220° Celsius. Serve.

Nutrition: Calories 108 Fat: 9g Carbohydrates: 2g Protein 6g

Bok Choy Samba

Preparation Time: 5 minutes **Cooking Time:** 15 minutes **Servings:** 3

1 onion
4 Bok choy
4 tablespoons coconut cream
Salt
Ground black pepper
60 grams Parmesan cheese

Toss Bok choy with salt and black pepper. Add oil to a large pan and sauté onion for 5 minutes. Stir in Bok choy and cream. Stir for 6 minutes. Toss in cheese and cover the skillet to cook on low for 3 minutes. Serve.

Nutrition: Calories 112 Fat: 4.9g Carbohydrates: 1.9g Protein 3g

Eggs with Watercress

Preparation Time: 10 minutes **Cooking Time:** 5 minutes **Servings:** 6

6 organic eggs
1 medium ripe avocado
43 ml. watercress
½ tablespoon lemon juice
Salt

Put water into the pot with the trivet inside—Cook for 3 minutes with high pressure. Spread the watercress in the trivet.
Drain the steamed watercress. Mix and mash and mix the watercress with lemon juice, salt, avocado, and yolks in a bowl.
Divide the egg yolk mixture at the center of all the egg whites. Serve.

Nutrition: Calories 132 Fat: 10.9g Carbohydrates: 3.3g Protein 6g

Banana Porridge

Preparation Time: 10 minutes **Cooking Time:** 5 minutes **Servings:** 2

60 grams walnuts
1 banana
hot water
2 tablespoons coconut butter
½ teaspoon cinnamon powder
2 teaspoons maple syrup

Pulse all the ingredients together using a blender, then transfer them to a saucepan. Warm-up over medium heat for 5 minutes, then share it into a large bowl and serve.

Nutrition: Calories: 269 Fat: 14g Carbohydrates: 21g Protein: 8g

Mushroom Sandwich

Preparation Time: 5 minutes **Cooking Time:** 10 minutes **Servings:** 1

2 Portobello mushroom caps
2 lettuce leaves
2 avocado slices
250 grams pound turkey meat, cooked
Olive oil

Cook the turkey meat, and for 4 minutes, transfer and drain excess oil.
Warm-up the pan with the olive oil, add mushroom caps, and cook for 2 minutes on each side.
Remove, arrange one mushroom cap on a plate, add turkey, avocado slices, and lettuce leaves, and serve.

Nutrition: Calories: 521 Fat: 15g Carbohydrates: 5g Protein: 47g

Bell Pepper Sandwich

Preparation Time: 5 minutes **Cooking Time:** 10 minutes **Servings:** 2

250 grams of bell peppers
½ tablespoon avocado oil
3 eggs
430 grams turkey breast
Olive oil

Warm-up oil over medium-high heat, add bell peppers, stir and cook for 5 minutes. Warm up another pan over medium heat, add the turkey meat, stir, cook for 3-4 minutes, and transfer. Mix the eggs, put them in the pan with the bell peppers, and cook for 7-8 minutes. Serve.

Nutrition: Calories: 411 Fat: 12g Carbohydrates: 19g Protein: 44g

Mushroom and Salmon Sliders

Preparation Time: 10 minutes **Cooking Time:** 15 minutes **Servings:** 3

3 Portobello mushroom caps
280 grams of turkey meat
3 eggs
300 grams smoked salmon
Olive oil

Warm up a pan over medium-high heat, add the turkey, cook for 4 minutes, and transfer. Warm-up pan with the olive oil over medium heat, place egg rings in the pan, crack an egg in each, cook for 6 minutes, and transfer. Warm up the pan again, add mushroom caps, cook for 5 minutes, and transfer. Top each mushroom cap with turkey slices, salmon, and eggs and serve.

Nutrition: Calories: 315 Fat: 12g Carbohydrates: 3g Protein: 33g

Beef and Squash Skillet

Preparation Time: 10 minutes **Cooking Time:** 20 minutes **Servings:** 3

430 grams beef
2 tablespoons ghee
3 garlic cloves
2 celery stalks
1 yellow onion
Sea salt
Black pepper
½ teaspoon coriander
1 teaspoon cumin
1 teaspoon garam masala
1/2 grams butternut squash
3 eggs
1 small avocado
430 grams spinach

Warm up a pan with the ghee over medium heat, add onion, garlic, celery, a pinch of salt and pepper, and cook for 3 minutes. Add beef, cumin, garam masala, and coriander. Cook for 5 minutes more. Add squash flesh and spinach, stir and make three holes in this mix. Break an egg into the pan, then bake at 220° Celsius for 15 minutes. Serve with avocado on top.

Nutrition: Calories: 594 Fat: 35g Carbohydrates: 19g Protein: 54g

Turkey and Veggies Mix

Preparation Time: 10 minutes **Cooking Time:** 15 minutes **Servings:** 4

20 ounces of turkey meat
4 tablespoons coconut oil
1 small green bell pepper
60 grams onion
2 garlic cloves
250 grams sweet potato
1 avocado
3 eggs
250 grams spinach

Warm-up a pan with the oil, add onion, stir and cook for 3 minutes. After that, add the garlic and bell pepper, and cook for 1 minute. Put the ground turkey, and cook for 15 minutes more. Put the sweet potato, and cook for 4 minutes. Put the spinach, and cook for 2 minutes. Make 3 holes in the batter, break an egg in each, place the pan under a preheated broiler, and cook for 3 minutes. Top with avocado slices and serve.

Nutrition: Calories: 619 Fat: 34g Carbohydrates: 29g Protein: 49g

Pork Skillet

Preparation Time: 10 minutes **Cooking Time:** 20 minutes **Servings:** 4

200 grams mushrooms
450 grams pork
Olives
2 courgettes
½ teaspoon garlic powder
½ teaspoon basil
Sea salt
Black pepper
2 tablespoons Dijon mustard

Warm up a pan with the oil over medium-high heat, add mushrooms, and cook for 4 minutes.
Put courgettes, salt, and black pepper and cook for 4 minutes more.
Put pork, garlic powder, and basil, and cook for 10 minutes.
Put the mustard, stir, and cook for 3 more minutes. Transfer and serve.

Nutrition: Calories: 226 Fat: 8g Carbohydrates: 5g Protein: 3g

Roasted Lemon Chicken Sandwich

Preparation Time: 15 minutes **Cooking Time:** 1 hour 30 minutes **Servings:** 12

A whole chicken, 1kg
5 tablespoons of butter
1 lemon (cut into wedges)
1 tablespoon garlic powder
Salt
Pepper
2 tablespoons mayonnaise
Keto-friendly bread

Preheat the oven to 220° Celsius. Grease a deep baking dish with butter. Ensure that the chicken is patted dry and that the gizzards have been removed. Combine the butter, garlic powder, salt, and pepper. Rub the entire chicken with it, including in the cavity. Place the lemon and onion inside the chicken and place the chicken in the prepared baking dish. Bake for about 160 grams hours, depending on the size of the chicken. Baste the chicken often with the drippings. If the drippings begin to dry, add water. The chicken is done when a thermometer inserts it into the thickest part of the thigh, reads 170° Celsius, or when the clear juices run when the widest part of the thigh is pierced. Allow the chicken to cool before slicing. To assemble the sandwich, shred some breast meat and mix it with the mayonnaise. Place the mixture between the two bread slices.

TIP: To save the chicken, refrigerate for up to 5 days or freeze for one month.

Nutrition: Calories: 214 **Fat:** 11.8g **Carbohydrates:** 1.6g **Protein:** 24.4g

Keto-Friendly Skillet Pepperoni Pizza

Preparation Time: 10 minutes **Cooking Time:** 6 minutes **Servings:** 4

FOR CRUST
60 grams almond flour
½ teaspoon of baking powder
8 large egg whites (whisked into stiff peaks)
Salt
Pepper
TOPPINGS
3 tablespoons unsweetened tomato sauce
60 grams shredded cheddar cheese
60 grams of pepperoni

Gently incorporate the almond flour into the egg whites. Stir in the remaining crust ingredients. Ensure that no lumps remain.
Heat a nonstick skillet over medium heat. Spray with nonstick spray. Pour the batter into the heated skillet to cover the bottom of the skillet. Cover the skillet with a lid and cook the pizza crust for 4 minutes or until bubbles appear on the top. Flip the dough and add the toppings, starting with the tomato sauce and ending with the pepperoni—Cook the pizza for two more minutes. Allow the pizza to cool slightly before serving.

TIP: It can be stored in the refrigerator for up to 5 days and frozen for one month.

Nutrition: Calories: 175 **Fat:** 12g **Carbohydrates:** 1.9g **Protein:** 14.3g

Cheesy Chicken Cauliflower

Preparation Time: 5 minutes **Cooking Time:** 10 minutes **Servings:** 4

250 grams of cauliflower florets (chopped)
60 grams of red bell pepper (chopped)
120 grams of roasted chicken, shredded (Lunch Recipes: Roasted Lemon Chicken Sandwich)
30 grams of shredded cheddar cheese
1 tablespoon of butter
1 tablespoon of sour cream
Salt and pepper (to taste)

Stir fry the cauliflower and peppers in the butter over medium heat until the veggies are tender. Add the chicken and cook until the chicken is warmed through. Add the remaining ingredients and stir until the cheese is melted. Serve warm.

Nutrition: Calories: 144 **Fat:** 8.5g **Carbohydrates:** 4g **Protein:** 13.2g

Lemon Baked Salmon

Preparation Time: 10 minutes **Cooking Time:** 30 minutes **Servings:** 4

450 grams salmon
1 tablespoon of olive oil
Salt and pepper to taste

1 tablespoon of butter
1 lemon (thinly sliced)
1 tablespoon of lemon juice

Preheat your oven to 220° Celsius. Grease a baking dish with olive oil and place the salmon skin-side down. Season the salmon with salt and pepper then top with the lemon slices. Slice half the butter and place it over the salmon. Bake for 20 minutes or until the salmon flakes easily. Melt the remaining butter in a saucepan. When it starts to bubble, remove it from heat and allow it to cool before adding the lemon juice. Drizzle the lemon butter over the salmon and serve warm.

Nutrition: Calories: 211 **Fat:** 13.5g **Carbohydrates:** 1.5g **Protein:** 22.2g

Baked Salmon

Preparation Time: 10 minutes **Cooking Time:** 10 minutes **Servings:** 4

Cooking spray
3 cloves of garlic (minced)
30 grams butter
1 teaspoon of lemon zest
2 tablespoons of lemon juice 4 salmon fillets
Salt
Pepper
2 tablespoons parsley, chopped

Preheat your oven to 220°Celsius. Grease the pan with cooking spray. In a bowl, mix the garlic, butter, lemon zest, and lemon juice. Sprinkle salt and pepper on salmon fillets. Drizzle with the lemon butter sauce. Bake in the oven for 12 minutes.
Garnish with parsley before serving.

Nutrition: Calories: 345 **Fat:** 22.7g **Carbohydrates:** 1.2g **Protein:** 34.9g

Buttered Cod

Preparation Time: 5 minutes **Cooking Time:** 5 minutes **Servings:** 4

450 grams cod fillets
6 tablespoons butter
¼ teaspoon of garlic powder
¾ teaspoon of ground paprika
Lemon slices
Salt
Pepper
Parsley, chopped

Mix the garlic powder, paprika, salt, and pepper in a bowl—season codpieces with the seasoning mixture. Add 10 grams of butter to a pan over medium heat. Let half of the butter melt. Add the cod and cook for 2 minutes per side. Top with the remaining slices of butter—Cook for 3 to 4 minutes. Garnish with parsley and lemon slices before serving.

Nutrition: Calories: 295 **Fat:** 19g **Carbohydrates:** 1.5g **Protein:** 30.7g

Tuna Salad

Preparation Time: 5 minutes **Cooking Time:** 0 minute
Servings: 2

2 tuna
56 gams mayonnaise
1 stalk of celery, diced
2 tablespoon red onion, diced
1 tablespoon chopped parsley, chives and/or other herbs
0.5 tablespoon Dijon mustard

Drain the liquid from the tuna cans. Then, add the tuna, mayonnaise, diced celery, diced red onion, herbs, Dijon mustard, salt and pepper to a mixing bowl. Stir all of the ingredients together until well combined. Enjoy, the tuna salad plain out of a bowl, wrapped up in lettuce, or a sandwich.

Nutrition: Calories: 130 **Fat:** 7.8g **Carbohydrates:** 8.5g **Protein:** 8.2g

Keto Frosty

Preparation Time: 45 minutes **Cooking Time:** 0 minutes **Servings:** 4

60 grams of heavy whipping cream
2 tablespoons of cocoa powder (unsweetened)
3 tablespoons of swerving
1 teaspoon of pure vanilla extract
Salt to taste

In a bowl, combine all the ingredients. Use a hand mixer and beat until you see stiff peaks forming. Place the mixture in a Ziploc bag. Freeze for 35 minutes. Serve in bowls or dishes.

Nutrition: **Calories:** 164 **Fat:** 17g **Carbohydrates:** 2.9g **Protein:** 1.4g

Coconut Crack Bars

Preparation Time: 2 minutes **Cooking Time:** 3 minutes **Servings:** 20

380 grams of coconut flakes (unsweetened)
120 grams of coconut oil
30 grams of maple syrup

Line a baking sheet with parchment paper. Put coconut in a bowl. Add the oil and syrup. Mix well. Pour the mixture into the pan. Refrigerate until firm. Slice into bars before serving.

Nutrition: **Calories:** 147 **Fat:** 14g **Carbohydrates:** 12g **Protein:** 6g

Strawberry Ice Cream

Preparation Time: 1 hour and 20 minutes **Cooking Time:** 0 minutes **Servings:** 4

200 ml. coconut milk
200 grams of frozen strawberries
2 tablespoons swerve
60 grams of fresh strawberries

Put all the ingredients except the fresh strawberries in a blender. Pulse until smooth. Put the mixture in an ice cream maker.
Use the ice cream maker according to the directions. Add the fresh strawberries a few minutes before the ice cream is done.
Freeze for 1 hour before serving.

Nutrition: **Calories:** 320 **Fat:** 25g **Carbohydrates:** 25g **Protein:** 2.9g

Trout and Chili Nuts

Preparation Time: 10 minutes **Cooking Time:** 0 minutes **Servings:** 3

1.5 kg of rainbow trout
300 grams of shelled walnuts
1 bunch of parsley
9 cloves of garlic
7 tablespoons Olive oil
2 fresh hot peppers
Lemon juice, 2 lemons

Clean and dry the trout, then place them in a baking tray. Then, chop the walnuts, parsley, and chilli peppers and mash the garlic cloves. Mix the ingredients by adding olive oil, lemon juice, and a pinch of salt. Stuff the trout with a part of the sauce, use the rest to cover the fish—Bake at 180° for 30/40 minutes. Serve the trout hot or cold.

Nutrition: Calories: 226 **Fat:** 5g **Carbohydrates:** 7g **Protein:** 8g

Five Greens Smoothie

Preparation Time: 10 minutes **Cooking Time:** 25 minutes **Servings:** 3

6 kale leaves (chopped)
3 stalks of celery (chopped)
1 ripe avocado (skinned, pitted, sliced)
120 grams of ice cubes
250 grams of spinach (chopped)
1 large cucumber (peeled and chopped)
Chia seeds to garnish

Add the kale, celery, avocado, and ice cubes to a blender, and blend for 45 seconds. Add the spinach and cucumber, and process for another 45 seconds until smooth. Pour the smoothie into glasses, garnish with chia seeds, and serve the drink immediately.

Nutrition: Calories: 124 **Fat:** 7.8g **Carbohydrates:** 2.9g **Protein:** 3.2g

Turkey and Cream Cheese Sauce

Preparation Time: 15 minutes **Cooking Time:** 25 minutes **Servings:** 5

2 tablespoons butter
1 kg of turkey breast
350 grams cream
40 grams cheese
1 tablespoon tamari soy sauce
Pepper
Salt
Capers

Warm up the oven to 170° Celsius, and dissolve half the butter in an iron skillet. Rub the breast of the turkey with pepper and salt. Fry for five minutes. Bake for ten minutes. Add the drippings of turkey in a pan, cream cheese, and whipping cream. Simmer. Put pepper, soy sauce, and salt. Sauté the small capers in the remaining butter. Slice and serve with fried capers and cream cheese sauce.

Nutrition: Calories: 810 Fat: 50g Carbohydrates: 6.9g Protein: 47.6g

Baked Salmon and Pesto

Preparation Time: 15 minutes **Cooking Time:** 30 minutes **Servings:** 4

For the green sauce:
4 tablespoons green pesto
130 grams mayonnaise
Half a Greek yoghurt
Pepper
Salt
For the salmon:
350 grams salmon
4 tablespoons green pesto
Pepper
Salt

Put the fillets on a greased baking dish with the skin side down. Add pesto on top. Add pepper and salt. Bake at 200° degrees for thirty minutes. Combine all the listed fixing for the green sauce in a bowl. Serve the baked salmon with green sauce on top.

Nutrition: Calories: 1010 Protein: 51.6g Carbohydrates: 3.1g Fat: 87.6g

Keto Chicken with Butter and Lemon

Preparation Time: 15 minutes **Cooking Time:** 1 hour & 30 minutes **Servings:** 2

A whole chicken
Pepper and salt
2 teaspoons barbecue seasoning
1 teaspoon water
One lemon
2 onions
500 ml. water

Warm-up oven to 170° degrees. Grease the baking dish. Rub the chicken with pepper, salt, and barbecue seasoning. Put in the baking dish. Arrange lemon wedges and onions surrounding the chicken and put slices of butter. Bake for 1 hour and 30 minutes. Slice and serve.

Nutrition: Calories: 980.3 Fat: 38g Carbohydrates: 55g Protein: 57g

Garlic Chicken

Preparation Time: 15 minutes **Cooking Time:** 40 minutes **Servings:** 4

50 grams butter
500 grams of chicken drumsticks
Pepper
Salt
lemon juice
2 tablespoons olive oil
7 garlic cloves
60 grams parsley, chopped

Warm up the oven to 250° degrees Celsius. Put the chicken in a baking dish. Add pepper and salt. Add olive oil with lemon juice over the chicken. Sprinkle parsley and garlic on top—Bake for forty minutes. Serve.

Nutrition: Calories: 540 Fat: 38.6g Protein: 41g Carbohydrates: 3.1g

Salmon Skewers Wrapped with Prosciutto

Preparation Time: 15 minutes **Cooking Time:** 4 minutes **Servings:** 4

30 grams basil
450 grams salmon
Black pepper
100 grams prosciutto
1 tablespoon olive oil
8skewers

Start by soaking the skewers in a bowl of water. Cut the salmon fillets lengthwise. Thread the salmon using skewers. Coat the skewers in pepper and basil. Wrap the slices of prosciutto around the salmon. Warm-up oil in a grill pan. Grill the skewers for four minutes. Serve.

Nutrition: Calories: 670.5 Carbohydrates: 1.2g Fat: 61.6g Protein: 27.2g

Buffalo Drumsticks and Chili Aioli

Preparation Time: 15 minutes **Cooking Time:** 40 minutes **Servings:** 4

For the chilli aioli:
60 grams mayonnaise
1 tablespoon smoked paprika powder
One clove garlic
for the chicken:
300 grams of chicken drumsticks
2 tablespoons white wine vinegar
Olive oil
2 tablespoons tomato paste
Salt
1 tablespoon paprika powder
1 tablespoon tabasco
Salt

Warm up the oven to 200° Celsius. Combine the listed marinade fixing. Marinate the chicken drumsticks for ten minutes. Arrange the chicken drumsticks in the tray—Bake for forty minutes. Combine the listed ingredients for the chilli aioli in a bowl. Serve.

Nutrition: Calories: 567.8 Fat: 43.2g Carbohydrates: 2.2g Protein: 41.3g

Slow Cooked Roasted Pork and Creamy Gravy

Preparation Time: 15 minutes **Cooking Time:** 8 hours & 15 minutes **Servings:** 6

For the creamy gravy:
200 grams of whipping cream
Roast juice

For the pork:
450 grams pork roast
Salt
Bay leaf

Five black peppercorns
600 ml. water
2 tablespoons thyme
2 cloves garlic
5 grams ginger, grated
10 grams of Paprika powder
Olive oil
Black pepper

Warm up your oven to 150° Celsius. Add the meat, salt, and water to a baking dish. Put peppercorns, thyme, and bay leaf. Put in the oven for 8hours. Remove—Reserve the juices. Adjust to 200° Celsius. Put ginger, garlic, pepper, herbs, and oil. Rub the herb mixture on the meat. Roast the pork for fifteen minutes. Slice the roasted meat. Strain the meat juices in a bowl—boil for reducing them by half. Add the cream. Simmer for twenty minutes. Serve with creamy gravy.

Nutrition: Calories: 586.9 Fat: 50.3g Carbohydrates: 2.6g Protein: 27.9g

Bacon-Wrapped Meatloaf

Preparation Time: 15 minutes **Cooking Time:** 1-hour **Servings:** 4

For the meatloaf:
2 tablespoons butter
One onion
450 grams beef
60 grams of whipping cream
30 grams cheese
One large egg
10 grams oregano
Salt
Black pepper
1 pack of bacon
For the gravy:
60 grams of whipping cream
Half a tablespoon of tamari soy sauce

Warm up the oven to 200° Celsius. Dissolve the butter in a pan. Add the onion—Cook for four minutes. Keep aside. Combine onion, ground meat, and the remaining fixing except for the bacon in a large bowl. Make a firm loaf. Use bacon strips for wrapping the loaf. Bake the meatloaf for forty-five minutes. Put the juices from the baking dish and cream, then boil. Simmer for ten minutes. Add the soy sauce. Slice and serve with gravy.

Nutrition: Calories: 1020.3 Fat: 88.9g Carbohydrates: 5.6g Protein: 46.7g

Lamb Chops and Herb Butter

Preparation Time: 15 minutes **Cooking Time:** 4 minutes **Servings:** 4

8lamb chops
Olive oil
Butter
Pepper
Salt
For the herb butter:
60 grams butter
One clove garlic
½ tablespoon Garlic powder
4 tablespoons parsley
Salt
1 teaspoon lemon juice

Season the lamb chops with pepper and salt—warm-up olive oil and butter in an iron skillet. Add the lamb chops. Fry for four minutes. Mix all the listed ingredients for the herb butter in a bowl. Cool. Serve with herb butter.

Nutrition: Calories: 722.3 Fat: 61.5g Carbohydrates: 0.4g Protein: 42.3g

Crispy Cuban Pork Roast

Preparation Time: 15 minutes **Cooking Time:** 4 minutes **Servings:** 6

2 kg. pork shoulder
Salt
2 teaspoons cumin
1 teaspoon black pepper
2 tablespoons oregano
1 red onion
4 garlic cloves
Orange juice
Lemon juice
60 ml. olive oil

Rub the pork shoulder with salt in a bowl. Mix all the remaining ingredients of the marinade in a blender. Marinate the meat for 8hours. Cook for forty minutes. Warm-up your oven to 200° Celsius. Roast the pork for thirty minutes. Remove the meat juice. Simmer for twenty minutes. Shred the meat. Pour the meat juice. Serve.

Nutrition: Calories: 910.3 Fat: 69.6g Carbohydrates: 5.3g Protein: 58.3g

Keto Barbecued Ribs

Preparation Time: 15 minutes **Cooking Time:** 1 hour & 10 minutes **Servings:** 4

60 grams of Dijon mustard
Apple cider vinegar
Butter
Salt
1.5 kg spareribs
2 tablespoons Paprika powder
2 teaspoons Chili powder
2 teaspoons Garlic powder
2 teaspoons Onion powder
2 teaspoons Cumin
2 teaspoons Black pepper

Warm-up a grill for thirty minutes. Mix vinegar and Dijon mustard in a bowl, put the ribs and coat. Mix all the listed spices. Rub the mix all over the ribs. Put aside. Put ribs on an aluminium foil. Add some butter over the ribs. Wrap with foil—grill for one hour. Remove and slice. Put the reserved spice mix. Grill again for ten minutes. Serve.

Nutrition: Calories: 980 Fat: 80.2g Carbohydrates: 5.8g Protein: 54.3g

Turkey Burgers and Tomato Butter

Preparation Time: 15 minutes **Cooking Time:** 15 minutes **Servings:** 4

For the chicken patties:
1 kg chicken (by choice)
One egg
Half an onion, chopped
Salt
Pepper
½ teaspoon thyme
40 grams butter

For the fried cabbage:
1 kg green cabbage
50 grams butter
Salt
Pepper

For the tomato butter:
50 grams butter
1 tablespoon tomato paste
1 teaspoon red wine vinegar
Pepper
Salt

Warm up your oven to 150° Celsius. Combine the listed ingredients for the patties in a large bowl. Shape the mixture into patties—Fry the chicken patties for five minutes on each side. Put the cabbage, plus pepper and salt—Fry for five minutes. Whip the ingredients for the tomato butter in a bowl using an electric mixer. Keep warm in the oven—warm-up butter in a pan.
Serve with a dollop of tomato butter from the top.

Nutrition: Calories: 830.4 Fat: 71.5g Carbohydrates: 6.7g Protein: 33.6g

Keto Hamburger

Preparation Time: 15 minutes **Cooking Time:** 70 minutes **Servings:** 4

For the burger buns:
260 grams Celsius grams almond flour
60 grams of ground psyllium husk powder
20 grams of baking powder
Salt
Water
2 tablespoons apple cider vinegar
Three egg whites
5 grams of sesame seeds
For the hamburger:
1 kg beef
Olive oil
Salt
Pepper
1 whole lettuce
One tomato
One red onion
50 grams mayonnaise
10 grams bacon

Warm up your oven to 150° Celsius. Mix the listed dry ingredients for the buns in a bowl. Boil the water. Put egg whites, water, and vinegar into the dry mix. Mix. Make individual pieces of buns, and put sesame seeds on the top. Bake for sixty minutes. Fry the slices of bacon. Keep aside. Mix beef, pepper, and salt in a bowl. Make patties. Grill the beef patties for five minutes on each side.
Cut the buns in half. Combine mayonnaise and lettuce in a bowl. Add beef patty, lettuce mix, onion slice, and a tomato slice. Top with bacon slices. Serve.

Nutrition: Calories: 1070.3 Fat: 85.3g Carbohydrates: 6.1g Protein: 53.4g

Chicken Wings and Blue Cheese Dressing

Preparation Time: 70 minutes **Cooking Time:** 25 minutes **Servings:** 4

30 grams mayonnaise
30 grams sour cream
3 teaspoons lemon juice

Salt
Garlic powder
50 grams of whipping cream
85 grams of blue cheese
For the chicken wings:
1 kg chicken wings
Olive oil
¼ teaspoon garlic powder
One clove garlic
Black pepper
Salt
20 grams parmesan cheese

Mix all the blue cheese dressing ingredients in a bowl. Chill for forty minutes. Combine the chicken with olive oil and spices. Marinate for thirty minutes. Bake in the oven for twenty-five minutes. Toss the chicken wings with parmesan cheese in a bowl.
Serve with blue cheese dressing by the side.

Nutrition: Calories: 839.3 Fat: 67.8g Carbohydrates: 2.9g Protein: 51.2g

Salmon Burgers with Lemon Butter and Mash

Preparation Time: 70 minutes **Cooking Time:** 15 minutes **Servings:** 4

For the salmon burgers:
1kg salmon
One egg
Half an onion, yellow
Salt
Pepper
60 grams butter
For the green mash:
500 grams broccoli
140 grams butter
40 grams of parmesan cheese

For the lemon butter:
120 grams butter
30 ml. lemon juice
Pepper
Salt

Warm-up your oven to 100° Celsius. Cut the salmon into small pieces. Combine all the burger ingredients with the fish in a blender—pulse for thirty seconds. Make 8patties. Warm-up butter in an iron skillet. Fry the burgers for five minutes. Boil water, along with some salt, in a pot, and put the broccoli florets. Cook for three to four minutes. Drain. Add parmesan cheese and butter. Blend the ingredients using an immersion blender. Add pepper and salt. Combine lemon juice with butter, pepper, and salt. Beat using an electric beater. Put a dollop of lemon butter on the top and green mash by the side. Serve.

Nutrition: Calories: 1025.3 Fat: 90.1g Carbohydrates: 6.8g Protein: 44.5g

Egg Salad Recipe

Preparation Time: 15 minutes **Cooking Time:** 20 minutes **Servings:** 6

3 tablespoons mayonnaise
3 tablespoons Greek yoghurt
2 tablespoons red wine vinegar
Kosher salt
Ground black pepper
8 hard-boiled eggs
8 strips bacon
One avocado
500 grams of crumbled blue cheese
500 grams of cherry tomatoes
2 tablespoons chives

Stir mayonnaise, cream, and red wine vinegar in a small bowl. Put pepper and salt. Mix the eggs, bacon, avocado, blue cheese, and cherry tomatoes in a large bowl. Fold in the mayonnaise dressing and put salt and pepper. Garnish with the chives and serve.

Nutrition: Calories: 200 Fat: 18g Carbohydrates: 3g Protein: 10g

Taco Stuffed Avocados

Preparation Time: 10 minutes **Cooking Time:** 25 minutes **Servings:** 8

4 ripe avocados
Lime juice
Olive oil
One onion
450 grams of ground beef
One packet of taco seasoning
Kosher salt
Ground black pepper
85 grams of Mexican cheese
500 grams lettuce
500 grams quartered grape tomatoes
Sour cream

Scoop a bit of avocado flesh. Put. Squeeze lime juice overall avocados —warm-up oil in a skillet over medium heat. Put onion, and cook for 5 minutes. Put ground beef and taco seasoning. Put salt and pepper, and cook for 6 minutes. Remove and drain.

Fill every half of the avocado with beef, then top with reserved avocado, cheese, lettuce, tomato, and a sour dollop of cream. Serve.

Nutrition: Calories: 324 Carbs: 16g Fat: 24g Protein: 15g

Buffalo Shrimp Lettuce Wraps

Preparation Time: 15 minutes **Cooking Time:** 20 minutes **Servings:** 4

¼ tablespoon butter
2 garlic cloves
20 ml. hot sauce
Olive oil
450 grams of shrimp tails removed
Kosher salt
Ground black pepper
One head romaine leaf
1/4 red onion
One rib celery
500 grams blue cheese

Make buffalo sauce:
Dissolve the butter over medium heat in a small saucepan. Put the garlic and cook for 1 minute. Put hot sauce and stir. Adjust to low.
Make shrimp:
Warm up the oil in a large skillet over medium heat. Put shrimp, salt, and pepper to the season: Cook for around 2 minutes per side. Remove, then put buffalo sauce, toss.
Assemble wraps:
Put a small scoop of shrimp in a roman leaf center, then top with red onion, celery, and blue cheese. Serve.

Nutrition: Calories: 242 Carbs: 7g Fat: 12g Protein: 25g

Broccoli Bacon Salad

Preparation Time: 15 minutes **Cooking Time:** 15 minutes **Servings:** 6

For the salad:
Kosher salt
3 heads broccoli
2 carrots
1/2 red onion
500 grams cranberries
500 grams almonds
Six slices bacon
For the dressing:
500 grams mayonnaise
3 tablespoons apple cider vinegar
Kosher salt
Ground black pepper

Boil 250 grams of salted water. Prepare a large bowl of ice water. Put broccoli florets in the heated water and cook for 1 to 2 minutes. Put the ice water in the prepared bowl. Drain. Combine broccoli, red onion, carrots, cranberries, nuts, and bacon in a large bowl. Mix vinegar and mayonnaise in a bowl and put salt plus pepper. Pour the broccoli mixture over the dressing. Mix and serve.

Nutrition: Calories: 280 Carbs: 9g Fat: 25g Protein: 6g

Keto Egg Salad

Preparation Time: 15 minutes **Cooking Time:** 15 minutes **Servings:** 4

3 tablespoons mayonnaise
2 teaspoons lemon juice
1 teaspoon chives
Ground black pepper
Kosher salt
Six hard-boiled eggs
One avocado
Lettuce
Cooked bacon

Mix the mayonnaise, lemon juice, and chives, and put pepper and salt. Add the eggs and the avocado to mix. Serve with bacon and lettuce.

Nutrition: Calories: 408 Carbs: 5g Fat: 39g Protein: 13g

Loaded Cauliflower Salad

Preparation Time: 15 minutes **Cooking Time:** 30 minutes **Servings:** 4

One large head of cauliflower
Six slices bacon
60 grams of sour cream
30 grams mayonnaise
1 tablespoon lemon juice
½ teaspoon garlic powder
Kosher salt
Ground black pepper
60 grams cheddar
60 grams chives

Boil ¼ water, put cauliflower, cover pan, and steam for 4 minutes. Drain and cool—Cook the pork for around 3 minutes per side. Drain, then cut. Mix the sour cream, mayonnaise, lemon juice, and garlic powder in a big bowl. Toss the cauliflower florets. Put salt, pepper, bacon, cheddar, and chives. Serve.

Nutrition: Calories: 440 Protein: 19g Carbohydrates: 13g Fiber: 4g Fat: 35g

Caprese Zoodles

Preparation Time: 15 minutes **Cooking Time:** 0 minutes **Servings:** 4

Four Courgettes
28 grams. extra-virgin olive oil
Kosher salt
Ground black pepper
300 grams cherry tomatoes halved
130 grams of mozzarella balls
60 grams of basil leaves
2 tablespoons balsamic vinegar

For the dressing:
500 grams mayonnaise
3 tablespoons apple cider vinegar
Kosher salt
Ground black pepper

Create zoodles out of courgettes using a spiralizer. Mix the zoodles, olive oil, salt, and pepper. Marinate for 15 minutes.
Put the tomatoes, mozzarella, and basil and toss. Serve with balsamic vinegar on top.

Nutrition: Calories: 417 Carbs: 11g Fat: 24g Protein: 36g

Sushi Courgettes

Preparation Time: 20 minutes **Cooking Time:** 0 minutes **Servings:** 6

2 courgettes
130 ml. cream cheese
1 teaspoon sriracha hot sauce
1 teaspoon lime juice
130 grams lump crab meat
60 grams carrot
60 grams avocado
60 grams cucumber
1 teaspoon toasted sesame seeds

Slice each courgette into thin flat strips. Put aside. Combine cream cheese, sriracha, and lime juice in a medium-sized bowl. Place two slices of courgettes horizontally flat on a cutting board. Place a thin layer of cream cheese over it, then top the left with a piece of lobster, carrot, avocado, and cucumber. Roll up courgettes. Serve with sesame seeds.

Nutrition: Calories: 450 Carbs: 23g Fat: 25g Protein: 35g

Asian Chicken Lettuce Wraps

Preparation Time: 15 minutes **Cooking Time:** 15 minutes **Servings:** 4

3 tablespoon hoisin sauce
2 tablespoon low-sodium soy sauce
2 tablespoon rice wine vinegar
1 tablespoon Sriracha
1 teaspoon sesame oil
1 tablespoon extra-virgin olive oil
2 cloves garlic
1 tablespoon grated ginger
450 grams of ground chicken
60 grams chestnuts
2 green onions
Kosher salt
Ground black pepper
Large leafy lettuce
Cooked white rice

Make the sauce: Mix the hoisin sauce, soy sauce, rice wine vinegar, sriracha, and sesame oil in a small bowl. Mix the olive oil in a large pan, put the onions, cook for 5 minutes, stir in garlic and ginger, and cook for 1-minute. Put ground chicken and cook. Set in the sauce and cook for 1 to 2 minutes. Turn off the heat and put in the green onions and chestnuts. Season with pepper and salt. Add spoon rice of and chicken mixture to the center of a lettuce leaf. Serve.

Nutrition: Calories: 315 Carbs: 5g Fat: 12g Protein: 34g

California Burger Bowls

Preparation Time: 15 minutes **Cooking Time:** 20 minutes **Servings:** 4

For the dressing:
60 grams c. extra-virgin olive oil
40 ml balsamic vinegar
3 tablespoons Dijon mustard
2 teaspoons honey
One clove garlic
Kosher salt
Ground black pepper

For the burger:
450 grams of grass-fed organic ground beef
One teaspoon Worcestershire sauce
½ teaspoon chilli powder
½ teaspoon onion powder
Kosher salt

Ground black pepper
1 package of butterhead lettuce
1 medium red onion
1 avocado
2 tomatoes

Make the dressing: Mix the dressing ingredients in a medium bowl. Make burgers: Combine beef and Worcestershire sauce, chilli powder, and onion powder in another large bowl. Put pepper and salt, and mix. Grill the onions for 3 minutes each. Form into four patties. Remove and detach burgers from the grill pan—Cook for 4 minutes per side. Assemble: Put lettuce in a large bowl and add the dressing. Finish with a patty burger, grilled onions, 60 grams slices of avocado, and tomatoes. Serve.

Nutrition: Calories: 407 Carbs: 33g Fat: 19g Protein: 26g

Parmesan Brussels Sprouts Salad

Preparation Time: 15 minutes **Cooking Time:** 25 minutes **Servings:** 6

Olive oil
2 tablespoons lemon juice
60 grams parsley
Salt
Pepper
1kg Brussels sprouts
60 grams of toasted almonds
60 grams of pomegranate seeds
Shaved Parmesan

Mix olive oil, lemon juice, parsley, 2 teaspoons of salt, and one teaspoon of pepper. Add the sprouts in Brussels and toss.
Let sit before serving for 20 minutes and up to 4 hours. Fold in almonds and pomegranate seeds and garnish with a rasped parmesan. Serve.

Nutrition: Calories: 130 Carbs: 8g Fat: 9g Protein: 4g

Chicken Taco Avocados

Preparation Time: 15 minutes **Cooking Time:** 20 minutes **Servings:** 6

For the filling:
130 grams of black beans
130 grams of canned corn
120 grams of green chilies
130 grams rotisserie chicken
130 grams Cheddar
One package of taco seasoning
30 grams cilantro
Three ripe avocados
For the dressing:
130 ml. ranch dressing
64 ml. lime juice
1 tablespoon cilantro
1 teaspoon Kosher salt
1 teaspoon ground black pepper

Warm up the broiler to cook.
For the filling: Mix black beans, corn, 60 grams can of green chillies, shredded chicken, cheddar, taco seasoning, and fresh cilantro in a bowl. Halve three avocados and split, eliminating the pit. Mash the flesh in a small bowl inside and set it aside. Fill the avocado boats with 43 grams of filling. Put cheddar and fresher cilantro, then broil for 2 minutes.
Dressing: Mix ranch dressing, lime juice, remaining green chillies, cilantro, salt, and pepper. Remove avocado. Fold in mashed avocados. Serve with dressing and cilantro.

Nutrition: Calories: 324 Carbs: 16g Fat: 24g Protein: 15g

Keto Quesadillas

Preparation Time: 15 minutes **Cooking Time:** 25 minutes **Servings:** 4

15 grams. extra-virgin olive oil
One bell pepper
60 grams yellow onion
25 grams of chili powder
Kosher salt
Ground black pepper
400 grams Monterey Jack
400 grams Celsius grams cheddar
500 grams chicken
1 avocado
1 green onion
Sour cream

Warm-up oven to 200° Celsius, and line 2 medium parchment paper baking sheets. Warm-up oil in a medium skillet. Put the onion and pepper, chili powder, salt, and pepper. Cook for 5 minutes. Stir cheeses in a medium-sized dish. Put 60 grams of mixed cheese on prepared baking sheets. Form a circle, the size of a tortilla flour. Bake the cheeses for 8 to 10 minutes. Put a batter of onion-pepper, shredded chicken, and slices of avocado to one half each. Cool and fold one side of the "tortilla" cheese over the side with the fillings. Bake for 3 to 4 more minutes. Serve with green onion and sour cream.

Nutrition: Calories: 473 Carbs: 5g Fat: 41g Protein: 21g

No-Bread Italian Subs

Preparation Time: 15 minutes **Cooking Time:** 15 minutes **Servings:** 6

60 grams mayonnaise
2 tablespoons red wine vinegar
Olive oil
One small garlic clove, grated
1 teaspoon Italian seasoning
6 slices ham
12 salami slices
12 pepperoni slices
Six provolone slices
130 grams romaine
60 grams roasted red peppers

Make creamy Italian dressing: Mix the mayo, vinegar, butter, garlic, and Italian seasoning. Assemble sandwiches: Stack a ham slice, 2 salami pieces, 2 pepperoni slices, and a provolone slice. Put a handful of romaine and a couple of roasted red peppers. Put creamy Italian sauce, then roll in and eat.

Nutrition: Calories: 390 Protein: 16g Carbohydrates: 3g Fat: 34g

Basil Avocado Frail Salad Wraps & Sweet Potato Chips

Preparation Time: 15 minutes **Cooking Time:** 30 minutes **Servings:** 4

For the sweet potato chips:
Kosher salt
Ground black pepper
cooking spray
2 -3 medium potatoes

For the shrimp salad:
60 grams small red onion
20 large frails
100 grams halved grape tomatoes
Cooking spray
2 avocados
Four fresh basil leaves
2 large heads of butterhead lettuce

For the marinade:
2 lemon juice
2 cloves garlic
Three basil leaves
2 tablespoons white wine vinegar
3 tablespoons extra-virgin olive oil
½ teaspoon paprika
Salt
Pepper

For sweet potato chips: Warm up the oven to 220° celsius, then grease a large baking sheet. Put the sweet potatoes wedge with salt and pepper. Roast for 15 minutes, then flip and roast for 15 minutes. Cool and put aside.
For shrimp salad: Grease a large skillet and cook the shrimp, stirring for 2 minutes per side. Set aside.
For the marinade: Mix the lemon juice, garlic, basil, vinegar, butter, and paprika, and put salt and pepper. Stir the tomatoes, onion, avocados, and basil. Fold in the shrimps. Mix.
Serve with lettuce cups.

Nutrition: Calories: 80 Carbs: 19g Fat: 0g Protein: 1g

Cauliflower Leek Soup

Preparation Time: 15 minutes **Cooking Time:** 45 minutes **Servings:** 2

½ tablespoons olive oil
½ tablespoon garlic
½ tablespoons butter
250 grams of vegetable broth
1 leek
Salt
120 grams cauliflower
black pepper
30 grams of double cream

Put the oil and butter in the pan to heat. Add garlic, cauliflower, and leek pieces and cook for 5 minutes on low. Add vegetable broth and boil. Cover the pan and cook on low for 45 minutes. Remove, then blend the soup in a mixer. Put heavy cream, salt, and pepper, and mix more. Serve with salt and pepper.

Nutrition: Calories: 155 kcal Fats: 13.1 g Carbohydrates: 8.3 g Proteins: 2.4 g

Sugar-Free Blueberry Cottage Cheese Parfaits

Preparation Time: 5 minutes **Cooking Time:** 5 minutes **Servings:** 2

225 g cheese, low fat
1/8 tablespoon cinnamon
60 grams vanilla extract
6 drops of stevia, liquid
150 grams berries

Blend cheese, vanilla extract, cinnamon, and stevia into the blender. Remove and pour these into bowls. Put the berries on top of the cheese parfaits. Serve.

Nutrition: Calories: 125 kcal Fats: 2.2 g Carbohydrates: 12.5 g Proteins: 14.8g Fiber: 1.5 g

Low-Carb Broccoli Leek Soup

Preparation Time: 15 minutes **Cooking Time:** 15 minutes **Servings:** 2

60 grams leek
100 grams of cream cheese
50 grams broccoli
60 grams of double cream
120 ml. water
60 grams tablespoon black pepper
60 grams vegetable bouillon cube
30 grams basil
5 grams garlic
Salt

Put water into a pan and put broccoli chopped, leek chopped, and salt—boil on high. Simmer on low. Put the remaining ingredients, and simmer for 1 minute. Remove. Blend the soup mixture into a blender. Serve.

Nutrition: Calories: 545 kcal Fats: 50 g Carbohydrates: 10 g Proteins: 15g

Low-Carb Chicken Taco Soup

Preparation Time: 10 minutes **Cooking Time:** 12 minutes **Servings:** 2

120 ml. chicken broth
60 grams tomatoes
60 grams of boneless chicken
4 green chilies
60 grams package of cream cheese
1 tablespoon seasoning

Put chicken broth, boneless chicken, cheese, tomatoes, and green chillies in a pressure cooker—Cook for 10 minutes. Remove. Shred the chicken. Put shredded chicken in the soup and stir. Put Italian seasoning. Serve.

Nutrition: Calories: 239 Fats: 12 g Carbohydrates: 3 g Proteins: 26 g

Keto Chicken & Veggies Soup

Preparation Time: 5 minutes **Cooking Time:** 30 minutes **Servings:** 2

1 tablespoon olive oil
130 ml. chicken broth
60 grams onion
¼ tablespoon Italian seasoning
2 bell peppers
1 tablespoon of Bay leaves
½ tablespoon garlic
Sea salt
30 grams of green beans
Black pepper
60 grams tomatoes
2 chicken breast pieces

Massage the chicken with salt and pepper and grill for 10 minutes. Put onions and bell pepper into heated oil and simmer for 5-6 minutes. Add all leftover ingredients and simmer for 15 minutes on low. Remove. Serve.

Nutrition: Calories: 79 Fats: 2g Carbohydrates: 11 g Proteins: 2g — Fiber: 3 g

Low-Carb Seafood Soup with Mayo

Preparation Time: 15 minutes **Cooking Time:** 40 minutes **Servings:** 2

¼ tablespoon olive oil
½ chopped onion
¼ tablespoon garlic
250 ml. fish broth
1 tomato
Thyme

Salt
Garlic Mayo
90 grams Whitefish
Olive oil
30 grams shrimps
Garlic clove

30 grams mussels
1 egg
30 grams scallops
½ tablespoon lemon juice
1/3 bay leaf
Salt
1/2 lime

Cook onions and garlic in heated olive oil. Put broth, bay leaf, tomatoes, and salt. After boiling, cover for 20 minutes on low flame. Add all fixing and cook for 4 minutes. Blend garlic mayo in the blender and put olive oil. Put the mayo on the top middle and serve with thyme and lime.

Nutrition: Calories: 592 kcal Fats: 47g Net Carbohydrates: 8 g Proteins: 27 g

Keto Tortilla Chips

Preparation Time: 10 minutes **Cooking Time:** 40 minutes **Servings:** 2

60 grams cube of mozzarella cheese
¼ teaspoon cumin powder
20 grams of almond flour
1 teaspoon coriander
1 tablespoon cream cheese
Chilli powder
1 egg
Salt

Microwave the mozzarella cheese, cream cheese, and flour for 30 seconds. Stir and set for 30 seconds more. Put spices and egg into the cheese mixture to make the dough. Put the dough in 2 pieces of parchment paper in a large rectangular form. Remove the parchment paper. Remove and cut into rectangular chips. Bake for 15 minutes to 200° Celsius-degree F. Bake the other side of the dough in the same way. Bake again for 2 minutes and serve.

Nutrition: Calories: 198 Fats: 16 g Carbohydrates: 4 g Proteins: 11 g

Chicken Alfredo

Preparation Time: 15 minutes **Cooking Time:** 30 minutes **Servings:** 2

100 grams of chicken breast
Basil
100 grams Courgettes
90 grams cauliflower
40 grams of cream cheese
Mayo
Black pepper
1 teaspoon olive oil
1 teaspoon garlic

Marinate chicken with basil, salt, and pepper. Grill the chicken and set it aside. Add oil, garlic, and zucchini and cook for 8 to 10 minutes. Put cream cheese in the courgettes with salt and pepper. Let the cauliflower steam in the water. Mash the steamed cauliflower and put salt, pepper, and herbs. Serve with mashed cauliflowers and enjoy an excellent lunch.

Nutrition: Calories: 262.4 Fats: 9.8 g Carbohydrates: 13.7 g Proteins: 30.2g Fiber: 3.8 g

Low Carbs Chicken Cheese

Preparation Time: 10 minutes **Cooking Time:** 20 minutes **Servings:** 2

150 grams of chicken breast
Salt
½ tablespoon Italian seasoning
Pepper
½ teaspoon paprika
½ onion
¼ teaspoon onion powder
1 teaspoon garlic
½ tablespoon olive oil
½ fire-roasted pepper
425 grams tomato
Red pepper flakes
½ tablespoon parsley
30 grams of mozzarella cheese

Marinate the chicken with salt, pepper, onion powder, and seasoning. Cook the chicken on low for 15 minutes. Put the onion and all fixing except cheese and simmer for 7 minutes. Put this sauce into a dish and place the cheese on the top of the chicken pieces. Warm-up for 1 to 2 minutes. Garnish with parsley and serve.

Nutrition: Calories: 309 Fats: 9 g Carbohydrates: 9 g Proteins: 37g Fiber: 3 g

Lemon Chicken Spaghetti Squash Boats

Preparation Time: 10 minutes **Cooking Time:** 1 hour and 10 minutes **Servings:** 2

60 grams spaghetti squash
60 grams onion
1 tablespoon olive oil
1 tablespoon garlic
500 grams of chicken breast
300 g cherry tomatoes
Sea Salt
60 grams of chicken broth
Black pepper
½ tablespoon lime
130 grams spinach

Combine the olive oil, salt, and pepper into the half squash—Bake for 40 minutes. Stir fry the chicken pieces in olive oil.

Remove the chicken and pour 11 teaspoons more olive oil with onions. Put garlic and stir. Put salt, pepper, and tomatoes, and simmer. Put the lemon juice and chicken broth, and cook for 15 minutes. Put chicken and spinach and cook for 3 to 4 minutes.

Shred the baked squash. Pour the sauce on the top of the shredded squash and serve.

Nutrition: Calories: 234 kcal Fats: 10 g Carbohydrates: 10 g Proteins: 26 g Fiber: 3 g

Stuffed Portobello Mushrooms

Preparation Time: 5 minutes **Cooking Time:** 10 minutes **Servings:** 2

¼ tablespoon butter
Balsamic glaze
1 clove garlic
100 g mozzarella cheese
1 teaspoon parsley
30 grams tomatoes
2 large Portobello mushrooms

Set the oven to 220° Celsius. Warm up the butter and stir the garlic. Grease the bottoms of the mushrooms with butter and place the butter side down on the baking dish. Fill in the mushrooms with the cheese slices and tomato slices. Broil in the microwave.

Top the mushrooms with salt, basil, and balsamic glaze. Serve.

Nutrition: Calories: 101 kcal Fats: 5 g Carbohydrates: 12 g Proteins: 2 g

Low Carbs Mexican Stuffed Bell Peppers

Preparation Time: 10 minutes **Cooking Time:** 20 minutes **Servings:** 2

1 large bell pepper
¼ teaspoon chipotle chili
1 teaspoon coconut oil
Cinnamon
250 g grounded beef
40 grams of Tomato puree
1 large onion
30 grams of cheddar cheese
1 teaspoon grounded cumin
Cilantro leaves
½ tablespoon chili powder

Bake the bell peppers in a baking dish for 5 minutes. Cook grounded beef and cook for 10 minutes. Put onions and mushrooms and cook. Put cumin, chilli powder, cinnamon, chipotle, and salt, then cook. Remove and put tomato puree, then stir. Fill the peppers with beef mixture and with cheese plus cilantro. Microwave for 1 minute, then serve.

Nutrition: Calories: 247 kcal Fats: 15 g Carbohydrates: 9 g Proteins: 22 g Fiber: 4 g

Low-Carb Broccoli Mash

Preparation Time: 10 minutes **Cooking Time:** 5 minutes **Servings:** 2

325 grams broccoli
60 grams clove garlic
60 grams parsley
Salt
½ teaspoon dried thyme
40 grams butter
Pepper

Put salt into the water and boil. Put broccoli florets and cook for a few minutes. Remove the water and separate the soft broccoli. Place all fixing in a blender and pulse. Serve.

Nutrition: Calories: 210 kcal Fats: 18 g Carbohydrates: 7 g Proteins: 5 g Fiber: 18 g

Roasted Tri-Color Vegetables

Preparation Time: 10 minutes **Cooking Time:** 30 minutes **Servings:** 2

150 grams of Brussels sprouts
Black pepper grounded
75 grams of cherry tomatoes

1 teaspoon dried thyme
75 grams mushrooms, chopped
3 tablespoons olive oil
Salt

Warm up the microwave oven to 220° Celsius. Put all vegetables in a baking dish. Mix in salt, pepper, and oil—Bake for 20 minutes. Serve.

Nutrition: Calories: 208 kcal Fats: 18 g Carbohydrates: 6 g Proteins: 4 g Fiber: 4g

Easy Keto Smoked Salmon Lunch Bowl

Preparation Time: 15 minutes **Cooking Time:** 0 minutes **Servings:** 2

340 grams of smoked salmon
4 tablespoons mayonnaise
56 grams spinach
1 teaspoon olive oil
1 medium lime
Pepper
Salt

PArrange the mayonnaise, salmon, and spinach on a plate. Sprinkle olive oil over the spinach. Serve with lime wedges and put salt plus pepper.

Nutrition: Calories: 457 Net Carbs: 1.9g Fats: 34.8g Protein: 32.3g

Easy One-Pan Ground Beef and Green Beans

Preparation Time: 15 minutes **Cooking Time:** 15 minutes **Servings:** 2

300 grams of ground beef
200 grams of green beans
Pepper
Salt
2 tablespoons sour cream
200 grams butter

Warm up the butter to a pan over high heat. Put the ground beef plus the pepper and salt. Cook. Reduce heat to medium. Add the remaining butter and the green beans, then cook for five minutes. Put pepper and salt, then transfer. Serve with a dollop of sour cream.

Nutrition: Net Carbs: 6.65g Calories: 787.5 Fats: 71.75g Protein: 27.5g

Easy Spinach and Bacon Salad

Preparation Time: 15 minutes **Cooking Time:** 15 minutes **Servings:** 4

250 grams spinach
4 large, hard-boiled eggs
150 grams bacon
2 medium red onions
250 grams of mayonnaise
Pepper
Salt
½ teaspoon dried thyme
40 grams butter
Pepper

Cook the bacon, then chop it into pieces and set it aside. Slice the hard-boiled eggs, and then rinse the spinach. Combine the lettuce, mayonnaise, and bacon fat into a large cup, and put pepper and salt. Add the red onion, sliced eggs, and bacon into the salad, then toss. Serve.

Nutrition: Fats: 45.9g Calories: 509.15 Net Carbs: 2.5g Protein: 19.75g

Easy Keto Italian Plate

Preparation Time: 15 minutes **Cooking Time:** 0 minutes **Servings:** 2

200 grams of mozzarella cheese
200 grams prosciutto
2 tomatoes
Olive oil
10 whole green olives
Pepper
Salt

Arrange the tomato, olives, mozzarella, and prosciutto on a plate. Season the tomato and cheese with pepper and salt. Serve with olive oil.

Nutrition: Calories: 780.98 Fat: 60.74g Carbohydrates: 5.9g Protein: 50.87g

Fresh Broccoli and Dill Keto Salad

Preparation Time: 15 minutes **Cooking Time:** 7 minutes **Servings:** 3

500 grams broccoli
60 grams mayonnaise
60 grams dill, chopped
Salt
Pepper

Boil salted water in a saucepan. Put the chopped broccoli in the pot and boil for 3-5 minutes. Drain and set aside. Once cooled, mix the rest of the fixing. Put pepper and salt, then serve.

Nutrition: Calories: 303.33 Fat: 28.1g Carbohydrates: 6.2g Protein: 4.03g

Keto Smoked Salmon Filled Avocados

Preparation Time: 15 minutes **Cooking Time:** 0 minutes **Servings:** 1

1 avocado
40 grams of smoked salmon
4 tablespoons sour cream
1 tablespoon lemon juice
Pepper
Salt

Cut the avocado into two equal pieces. Put pepper and salt, and squeeze lemon juice over the top. Place the sour cream in the hollow parts of the avocado with smoked salmon. Serve.

Nutrition: Calories: 517 Carbohydrates: 6.7g Fat: 42.6g Protein: 20.6g

Low-Carb Broccoli Lemon Parmesan Soup

Preparation Time: 15 minutes **Cooking Time:** 15 minutes **Servings:** 4

380 ml. of water
120 ml. unsweetened almond milk
356 grams of broccoli florets
120 ml. heavy whipping cream
40 grams Parmesan cheese
Salt
Pepper
2 tablespoons lemon juice

Cook broccoli with water over medium-high heat. Take out 120 grams of the cooking liquid and remove the rest. Blend half the broccoli, reserved cooking oil, unsweetened almond milk, heavy cream, and salt plus pepper in a blender. Put the blended ingredients into the remaining broccoli and stir with Parmesan cheese and lemon juice. Cook until heated through. Serve with Parmesan cheese on the top.

Nutrition: Calories: 371 Fat: 28.38g Carbohydrates: 11.67g Protein: 14.63g

Prosciutto and Mozzarella Bomb

Preparation Time: 15 minutes **Cooking Time:** 10 minutes **Servings:** 4

120 grams sliced prosciutto
230 grams of mozzarella balls
Olive oil

Layer half of the prosciutto vertically. Lay the remaining slices horizontally across the first set of slices. Place the mozzarella ball, upside down, onto the crisscrossed prosciutto slices. Wrap the mozzarella ball with the prosciutto slices. Warm up the olive oil in a skillet, crisp the prosciutto, and serve.

Nutrition: Calories: 253 Fat: 19.35g Carbohydrates: 1.08g Protein: 18g

Summer Tuna Avocado Salad

Preparation Time: 15 minutes **Cooking Time:** 0 minutes **Servings:** 2

1 can tuna flake
1 medium avocado
1 medium cucumber
30 grams cilantro
1 tablespoon lemon juice
1 tablespoon olive oil
Olive oil
Pepper
Salt

Chop the tuna flake, avocado, cucumber, and cilantro, and transfer it into a salad bowl. Toss well to combine. Sprinkle with the lemon and olive oil. Serve.

Nutrition: Calories 303 Fat: 22.6g Carbohydrates: 5.2g Protein: 16.7g

Mushrooms & Goat Cheese Salad

Preparation Time: 15 minutes **Cooking Time:** 10 minutes **Servings:** 1

1 tablespoon butter
56 grams cremini mushrooms
Pepper
Salt
120 grams spring mix
30 grams cooked bacon
30 grams goat cheese
1 tablespoon olive oil
1 tablespoon balsamic vinegar

Sautee the mushrooms, and put pepper and salt. Place the salad greens in a bowl. Top with goat cheese and crumbled bacon.
Whisk the olive oil in a small bowl and balsamic vinegar. Mix these in the salad once the mushrooms are done. Put the salad on top and serve.

Nutrition: Calories: 243 Fat: 21g Carbohydrates: 8g Protein: 20g

Keto Bacon Sushi

Preparation Time: 15 minutes **Cooking Time:** 13 minutes **Servings:** 4

6 slices bacon
1 avocado
2 cucumbers
2 medium carrots
120 grams of cream cheese

Warm-up oven to 200° Celsius. Line a baking sheet. Place bacon halves in an even layer and bake for 11 to 13 minutes. Meanwhile, slice cucumbers, avocado, and carrots into parts roughly the width of the bacon. Spread an even layer of cream cheese in the cooled-down bacon. Divide vegetables evenly and place them on one end. Roll up vegetables tightly. Garnish and serve.

Nutrition: Calories: 345 Fat: 30g Carbohydrates: 11g Protein: 28g

Cole Slaw Keto Wrap

Preparation Time: 15 minutes **Cooking Time:** 0 minutes **Servings:** 2

300 grams of Red Cabbage
150 grams of Green Onions
50 grams Mayonaise
6 ml. Apple Cider Vinegar
Salt
16 collard greens
500 grams Ground Meat, cooked
Alfalfa Sprouts
Toothpicks

Mix slaw ingredients with a spoon in a large-sized bowl. Place a collard green on a plate and scoop a tablespoon of coleslaw on the edge of the leaf. Top it with a scoop of meat and sprouts. Roll and tuck the sides. Insert the toothpicks. Serve.

Nutrition: Calories: 409 Fat: 42g Carbohydrates: 4g Protein: 2g

Keto Chicken Club Lettuce Wrap

Preparation Time: 15 minutes **Cooking Time:** 15 minutes **Servings:** 1

1 head of iceberg lettuce
1 tablespoon mayonnaise
6 slices of organic chicken
Bacon
Tomato

Cut it in half. Layer 6-8 large lettuce leaves in the center of the parchment paper, around 9-10 inches. Spread the mayo in the center and lay with chicken, bacon, and tomato. Roll the wrap halfway through, then roll tuck in the ends of the wrap. Serve.

Nutrition: Calories: 837 Fat: 78g Carbohydrates: 15g Protein: 28g

Keto Broccoli Salad

Preparation Time: 10 minutes **Cooking Time:** 0 minutes **Servings:** 4-6

For salad:
2 broccoli
2 red cabbage
5 c sliced almonds
1 green onion
20 grams raisins
For the orange almond dressing
33 c orange juice
25 c almond butter
1 tablespoon coconut aminos
1 shallot
Salt

Using a blender, pulse the salt, shallot, amino, nut butter, and orange juice. Combine other fixing in a bowl. Toss it with dressing and serve.

Nutrition: Calories: 1022 Fat: 94g Carbohydrates: 13g Protein: 22g

Keto Sheet Pan Chicken and Rainbow Veggies

Preparation Time: 15 minutes **Cooking Time:** 25 minutes **Servings:** 4

Nonstick spray
500 grams of Chicken Breasts
Sesame oil
Soy sauce
30 grams Honey
2 Red Peppers
2 Yellow Peppers
3 Carrots
60 grams broccoli
2 Red Onions
1 tablespoon EVOO
Pepper & salt
Parsley

Grease the baking sheet, and warm up the oven to 200° Celsius. Put the chicken in the middle of the sheet. Separately, combine the oil and the soy sauce. Brush over the chicken. Separate veggies across the plate. Sprinkle with oil and then toss. Put pepper & salt. Set tray into the oven and cook for 25 minutes. Garnish using parsley. Serve.

Nutrition: Calories: 437 Carbohydrates: 9g Fat: 30g Protein: 30g

Skinny Bang-Bang Courgette Noodles

Preparation Time: 15 minutes **Cooking Time:** 15 minutes **Servings:** 4

For the noodles:
4 medium courgettes spiraled
1 tablespoon olive oil
For the sauce:
2 tablespoons plain Greek yoghurt
2 tablespoons mayo
2 tablespoons Thai sweet chili sauce
1.5 teaspoons Honey
1.5 teaspoons Sriracha
2 teaspoons Lime Juice

Pour the oil into a large skillet at medium temperature. Stir in the spirallased courgettes noodles. Cook well until they get soft.
Combine sauce ingredients into a bowl. Mix the noodles into the sauce. Remove, then drain, and let it rest for 10 minutes. Serve.
Nutrition: Calories: 189 Fat: 1g Carbohydrates: 18g Protein: 9g

Keto Caesar Salad

Preparation Time: 15 minutes **Cooking Time:** 0 minutes **Servings:** 4

5 grams Mayonnaise
3 tablespoons Apple Cider Vinegar
1 teaspoon Dijon Mustard
4 Anchovy Fillets
24 Romaine Heart Leaves
200 grams of Pork Rinds
Parmesan

Process the mayo with ACV, mustard, and anchovies into a blender. Prepare romaine leaves and pour the dressing. Top with pork rinds and serve.

Nutrition: Calories: 993 Fat: 86g Carbohydrates: 4g Protein: 47g

Keto Buffalo Chicken Empanadas

Preparation Time: 20 minutes **Cooking Time:** 30 minutes **Servings:** 6

For the empanada dough:
150 grams of mozzarella cheese
90 grams of cream cheese
One whisked egg
250 grams of almond flour
For the buffalo chicken filling:
250 grams of shredded chicken
2 tablespoons butter
20 grams of Hot Sauce

Warm-up oven, 220° Celsius. Microwave the cheese & cream cheese for 1-minute. Stir the flour and egg into the dish. With another bowl, combine the chicken with sauce and set aside.   Cover a flat surface with plastic wrap and sprinkle with almond flour. Grease a rolling pin, and press the dough flat. Make the circle shapes out of this dough with a lid. Portion spoonfuls of filling into these dough circles. Fold the other half over to close up into half-moon shapes—Bake for 9 minutes. Serve.

Nutrition: Calories: 1217 Fat: 96g Carbohydrates: 20g Protein: 74g

Pepperoni and Cheddar Stromboli

Preparation Time: 15 minutes **Cooking Time:** 20 minutes **Servings:** 3

150 grams of Mozzarella Cheese
50 grams of Almond Flour
3 tablespoons Coconut Flour
1 teaspoon Italian Seasoning
1 Egg
150 grams Deli Ham
90 grams Pepperoni
190 grams of Cheddar Cheese
1 tablespoon butter
600 grams Salad Greens

Warm up the oven to 200° Celsius. Melt the mozzarella—mix flours & Italian seasoning in a separate bowl. Dump in the melty cheese and mix with pepper and salt. Stir in the egg and process the dough. Pour it onto that prepared baking tray.   Roll out the dough. Cut slits that mark out four equal rectangles. Put the ham and cheese, then brush with butter and close up. Bake for 17 minutes. Slice and serve.

Nutrition: Calories: 240 Fat: 13g Carbohydrates: 20g Protein: 11g

Tuna Casserole

Preparation Time: 15 minutes **Cooking Time:** 10 minutes **Servings:** 4

1 can tuna
50 grams butter
Salt
Black pepper
1 teaspoon chili powder
6 stalks celery
1 bell pepper, green
1 yellow onion
115 grams of parmesan cheese
130 grams mayonnaise

Warm-up oven to 200° Celsius. Fry the onion, bell pepper, and celery chops in the melted butter for five minutes. Mix with chilli powder, parmesan cheese, tuna, and mayonnaise. Grease a baking pan. Add the tuna mixture to the fried vegetables.
Bake for twenty minutes. Serve.

Nutrition: Calories 953 Fat: 83g Carbohydrates: 5g Protein: 43g

Brussels Sprout and Hamburger Gratin

Preparation Time: 15 minutes **Cooking Time:** 20 minutes **Servings:** 4

500 grams of ground beef
150 grams bacon
150 grams of brussels sprouts
Salt
Black pepper
½ teaspoon thyme
130 grams cheese, cheddar
1 tablespoon Italian seasoning
2 tablespoons butter
4 tablespoons sour cream

Warm-up oven to 200° Celsius. Fry bacon and Brussel sprouts in butter for five minutes. Stir in the sour cream and put it into a greased baking pan. Cook the ground beef and put salt and pepper, then add this mix to the baking pan. Top with the herbs and the shredded cheese. Bake for twenty minutes. Serve.

Nutrition: Calories: 770 Fat: 62g Carbohydrates: 8g Protein: 42g

Carpaccio

Preparation Time: 15 minutes **Cooking Time:** 5 minutes **Servings:** 4

100 grams smoked prime rib
30 grams Rocket
20 grams Parmesan cheese
10 grams of pine nuts
7 grams of butter
3 tablespoons olive oil with orange
1 tablespoon lemon juice
Pepper
Salt

Arrange the meat slices on a plate. Place the rocket on top of the meat —spread Parmesan cheese over the missile. Put the butter in a frying pan. Add the pine nuts, bake for a few minutes over medium heat and then sprinkle them over the carpaccio. Mix the lemon juice into the olive oil for the vinaigrette, put pepper and salt, and drizzle over the carpaccio. Serve.

Nutrition: Calories: 350 Fat: 24g Carbohydrates: 2g Protein: 31g

Keto Croque Monsieur

Preparation Time: 15 minutes **Cooking Time:** 7 minutes **Servings:** 4

2 eggs
25 grams of grated cheese
25 grams ham
40 ml of cream
40 grams mascarpone
30 grams of butter
Pepper
Salt
Basil leaves

Beat eggs in a bowl, and put salt and pepper. Add the cream, mascarpone, and grated cheese and mix. Melt the butter over medium heat. Adjust the heat to low. Add half of the omelet mixture to the frying pan, and then place the slice of ham. Put the rest of the omelet mixture over the ham. Fry for 2-3 minutes over low heat. Then put the omelet back in the frying pan to fry for another 1-2 minutes. Garnish with a few basil leaves. Serve.

Nutrition: Calories: 350 Fat: 24g Carbohydrates: 2g Protein: 31g

Keto Wraps with Cream Cheese and Salmon

Preparation Time: 15 minutes **Cooking Time:** 10 minutes **Servings:** 4

80 grams of cream cheese
1 tablespoon dill
30 grams smoked salmon
1 egg
15 grams of butter
Pinch cayenne pepper
Pepper
Salt

Beat the egg well in a bowl. Dissolve the butter over medium heat in a small frying pan. Put half of the beaten egg into the pan. Carefully loosen the egg on the edges with a silicone spatula and turn the wafer-thin omelet for about 45 seconds on each side. Remove. Cut the dill into small pieces and put them in a bowl. Add the cream cheese and the salmon, and cut into small pieces. Mix. Put a cayenne pepper and mix. Put salt and pepper. Spread a layer on the wrap and roll it up. Cut the wrap in half and serve.

Nutrition: Calories: 479 Fat: 45g Carbohydrates: 4g Protein: 16 g

Savory Keto Broccoli Cheese Muffins

Preparation Time: 15 minutes **Cooking Time:** 10 minutes **Servings:** 4

4 eggs
75 grams Parmesan cheese
125 grams of young cheese
125 grams mozzarella
75 grams of broccoli
1.5 teaspoon baking powder
0.25 teaspoon garlic powder
0.25 teaspoon mustard

Warm up the oven to 160° Celsius. Boil water into a saucepan, and put the broccoli pieces for 1 minute. Drain. Grate the Parmesan cheese and the young cheese. Cut the mozzarella into small pieces. Beat the eggs, and put the broccoli, cheese, and mustard. Then add the garlic powder and baking powder and mix. Add baking powder and garlic powder. Fill a silicone muffin tray with the broccoli-cheese egg batter and bake for 10 minutes. Serve.

Nutrition: Calories: 349 Fat: 25g Carbohydrates: 3g Protein: 28g

Keto Rusk

Preparation Time: 15 minutes **Cooking Time:** 9 minutes **Servings:** 6

35 grams of almond flour
1 egg
1 tablespoon butter
0.5 teaspoon baking powder
1/8 teaspoon salt

Warm-up oven to 200° Celsius. Put all the fixing in a cup and mix—microwave for 90 seconds. Cooldown and cut the dough into 5 equal slices and place it on a sheet with baking paper. Bake for 5-6 minutes, then serve.

Nutrition: Calories: 256 Fat: 4g Protein: 22g Carbohydrates: 25g

Flaxseed Hemp Flour Bun

Preparation Time: 15 minutes **Cooking Time:** 8 minutes **Servings:** 4

1 teaspoon hemp flour
1 teaspoon linseed flour
1 teaspoon psyllium
1 teaspoon baking powder
1 egg
0.5 teaspoon butter

Warm-up oven to 180°C. Put all dry ingredients in a large bowl, and mix. Add the egg and the butter, then remix it—microwave for 1 minute. Remove the sandwich and cut it into three slices. Bake those slices for 5 minutes.
Serve.

Nutrition: Calories: 182 Fat: 15g Carbohydrates: 14g Protein: 11g

Keto Wrap

Preparation Time: 15 minutes **Cooking Time:** 5 minutes **Servings:** 2

1 egg
0.5 teaspoon coconut fat
0.5 teaspoon curry powder

Warm-up coconut fat in a small frying pan over high heat. Beat the egg plus the curry powder with salt in a bowl. Put the batter into the frying pan. Bake this wafer-thin omelet for 10-20 seconds. Turn the wrap over and bake for a few seconds. Serve.

Nutrition: Calories: 128 Protein: 6g Fat: 12g Carbohydrates: 1 g

Savory Keto Muffins

Preparation Time: 15 minutes **Cooking Time:** 20 minutes **Servings:** 5

4 eggs
1 forest outing
100 grams chorizo
75 grams mascarpone
100 grams grated cheese
Salt
Pepper

Warm-up oven to 175° Celsius. Beat the eggs with the mascarpone. Add the spring onion, cheese, and chorizo to the egg batter. Put salt and pepper. Mix. Bake for 9 - 14 minutes. Cooldown and serve.

Nutrition: Calories: 315 Protein: 17g Fat: 26g Carbohydrates: 4g

Quick Pumpkin Soup

Preparation Time: 10 minutes **Cooking Time:** 20 minutes **Servings:** 4-6

120 ml. coconut milk
250 ml. chicken broth
600 grams of baked pumpkin
1 teaspoon garlic powder
1 teaspoon ground cinnamon
1 teaspoon dried ginger
1 teaspoon nutmeg
1 teaspoon paprika
Salt and pepper (to taste)
Sour cream or coconut yoghurt (for topping)
Pumpkin seeds (toasted for topping)

Combine the coconut milk, broth, baked pumpkin, and spices in a soup pan (use medium heat). Stir occasionally and simmer for 15 minutes. With an immersion blender, blend the soup mixture for 1 minute. Top with sour cream or coconut yoghurt and pumpkin seeds.

Nutrition: Calories: 569 **Fat:** 9.8g **Carbohydrates:** 8.1g **Protein:** 3.1g

Fresh Avocado Soup

Preparation Time: 5 minutes **Cooking Time:** 10 minutes **Servings:** 2

1 ripe avocado
2 romaine lettuce leaves (washed and chopped)
130 ml. of coconut milk (chilled)
1 tablespoon lime juice
20 fresh mint leaves
Salt (to taste)

Mix all your ingredients thoroughly in a blender. Chill in the fridge for 5-10 minutes.

Nutrition: Calories: 280 **Fat:** 26g **Carbohydrates:** 12g **Protein:** 4g

Creamy Garlic Chicken

Preparation Time: 5 minutes **Cooking Time:** 15 minutes **Servings:** 4

4 chicken breasts (finely sliced)
1 teaspoon garlic powder
1 teaspoon paprika
2 tablespoon butter
1 teaspoon salt
130 grams of heavy cream
60 grams of sun-dried tomatoes
2 cloves garlic (minced)
130 grams of spinach (chopped)

Blend the paprika, garlic powder, and salt and sprinkle over both sides of the chicken. Melt the butter in a frying pan (choose medium heat). Add the chicken breast and fry for 5 minutes on each side. Set aside. Add the heavy cream, sun-dried tomatoes, and garlic to the pan and whisk well to combine—Cook for 2 minutes. Add spinach and sauté for an additional 3 minutes. Return the chicken to the pan and cover it with the sauce.

Nutrition: Calories: 330 **Fat:** 26g **Carbohydrates:** 12g **Protein:** 36g

Shrimp Scampi with Garlic

Preparation Time: 5 minutes **Cooking Time:** 10 minutes **Servings:** 4

500 grams of shrimp
3 tablespoons olive oil
1 bulb of shallot (sliced)
4 cloves of garlic (minced)
64 ml. pinot grigio
4 tablespoon salted butter
1 tablespoon lemon juice
½ teaspoon sea salt
¼ teaspoon black pepper
¼ teaspoon red pepper flakes
30 grams of parsley (chopped)

Pour the olive oil into the heated frying pan. Add the garlic and shallots and fry for about 2 minutes. Combine the Pinot Grigio, salted butter, and lemon juice. Pour this mixture into the pan and cook for 5 minutes. Put the parsley, black pepper, red pepper flakes, and sea salt into the pan and whisk well. Add the shrimp and fry until they are pink (about 3 minutes).

Nutrition: Calories: 344 **Fat:** 7g **Carbohydrates:** 7g **Protein:** 32g

Chinese Pork Bowl

Preparation Time: 5 minutes **Cooking Time:** 15 minutes **Servings:** 4

160 grams pounds of pork belly (cut into bite-size pieces)
2 tablespoons tamari soy sauce
1 tablespoon rice vinegar
2 cloves of garlic (smashed)
60 grams butter
500 grams of Brussels sprouts (rinsed, trimmed, halved, or quartered)
60 grams leek (chopped)
Salt
Pepper

Fry the pork over medium-high heat until it starts to turn golden brown. Combine the garlic cloves, butter, and Brussels sprouts. Add to the pan, whisk well and cook until the sprouts turn golden brown. Stir the soy sauce and rice vinegar together and pour the sauce into the pan. Sprinkle with salt and pepper. Top with chopped leek.

Nutrition: Calories: 993 **Fat:** 97g **Carbohydrates:** 7g **Protein:** 19g

Chicken Pan with Veggies and Pesto

Preparation Time: 10 minutes **Cooking Time:** 20 minutes **Servings:** 4

2 tablespoons olive oil
500 grams of chicken thighs (skinless, boneless, sliced into strips)
90 grams of oil-packed sun-dried tomatoes (chopped)
500 grams of asparagus ends
30 grams of basil pesto
120 grams of cherry tomatoes (red and yellow, halved)
Salt (to taste)

Heat olive oil in a frying pan over medium-high heat. Put salt on the chicken slices and then put it into a skillet, add the sun-dried tomatoes and fry for 5–10 minutes. Remove the chicken slices and season with salt. Add asparagus to the skillet. Cook for additional 5–10 minutes. Place the chicken back in the skillet, pour in the pesto, and whisk. Fry for 1–2 minutes. Remove from the heat. Add the halved cherry tomatoes and pesto. Stir well and serve.

Nutrition: Calories: 423 **Fat:** 32g **Carbohydrates:** 12g **Protein:** 2g

Cabbage Soup with Beef

Preparation Time: 15 minutes **Cooking Time:** 20 minutes **Servings:** 4

2 tablespoons olive oil
1 medium onion (chopped)
500 grams of fillet steak (cut into pieces)
60 grams stalk celery (chopped)
1 carrot (peeled and chopped)
60 grams head of small green cabbage (cut into pieces)
2 cloves of garlic (minced)

500 ml. of beef broth
2 tablespoons of fresh parsley (chopped)
1 teaspoon dried thyme
1 teaspoon dried rosemary
1 teaspoon garlic powder
Salt and black pepper (to taste)

Heat olive oil in a frying pan over medium-high heat. Put salt on the chicken slices and then put it into a skillet, add the sun-dried tomatoes and fry for 5–10 minutes. Remove the chicken slices and season with salt. Add asparagus to the skillet. Cook for additional 5–10 minutes. Place the chicken back in the skillet, pour in the pesto, and whisk. Fry for 1–2 minutes. Remove from the heat. Add the halved cherry tomatoes and pesto. Stir well and serve.

Nutrition: Calories: 423 **Fat:** 32g **Carbohydrates:** 12g **Protein:** 2g

Cauliflower Rice Soup with Chicken

Preparation Time: 10 minutes **Cooking Time:** 1-hour **Servings:** 5

300 grams of chicken breasts (boneless and skinless)
8 tablespoons butter
30 grams celery (chopped)
70 grams onion (chopped)
4 cloves garlic (minced)
200 grams of cauliflower rice
1 tablespoon parsley (chopped)
2 teaspoons of poultry seasoning
70 grams carrots, grated
¾ teaspoon rosemary
Salt
¾ teaspoon pepper
150 grams of cream cheese
200 ml. chicken broth

Put shredded chicken breasts into a saucepan and pour in the chicken broth. Add salt and pepper. Cook for 1 hour. In another pot, melt the butter. Add the onion, garlic, and celery. Sauté until the mix is translucent. Add the riced cauliflower, rosemary, and carrot. Mix and cook for 7 minutes. Add the chicken breasts and broth to the cauliflower mix. Put the lid on & simmer for 15 minutes.

Nutrition: Calories: 415 **Fat:** 30g **Carbohydrates:** 6g **Protein:** 27g

Baked Courgettes Noodles with Feta

Preparation Time: 15 minutes **Cooking Time:** 15 minutes **Servings:** 1

1 plum tomato
2 courgettes
8 cubes of Feta cheese
1 teaspoon pepper
1 tablespoon olive oil

Set the oven temperature to reach 170° Celsius. Slice the noodles with a spiralizer and put the olive oil, tomatoes, pepper, and salt—Bake for 10 to 15 minutes. Transfer, then put cheese cubes, toss. Serve.

Nutrition: Calories: 447 Carbohydrates: 44g Protein: 4g Fat: 8g

Brussels Sprouts With Bacon

Preparation Time: 15 minutes   **Cooking Time:** 40 minutes **Servings:** 6

450 grams Bacon
450 grams Brussels sprouts
Black pepper

Warm the oven to reach 200° Celsius. Put the sprouts and bacon with pepper. Slice the bacon into small lengthwise pieces. Bake for 35 to 40 minutes. Serve.

Nutrition: Calories: 258 Carbohydrates: 12g Protein: 6g Fat: 4g

Burger - Keto Style

Preparation Time: 15 minutes   **Cooking Time:** 25 minutes **Servings:** 6

0,5 kg. Ground beef
1 tablespoon Worcestershire sauce
1 tablespoon steak seasoning
2 tablespoons olive oil
115 grams onion

Grill the burger. Mix the beef, olive oil, Worcestershire sauce, and seasonings. Prepare the onions by adding one tablespoon of oil in a skillet to med-low heat. Sauté. Serve.

Nutrition: Calories: 479 Carbohydrates: 2g Protein: 26g Fat: 40g

Coffee BBQ Pork Belly

Preparation Time: 15 minutes   **Cooking Time:** 60 minutes **Servings:** 4

300 ml. Beef stock
1 kg. Pork belly
4 tablespoons Olive oil
Low-carb barbecue dry rub
2 tablespoons Instant Espresso Powder

Set the oven to 190° Celsius. Heat the beef stock in a small saucepan. Mix in the dry barbecue rub and espresso powder.
Put the pork belly and skin side up in a shallow dish and drizzle half of the oil over the top. Put the hot stock around the pork belly. Bake for 45 minutes. Sear each slice for three minutes per side. Serve.

Nutrition: Calories: 644 Carbohydrates: 2.6g Protein: 2 g Fat: 68g

Garlic & Thyme Lamb Chops

Preparation Time: 15 minutes   **Cooking Time:** 10 minutes **Servings:** 6

400 grams of Lamb chops
4 garlic cloves
2 thyme sprigs
1 teaspoon ground thyme
3 tablespoons olive oil

Warm a skillet. Put the olive oil. Rub the chops with the spices. Put the chops in the skillet with the garlic and sprigs of thyme. Sauté for 3 to 4 minutes and serve.

Nutrition: Calories: 252 Carbohydrates: 33g Protein: 14g Fat: 21g

Jamaican Jerk Pork Roast

Preparation Time: 15 minutes **Cooking Time:** 4 hours **Servings:** 12

1 tablespoon Olive oil
2 kg. Pork shoulder
250 ml. Beef Broth
30 grams Jamaican Jerk spice blend

Rub the roast well with the oil and the jerk spice blend. Sear the roast on all sides. Put the beef broth. Simmer for four hours on low. Shred and serve.

Nutrition: Calories: 282 Carbohydrates: 17g Protein: 23g Fat: 20g

Keto Meatballs

Preparation Time: 15 minutes **Cooking Time:** 20 minutes **Servings:** 10

1 egg
150 grams Grated parmesan
150 grams of Shredded mozzarella
450 grams of Ground beef
15 grams garlic

Warm up the oven to reach 200° Celsius. Combine all of the ingredients. Shape into meatballs. Bake for 18-20 minutes. Cool and serve.

Nutrition: Calories: 223 Carbohydrates: 4g Protein: 12.2g Fat: 10.9g

Mixed Vegetable Patties - Instant pot

Preparation Time: 15 minutes **Cooking Time:** 10 minutes **Servings:** 4

120 grams cauliflower florets
1 bag vegetables
200 ml. Water
120 grams of Flax meal
Olive oil

Steam the veggies to the steamer basket for 4 to 5 minutes—Put in the flax meal. Shape into four patties. Took the patties for 3 minutes per side. Serve.

Nutrition: Calories: 220 Carbohydrates: 3 grams Protein: 4 grams Fat: 10 grams

Roasted Leg of Lamb

Preparation Time: 15 minutes **Cooking Time:** 1 hour & 30 minutes **Servings:** 6

50 ml. Reduced-sodium beef broth
2 kg. lamb leg
6 garlic cloves
1 tablespoon rosemary leaves
1 teaspoon black pepper

Warm up the oven temperature to 200° Celsius. Put the lamb in the pan and put the broth and seasonings. Roast for 30 minutes and lower the heat to 220° Celsius. Cook for one hour. Cool and serve.

Nutrition: Calories: 223 Carbohydrates: 15g Protein: 22g Fat: 13g

Salmon Pasta

Preparation Time: 15 minutes **Cooking Time:** 1 hour & 30 minutes **Servings:** 2

2 tablespoons coconut oil
2 courgettes
230 grams of Smoked salmon
30 grams Keto-friendly mayo

Make noodle-like strands from the courgettes. Warm up the oil, put the salmon and sauté for 2 to 3 minutes. Stir in the noodles and sauté for 1 to 2 more minutes. Stir in the mayo and serve.

Nutrition: Calories: 470 Carbohydrates: 3g Protein: 21g Fat: 42g

Skillet Fried Cod

Preparation Time: 15 minutes **Cooking Time:** 30 minutes **Servings:** 4

6 garlic cloves
3 tablespoons Ghee
4 cod fillets
Optional: Garlic powder

Put the fillets in the pan, and put garlic, pepper, and salt. Toss half of the garlic into a skillet with the ghee. Turn it over, and add the remainder of the minced garlic. Cook. Serve with garlic.

Nutrition: Calories: 446 Carbohydrates: 15g Protein: 21g Fat: 7g

Slow-Cooked Kalua Pork & Cabbage

Preparation Time: 15 minutes **Cooking Time:** 11 hours **Servings:** 12

1,5 kg. pork shoulder butt
1 medium cabbage
7 strips bacon
Sea salt

Trim the fat from the roast—layer most of the bacon in the cooker. Put salt over the roast and add to the slow cooker on top of the bacon. Cook on low for 8to ten hours. Put in the cabbage and cook for an hour. Shred the roast. Serve with cabbage and slow cooker juice.

Nutrition: Calories: 369 Carbohydrates: 16g Protein: 22g Fat: 13g

Steak Pinwheels

Preparation Time: 15 minutes **Cooking Time:** 25 minutes **Servings:** 6

1 kg. Flank steak
230 grams of Mozzarella cheese
1 bunch Spinach

Warm up the oven to reach 220° Celsius. Slice the steak into six portions. Beat until thin with a mallet. Shred the cheese using a food processor and sprinkled the steak. Roll it up and tie it with cooking twine. Line the pan with the pinwheels and place it on a layer of spinach—Bake for 25 minutes.

Nutrition: Calories: 414 Carbohydrates: 11g Protein: 55g Fat: 22g

Tangy Shrimp

Preparation Time: 15 minutes **Cooking Time:** 15 minutes **Servings:** 2

3 garlic cloves
Olive oil
250 grams Jumbo shrimp
1 lemon
Cayenne pepper

Sauté the garlic and cayenne with olive oil. Peel and devein the shrimp. Cook for 2 to 3 minutes per side. Put pepper, salt, and lemon wedges. Use the rest of the garlic oil for a dipping sauce. Serve.

Nutrition: Calories: 335 Carbohydrates: 3g Protein: 23g Fat: 27g

Chicken Salad with Champagne Vinegar

Preparation Time: 15 minutes **Cooking Time:** 10 minutes **Servings:** 3

60 grams sliced red onion
64 ml. champagne vinegar
1 package of Chipotle Adobo flavour
250 grams of mixed greens
250 grams of sweet butter lettuce
60 grams of cooked; then crumbled bacon
120 grams of halved cherry tomatoes
60 grams of almond flour
60 grams sliced Avocado
120 ml. avocado Lime Green Goddess Dressing
2 sliced hard-boiled eggs

Put the red onion and the vinegar in a bowl. Open the bag of the chipotle adobo flavour, then toss the almond flour in the bag; then add in the chicken and shake it very well. Toss the chicken in your Air Fryer basket and lock the lid. Set the timer to about 8 to 10 minutes at about 220° Celsius. When the timer beeps, turn off your Air Fryer. Transfer the chicken to a bowl and add the lettuce, the bacon, the greens, the tomatoes, and the avocado. Toss your ingredients very well with the dressing. Top your salad with the pickled onion, the hard-boiled eggs, and the baked chicken shakers!

Nutrition: Calories: 565 Carbohydrates: 11g Protein: 8.9g Fat: 4.6g

Mexican Beef Salad

Preparation Time: 15 minutes **Cooking Time:** 12 minutes **Servings:** 6

0,5 kg ground beef
1 tablespoon taco seasoning
220 grams grape tomatoes, halved
60 grams scallion, chopped
43 ml. salsa
Olive oil
230 grams lettuce, chopped
1 large cucumber, chopped
30 grams cheddar cheese, shredded
43 grams of sour cream

Warm-up oil over high heat and stir fry the beef for about 8-10 minutes, breaking up the pieces with a spatula. Stir in the taco seasoning and remove from the heat. Set aside to cool slightly. Meanwhile, in a large bowl, add the remaining ingredients and mix well. Add the ground beef and toss to coat well. Serve immediately.

Nutrition: Calories: 263 Carbohydrates: 7g Protein: 28.1g Fat: 13.1g

Cherry Tomatoes Tilapia Salad

Preparation Time: 15 minutes **Cooking Time:** 18 minutes **Servings:** 3

400 grams of mixed greens
120 grams of cherry tomatoes
1 red onion, chopped
1 medium avocado
2 to 3 Tortilla Crusted Tilapia fillet

Spray the tilapia fillet with a little bit of cooking spray. Put the fillets in your Air Fryer basket. Lock the lid of your Air Fryer and set the timer for about 18 minutes and the temperature to about 220° Celsius. Turn off your Air Fryer when the timer beeps and transfer the fillet to a bowl. Add about half of the fillets to a large bowl, then toss it with the tomatoes, the greens, and the red onion. Add the lime dressing and mix again. Turn off your Air Fryer when the timer beeps, and transfer the fish to the veggie salad. Serve and enjoy your salad!

Nutrition: Calories: 271 Carbohydrates: 10.1g Protein: 18.5g Fat: 8g

Crunchy Chicken Milanese

Preparation Time: 15 minutes **Cooking Time:** 10 minutes **Servings:** 2

Chicken breasts (2, skinless, boneless)
60 grams of coconut flour
1 egg, lightly beaten
60 grams crushed pork rinds
Olive oil

Pound the chicken breasts using a heavy mallet. Prepare 2 separate prep plates and one small, shallow bowl. On plate 1, put the coconut flour, cayenne pepper, pink salt, and pepper. Mix. On plate 2, put the crushed pork rinds. Warm up the olive oil, then dredge chicken breasts in flour mixture, then egg and finish with pork rinds. Set a skillet with oil over medium heat and add your coated chicken. Cook the chicken for 10 minutes and serve.

Nutrition: Calories: 604 Carbohydrates: 17g Protein: 65g Fat: 29g

Parmesan Baked Chicken

Preparation Time: 15 minutes **Cooking Time:** 20 minutes **Servings:** 2

2 tablespoons ghee
2 boneless skinless chicken breasts
60 grams mayonnaise
30 grams grated Parmesan cheese
30 grams crushed pork rinds

Preheat the oven to 200° Celsius. Put both chicken breasts in a large baking dish and coat it with ghee. Pat dry the chicken breasts with a paper towel, season with pink salt and pepper, and place in the prepared baking dish. Mix combine the mayonnaise, Parmesan cheese, and Italian seasoning in a small bowl. Slather the mayonnaise mixture evenly over the chicken breasts and sprinkle the crushed pork rinds on top of the mayonnaise mixture. Bake until the topping is browned, about 20 minutes, and serve.

Nutrition: Calories: 850 Carbohydrates: 2g Protein: 60g Fat: 67g

Cheesy Bacon and Broccoli Chicken

Preparation Time: 15 minutes **Cooking Time:** 1-hour **Servings:** 2

2 boneless skinless chicken breasts
4 bacon slices
180 grams cream cheese, room temp.
250 grams frozen broccoli florets thawed
90 grams of shredded Cheddar cheese

Warm up the oven to 220° Celsius, then choose a baking dish that is large enough to hold both chicken breasts and coat it with the ghee. Pat dry the chicken breasts with a paper towel and season with pink salt and pepper. Place the chicken breasts and the bacon slices in the baking dish and bake for 25 minutes. Shred the chicken. Season it again with pink salt and pepper. Place the bacon on a paper towel–lined plate to crisp up and then crumble it. Mix the cream cheese, shredded chicken, broccoli, and half of the bacon crumble in a medium bowl. Transfer the chicken mixture, and top with the cheddar and the remaining half of the bacon crumbles. Bake for about 35 minutes and serve.

Nutrition: Calories: 935 Carbohydrates: 10g Protein: 75g Fat: 66g

Buttery Garlic Chicken

Preparation Time: 15 minutes **Cooking Time:** 40 minutes **Servings:** 2

2 tablespoons ghee melted
2 boneless skinless chicken breasts
4 tablespoons butter
2 garlic cloves minced
30 grams grated Parmesan cheese

Warm up the oven to 220° Celsius, then choose a baking dish that is large enough to hold both chicken breasts and coat it with the ghee. Pat dry the chicken breasts and season with pink salt, pepper, and Italian seasoning. Place the chicken in the baking dish. Dissolve the butter in a skillet. Put the minced garlic and cook for 5 minutes, then remove the butter-garlic mixture from the heat and pour it over the chicken breasts. Roast the chicken in the oven for 30 to 35 minutes until cooked through. Sprinkle some of the Parmesan cheese on top of each chicken breast. Let it rest in the baking dish for 5 minutes, spoon the butter sauce over the chicken, and serve.

Nutrition: Calories: 642 Carbohydrates: 2g Protein: 57g Fat: 45g

Creamy Slow Cooker Chicken

Preparation Time: 15 minutes **Cooking Time:** 4 hours & 15 minutes **Servings:** 2

2 boneless skinless chicken breasts
120 ml. Alfredo Sauce
30 grams chopped sun-dried tomatoes
30 grams Parmesan cheese, grated
250 grams of fresh spinach

Dissolve the ghee in a skillet, then put the chicken and cook for about 4 minutes on each side. Transfer the chicken to your slow cooker with the crock insert in place. Set your slow cooker to low. Mix the Alfredo sauce, sun-dried tomatoes, Parmesan cheese, salt, and pepper in a small bowl. Pour the sauce over the chicken—cover, and cook on low for 4 hours. Add the fresh spinach. Cover and cook for 5 minutes more, until the spinach is slightly wilted, and serve.

Nutrition: Calories: 900 Carbohydrates: 9g Protein: 70g Fat: 66g

Braised Chicken Thighs with Kalamata Olives

Preparation Time: 15 minutes **Cooking Time:** 40 minutes **Servings:** 2

4 chicken thighs, skin on
70 ml. chicken broth
1 lemon, sliced
50 ml. lemon juice
70 grams pitted Kalamata olives
2 tablespoons butter

Warm up the oven to 220° Celsius, dry the chicken and season to taste. Melt butter in a medium oven-safe skillet or high-sided baking dish over medium-high heat. When the butter has melted and is hot, add the chicken thighs, skin-side down, and leave them for about 8 minutes, or until the skin is brown and crispy. Turn over the chicken and cook for 2 minutes on the second side. Around the chicken thighs, pour in the chicken broth, and add the lemon slices, lemon juice, and olives.
Bake in the oven for about 30 minutes, until the chicken is cooked through. Add the butter to the broth mixture. Divide the chicken and olives between 2 plates and serve.

Nutrition: Calories: 567 Carbohydrates: 4g Protein: 33g Fat: 47g

Baked Garlic and Paprika Chicken Legs

Preparation Time: 15 minutes **Cooking Time:** 55 minutes **Servings:** 2

450 grams chicken drumsticks, skin on
2 tablespoons paprika
2 garlic cloves minced
60 grams pound fresh green beans
1 tablespoon olive oil

Set the oven to 220° Celsius. Combine all the ingredients in a large bowl, toss to mix, and transfer to a baking dish. Bake for 60 minutes until crisp and thoroughly cooked.

Nutrition: Calories: 700 Carbohydrates: 10g Protein: 63g Fat: 45g

Chicken Curry with Masala

Preparation Time: 15 minutes **Cooking Time:** 30 minutes **Servings:** 4

2 tablespoons olive oil
4 tablespoons minced jalapeno
500 grams of chopped boneless skinless chicken thighs
1 teaspoon garam masala
30 grams of chopped cilantro
2 tablespoons diced ginger
120 grams of chopped tomatoes
1 teaspoon turmeric
2 tablespoons lemon juice
28 ml. of lemon juice

Heat your Air Fryer to a temperature of about 200° Celsius. Grease the Air Fryer pan with the cooking spray. Add the jalapenos and the ginger. Add in the chicken and the tomatoes and stir. Add the spices and 15 grams. of oil, and 15 ml. of water.
3. Place the pan in Air Fryer and set the temperature to 200° Celsius. Now, set the timer to 30 minutes. When the timer beeps, turn off your Air Fryer. Serve and enjoy your lunch!

Nutrition: Calories: 254 Carbohydrates: 9g Protein: 27.8g Fat: 14g

Chicken Quesadilla

Preparation Time: 15 minutes **Cooking Time:** 5 minutes **Servings:** 2

1 tablespoon olive oil
2 low-carbohydrate tortillas
60 grams shredded Mexican blend cheese
56 grams of shredded chicken
2 tablespoons sour cream

Warm up the olive oil in a large skillet, put a tortilla, then top with 30 grams of cheese, the chicken, the Tajin seasoning, and the remaining 30 grams of cheese. Top with the second tortilla. Once the bottom tortilla gets golden and the cheese begins to melt, after about 2 minutes, flip the quesadilla over. The second side will cook faster, about 1 minute. Once the second tortilla is crispy and golden, transfer the quesadilla to a cutting board and sit for 2 minutes. Cut the quesadilla into 4 wedges using a pizza cutter or chef's knife. Transfer half the quesadilla to each of the 2 plates. Put 15 grams of sour cream and serve hot.

Nutrition: Calories: 414 Carbohydrates: 24g Protein: 26g Fat: 28g

Slow Cooker Barbecue Ribs

Preparation Time: 15 minutes **Cooking Time:** 4 hours **Servings:** 2

1 kg. pork ribs
Salt
Freshly ground black pepper
10 grams package of dry rib-seasoning rub
11 teaspoon sugar-free barbecue sauce

With the crock insert in place, preheat your slow cooker to high. Generously season the pork ribs with pink salt, pepper, and a dry rib-seasoning rub. Stand the ribs up along the walls of the slow-cooker insert, with the bonier side facing inward. Pour the barbecue sauce on both sides of the ribs, using just enough to coat. Cover, cook for 4 hours and serve.

Nutrition: Calories: 956 Carbohydrates: 5g Protein: 68g Fat: 72g

Barbacoa Beef Roast

Preparation Time: 15 minutes **Cooking Time:** 8 hours **Servings:** 4

450 grams beef chuck roast
4 chipotle peppers in adobo sauce
1 can green jalapeño chilis
2 tablespoons apple cider vinegar
70 ml. beef broth

with the crock insert in place, preheat your slow cooker to low. Massage the beef chuck roast on both sides with pink salt and pepper. Put the roast in the slow cooker. Pulse the chipotle peppers and their adobo sauce, jalapeños, and apple cider vinegar in a blender. Add the beef broth and pulse a few more times. Pour the chilli mixture over the top of the roast.
Cover and cook on low for 8 hours, then shred the meat. Serve hot.

Nutrition: Calories: 723 Carbohydrates: 7g Protein: 66g Fat: 46g

Cauliflower and Pumpkin Casserole

Preparation Time: 15 minutes **Cooking Time:** 1 hour & 30 minutes **Servings:** 4

2 tablespoons Olive oil
1 onion, chopped
150 grams kale
1 little clove of garlic, minced
Salt
Pepper
200 ml. low sodium chicken broth
250 grams pumpkin
250 grams courgettes
2 tablespoons mayonnaise
380 grams frozen, thawed brown rice
120 grams grated Swiss cheese
43 grams grated Parmesan
120 grams of panko flour
1 large beaten egg
Cooking spray

Preheat the oven to 200° Celsius. Heats the oil in a large non-stick skillet over medium heat. Add onions and cook, occasionally stirring, until browned and tender (about 5 minutes). Add the cabbage, garlic, 60 grams teaspoon salt, and 60 grams teaspoon pepper and cook until the cabbage is light (about 2 minutes). Put the stock and cook for 5 minutes, then put the squash, zucchini, and 60 grams teaspoon Salt and mix well. Continuously cooking for 8 minutes. Remove from heat and add mayonnaise. In a bowl, combine cooked vegetables, brown rice, cheese, 60 grams of flour, and a large egg and mix well. Spray a 2-litre casserole with cooking spray. Put the mixture in the pan and cover with the remaining flour, 1.21 teaspoon salt, and a few pinches of pepper. Bake until the squash and courgettes are tender and the top golden and crispy (about 35 minutes). Serve hot.

Advanced Preparation Tip: Freeze the casserole for up to 2 weeks. Cover with aluminium foil and heat at 180 ° C until warm (35 to 45 minutes).

Nutrition: Calories: 966 Carbohydrates: 11g Fat: 3g Protein: 5g

Thai Beef Salad

Preparation Time: 15 minutes **Cooking Time:** 30 minutes **Servings:** 4 **Ingredients:**

800 grams of beef tenderloin

For the marinade:
2 tablespoons soy sauce
1 tablespoon soup of honey
1 pinch of the pepper mill

For the sauce:
1 small bunch of fresh coriander
1 small bouquet of mint
3 tablespoons fish sauce soup
1 lime
1 clove of garlic
2 tablespoons sugar palm
10 drops of tabasco sauce
1 small glass of raw Thai rice to make grilled rice powder
200 grams of arugula or young shoots of salad

Cut the beef tenderloin into strips and put it in a container. Sprinkle with two tablespoons of soy sauce, 15 grams of honey, and pepper. Soak thoroughly and let marinate for 1 hour at room temperature. Meanwhile, prepare the roasted rice powder. Pour a glass of Thai rice into an anti-adhesive pan. Dry colour the rice, constantly stirring to avoid burning. When it has a lovely colour, get rid of it on a plate and let it cool. When it has cooled, reduce it to powder. Wash and finely chop mint and coriander. Put in a container and add lime juice, chopped garlic clove, 50 grams mam, 50 grams brown sugar, 50 ml. water, 11 teaspoon sauce soy, and a dozen drop of Tabasco. Mix well and let stand when the sugar melts and the flavours mix. Place a bed of salad on a dish. Cook the beef strips and put them on the salad. Sprinkle with a spoonful of sauce and roasted rice powder. To be served as is or with a Thai cooked white rice scented.

Nutrition: Calories: 687 Carbohydrates: 33g Fat: 22g Protein: 30g

Stuffed Apples with Shrimp

Preparation Time: 15 minutes **Cooking Time:** 30 minutes **Servings:** 4

6 medium apples
1 lemon juice
60 grams butter

Filling:
300 grams of shrimp
1 onion minced
60 grams chopped parsley
2 tablespoons flour
1 can of cream
100 grams of curd
1 tablespoon butter
1 tablespoon pepper sauce
Salt
2 tablespoons mayonnaise
380 grams frozen, thawed brown rice
120 grams grated Swiss cheese
43 grams grated Parmesan
120 grams of panko flour
1 large beaten egg
Cooking spray

Cut a cap from each apple, remove the seeds a little from the pulp on the sides, and put the pulp in the bottom, leaving a cavity. Pass a little lemon and some butter on the apples, and bake them in the oven. Remove from oven, let cool and bring to freeze. Prepare the shrimp sauce in a pan by mixing the butter with the flour, onion, parsley, and pepper sauce. Then add the prawn shrimp to the sauce. When boiling, mix the cream cheese and sour cream. Stuff each apple. Serve hot or cold, as you prefer.

Nutrition: Calories: 741 Carbohydrates: 44g Fat: 15g Protein: 36g

Grilled Chicken Salad with Oranges

Preparation Time: 15 minutes **Cooking Time:** 15 minutes **Servings:** 4

75 ml. orange juice
30 ml. lemon juice
3 tablespoons extra virgin olive oil
1 tablespoon Dijon mustard
2 cloves of garlic, chopped
Salt
Pepper
450 grams skinless chicken breast, trimmed
25 grams pistachio or flaked almonds, toasted
600 grams of mesclun, rinsed and dried
75 grams minced red onion
2 medium oranges, peeled, quartered, and sliced

Preheat the barbecue over medium heat. Place the orange juice, lemon juice, oil, mustard, garlic, salt, and pepper in a small bowl or jar with an airtight lid; whip or shake to mix—Reserve 75 millilitres of this salad vinaigrette and 45 millilitres for basting. Place the vinaigrette rest in a shallow glass dish or resealable plastic bag. Add the chicken and turn it over to coat. Cover or close and marinate in the refrigerator for at least 20 minutes or 2 hours. Lightly oil the grill by rubbing it with a crumpled paper towel soaked in oil.

Grill the chicken 10 to 15 centimetres (four to six inches) from the heat source, basting the cooked sides with the basting vinaigrette until it is no longer pink in the centre; an Instant-read thermometer inserted in the thickest part records 175° Celsius, four six minutes on each side. Transfer and let the rest for five minutes.

Meanwhile, grill almonds in a small, dry pan on medium-low heat, stirring constantly, until lightly browned, about 2 to three minutes. Transfer them to a bowl and let them cool. Place the salad and onion mixture in a large bowl, then mix with the vinaigrette reserved for the salad. Slice chicken and spread on salads. Sprinkle orange slices on top and sprinkle with pistachios.

Nutrition: Calories: 654 Carbohydrates: 21g Fat: 14g Protein: 25g

Red Curry with Vegetables

Preparation Time: 15 minutes   **Cooking Time:** 30 minutes **Servings:** 4

600 grams of sweet potatoes
200 grams of canned chickpeas
2 leek whites
2 tomatoes
100 grams of spinach shoots
1 can of Greek yoghurt
1 lime
3 cm fresh ginger
1 small bunch of coriander
60 grams of red onion
2 cloves garlic
4 tablespoons red curry paste
Salt
40 ml. of coconut milk

Cut the sweet potatoes into pieces. Clean the leek whites and cut them into slices. Peel and seed the tomatoes. Mix the Greek yoghurt with a drizzle of lime juice, chopped onion, salt, and half of the coriander leaves. Heat 11 teaspoons of coconut milk in a frying pan until it reduces and forms many tiny bubbles. Brown curry paste with chopped ginger and garlic. Add vegetables, drained chickpeas, remaining coconut milk, and salt. Cook for 20 min covered, then 5 min without a lid for the sauce to thicken. When serving, add spinach sprouts and the remaining coriander. Serve with the yoghurt sauce.

Nutrition: Calories: 254 Carbohydrates: 13g Fat: 4g Protein: 3g

Baked Turkey Breast with Cranberry Sauce

Preparation Time: 15 minutes   **Cooking Time:** 1 hour & 30 minutes **Servings:** 3

2 kg. of whole turkey breast
1 tablespoon olive oil
40 grams onion
2 cloves of garlic
5 grams of dried thyme
5 grams poultry seasonings
Salt
30 grams butter
30 grams minced shallot
30 grams chopped onion
1 clove garlic
2 tablespoons flour
100 grams blueberries
250 grams of apple cider
2 tablespoons maple honey
Pepper

Grind in the blender 30 grams of onion, and 2 garlic with herbs. Grease the breast with oil. Put in the baking tray, add half a citron, and bake at 190° Celsius. Bring the citron to a boil, add the blueberries, and leave a few minutes. In the butter (2 tablespoons), fry the onion (60 grams), shallot, and garlic (1 clove). Add the flour to the onion and shallot and leave a few minutes. Add the citron, cranberries, and honey and leave on low heat. Season with salt and pepper, and let the blueberries get soft. If you want to strain, use the processor. Let it thicken slightly. Slice the thin turkey breast and serve with the blueberry sauce.

Nutrition: Calories: 1258 Carbohydrates: 77g Fat: 17g Protein: 23g

Italian Keto Casserole

Preparation Time: 15 minutes **Cooking Time:** 1-hour **Servings:** 4

200 grams of Shirataki noodles
2 tablespoons olive oil
1 small onion, chopped
2 garlic cloves, finely chopped
1 teaspoon dried marjoram
450 grams of ground beef
Salt
Pepper
2 chopped tomatoes
120 grams of fat cream
340 grams ricotta cheese
100 grams grated parmesan
1 egg
30 grams parsley, roughly chopped

Preheat the oven to 190° Celsius. Prepare the shirataki noodles as indicated on the packaging, strain well, and set aside. Cook oil, onion, garlic, and marjoram, and fry for 2-3 minutes, until the onion is soft. Add ground beef, salt, pepper, and simmer, stirring, while the mixture is browned. Add tomatoes and fat cream and cook for 5 minutes. Remove from heat and mix with noodles. Transfer the mixture to a baking dish: mix ricotta, parmesan, egg, and parsley. Spoon over the casserole. Bake for about 35-45 minutes until golden brown.

Nutrition: Calories: 369 Carbohydrates: 44g Fat: 10g Protein: 20g

Salmon Keto Cutlets

Preparation Time: 15 minutes **Cooking Time:** 10 minutes **Servings:** 4

450 g canned salmon
60 grams almond flour
30 grams shallots, finely chopped
2 tablespoons parsley, finely chopped
1 tablespoon dried chopped onions
2 large eggs
Zest of 1 lemon
1 clove of garlic, finely chopped
½ teaspoon salt
½ teaspoon ground white pepper
3 tablespoons olive oil

Put all the fixing except the oil in a large bowl and mix well. Form 8, identical cutlets. Fry salmon cutlets in portions, adding more oil for 2-3 minutes on each side. Serve the cutlets warm or cold with lemon wedges and low carbohydrate mayonnaise.

Nutrition: Calories: 456 Carbohydrates: 55g Fat: 19g Protein: 35g

Baked Cauliflower

Preparation Time: 15 minutes **Cooking Time:** 60 minutes **Servings:** 2

1 medium cauliflower
113 grams of salted butter
100 grams finely grated parmesan
3 tablespoons Dijon mustard
2 minced garlic cloves
Zest of 1 lemon
Salt
Pepper
40 grams of fresh Parmesan
1 tablespoon chopped parsley

Preheat the oven to 190° Celsius. Put the cauliflower in a small baking dish. Put the remaining ingredients in a small saucepan, except for fresh parmesan and parsley, and put on low heat until they melt. Whip together. Lubricate cauliflower ⅓ of the oil mixture. Bake for 20 minutes, then remove from the oven and pour another quarter of the oil mixture. Bake for another 20 minutes and pour over the remaining oil mixture. Cook for another 20-30 minutes until the core is soft. Put on a plate, sprinkle a drop of oil from the mould, grate fresh parmesan and sprinkle with parsley.

Nutrition: Calories: 420 Carbohydrates: 41g Fat: 11g Protein: 19g

Risotto with Mushrooms

Preparation Time: 15 minutes **Cooking Time:** 25 minutes **Servings:** 2

2 tablespoons olive oil
2 minced garlic cloves
1 small onion, finely chopped
Salt
White Pepper
200 grams of chopped mushrooms
30 grams chopped oregano leaves
255 grams cauliflower rice
40 grams of vegetable broth
2 tablespoons butter
100 grams grated parmesan

Sauté oil, garlic, onions, salt, pepper, and sauté for 5-7 minutes until the onions become transparent. Add mushrooms and oregano and cook for 5 minutes. Add cauliflower rice and vegetable broth, then reduce heat to medium. Cook the risotto, frequently stirring, for 10-15 minutes, until the cauliflower is soft. Remove from heat and mix with butter and parmesan.
Try and add more seasoning if you want.

Nutrition: Calories: 362 Carbohydrates: 31g Fat: 7g Protein: 4g

Low Carb Green Bean Casserole

Preparation Time: 15 minutes **Cooking Time:** 60 minutes **Servings:** 4

2 tablespoons butter
1 small chopped onion
2 minced garlic cloves
230 grams of chopped mushrooms
Salt
Pepper
90 ml. chicken stock
50 grams fat cream
½ teaspoon xanthan gum
450 grams of green beans (with cut ends)
60 grams crushed cracklings

Preheat the oven to 190° degrees. Add oil, onion, and garlic to a non-stick pan over high heat. Fry until the onion is transparent. Add mushrooms, salt, and pepper. Cook for 7 minutes until the mushrooms are tender. Add chicken stock and cream and bring to a boil. Sprinkle with xanthan gum, mix and cook for 5 minutes. Add the string beans to the creamy mixture and pour it into the baking dish. Cover with foil and bake for 20 minutes. Remove the foil, sprinkle with greaves and bake for another 10-15 minutes.

Nutrition: Calories: 554 Carbohydrates: 6g Fat: 18g Protein: 8g

Avocado Low Carb Burger

Preparation Time: 15 minutes **Cooking Time:** 25 minutes **Servings:** 4

1 avocado
1 leaf lettuce
2 slices of prosciutto or any ham
1 slice of tomato
1 egg
Olive oil
For the sauce:
1 tablespoon low carb mayonnaise
¼ teaspoon low carb hot sauce
¼ teaspoon mustard
¼ teaspoon Italian seasoning
½ teaspoon sesame seeds

Combine keto-friendly mayonnaise, mustard, hot sauce, and Italian seasoning in a small bowl. Heat 60 grams tablespoon of olive oil in a pan and cook an egg. The yolk must be fluid. Cut the avocado in half, and remove the peel and bone. Cut the narrowest part of the avocado so that the fruit can stand on a plate. Fill the hole in one-half of the avocado with the prepared sauce. Cover the other half of the avocado and sprinkle with sesame seeds (optional). Top with lettuce, prosciutto strips, a slice of tomato, and a fried egg.

Nutrition: Calories: 416 Carbohydrates: 15g Fat: 55g Protein: 35g

Protein Gnocchi with Basil Pesto

Preparation Time: 15 minutes **Cooking Time:** 30 minutes **Servings:** 4

400 grams potatoes
60 grams protein powder, neutral
50 grams of wheat flour
Salt
20 grams Nutmeg
2 tablespoons flour for the work surface
One bunch basil
30 grams pine nuts
1 clove of garlic
100 ml olive oil
Salt
Pepper

The recipe is a bit tricky. So, take your time. Slice the potatoes into small pieces and cook for 20-25 minutes. Let the potatoes cool off. Put the pieces of potato, the protein powder, the flour, and the spices together in a blender and mix everything properly. Put flour on the work surface and divide the dough into four parts: form long, round snakes out of the dough.

5. Slice the snakes every 1.5-2 cm, press briefly with a fork to keep the pesto better, and you're done with the raw gnocchi.

6. Now, put the gnocchi together in lightly boiling water for 3-4 minutes and wait until they float up. Serve.

Nutrition: Calories: 347 Carbohydrates: 33g Fat: 11g Protein: 7g

Summery Bowls with Fresh Vegetables and Protein Quark

Preparation Time: 15 minutes **Cooking Time:** 10 minutes **Servings:** 4

100 grams of green salad
100 grams radish
200 grams kohlrabi
70 grams carrots
70 grams Red lenses
50 grams tomatoes
2 spring onions
20 grams of Nuts/seeds
150 grams of soy yoghurt
2 tablespoons mixed herbs
1 teaspoon lemon juice
20 grams Nutri-Plus Shape & Shake, neutral
Salt
Pepper

Wash the salad and the vegetables and peel the kohlrabi. Simmer the red lentils for about 7 minutes. In time, grate the vegetables. Mix the soy yoghurt with lemon juice, protein powder, salt, and herbs. Arrange all ingredients together in a deep plate or bowl and top with the spring onions and nuts.

Nutrition: Calories: 357 Carbohydrates: 10g Fat: 16g Protein: 80g

Beef and Kale Pan

Preparation Time: 10 minutes **Cooking Time:** 20 minutes **Servings:** 4

500 grams beef stew meat, cubed
1 red onion, chopped
1 tablespoon olive oil
2 garlic cloves, minced
120 grams kale, torn
120 ml. beef stock
1 teaspoon chilli powder
½ teaspoon sweet paprika
1 teaspoon rosemary, dried
1 tablespoon cilantro, chopped

Ensure that you heat the pan; add the onion and the garlic. Stir and sauté for 2 minutes. Add the meat and brown it for 5 minutes. Put the rest of the fixing, simmer, and then cook over medium heat for 13 minutes more. Divide the mix between plates and serve for lunch.

Nutrition: Calories: 477g Fat: 10g Fiber: 3g Carbohydrates: 1g Protein: 12g

Salmon and Lemon Relish

Preparation Time: 10 minutes **Cooking Time:** 1-hour **Servings:** 2

2 medium salmon fillets
Salt
Black pepper
A drizzle of olive oil
1 shallot, chopped
1 teaspoon lemon juice
1 big lemon
30 ml. olive oil
2 tablespoons parsley

Grease salmon fillets with olive oil, put salt and pepper, place on a lined baking sheet, stand in the oven at 200° Celsius, and bake for 1 hour. Stir 11 teaspoons of lemon juice, salt, and pepper in a bowl, and leave aside for 10 minutes. Cut the whole lemon in wedges and then very thinly. Put this to shallots, parsley, and 32 ml. olive oil and stir. Break the salmon into medium pieces and serve with the lemon relish on the side.

Nutrition: Calories: 500g Fat: 10g Carbohydrates: 5g Protein: 20g

Mustard Glazed Salmon

Preparation Time: 10 minutes **Cooking Time:** 20 minutes **Servings:** 1

1 big salmon fillet
Salt
Black Pepper
60 grams mustard
1 tablespoon coconut oil
1 tablespoon maple extract

Mix maple extract with mustard in a bowl. Massage salmon with salt and pepper and ½ of mustard mix. Heat a pan to high heat, place salmon flesh side down and cook for 5 minutes. Rub salmon with the rest of the mixture, transfer to a baking dish, place in the oven at 200° Celsius degrees F and bake for 15 minutes. Enjoy! Serve with a tasty side salad.

Nutrition: Calories: 666 Fat: 7g Carbohydrates: 35g Protein: 23g

Turkey and Tomatoes

Preparation Time: 10 minutes **Cooking Time:** 30 minutes **Servings:** 4

2 shallots, chopped
1 tablespoon ghee, melted
120 ml. chicken stock
500 grams turkey breast, skinless, boneless, and cubed
120 grams cherry tomatoes, halved
1 tablespoon rosemary, chopped

Ensure that the pan containing ghee is heated, add the shallots and the meat, and brown for 5 minutes. Put the rest of the fixing, simmer, and cook over medium heat for 25 minutes, stirring often. Divide into bowls and serve.

Nutrition: Calories: 411 Fat: 44g Carbohydrates: 33g Protein: 10g

Salmon Bowls

Preparation Time: 10 minutes **Cooking Time:** 15 minutes **Servings:** 4

500 kg. salmon fillets, boneless, skinless, and roughly cubed
130 ml. chicken stock
2 spring onions, chopped
1 tablespoon olive oil
120 grams kalamata olives, pitted and halved
1 avocado, pitted, peeled, and roughly cubed
120 grams of baby spinach
30 grams cilantro, chopped
1 tablespoon basil, chopped
1 teaspoon lime juice

Ensure that you heat the pan, add the spring onions and the salmon, toss gently, and then cook for 5 minutes. Add the olives and the other ingredients, then cook over medium heat for 10 minutes more. Divide the mix into bowls and serve for lunch.

Nutrition: Calories: 254 Fat: 17g Carbohydrates: 6g Protein: 20g

Shrimp and Cauliflower Delight

Preparation Time: 10 minutes **Cooking Time:** 15 minutes **Servings:** 2

1 tablespoon ghee
1 tablespoon parsley
1 cauliflower head, florets separated
500 grams shrimp, peeled and deveined
32 ml. of coconut milk
250 grams mushrooms, roughly chopped
A pinch of red pepper flakes
Black pepper
Salt
2 garlic cloves, minced
4 bacon slices
70 ml. beef stock
1 tablespoon chives, chopped

Heat a pan, add bacon, cook until it's crispy, transfer to paper towels, and leave aside. Heat 11 teaspoons of bacon fat on another pan over medium-high heat, add shrimp, cook for 2 minutes on each side and transfer to a bowl. Cook mushrooms, stir and cook for 3-4 minutes. Put garlic and pepper flakes, and cook for 1 minute. Put beef stock, salt, pepper, and return shrimp to pan. Stir. Mince cauliflower in the food processor. Cook for 5 minutes. Add ghee and butter, stir and blend using an immersion blender. Put salt and pepper, and stir. Top with shrimp mixture and serve with parsley and chives sprinkled all over. Enjoy!

Nutrition: Calories: 432 Fat: 8g Carbohydrates: 6g Protein: 20g

Scallops and Fennel Sauce

Preparation Time: 10 minutes **Cooking Time:** 10 minutes **Servings:** 2

6 scallops
1 fennel, trimmed, leaves chopped, and bulbs cut in wedges
Lime juice
1 lime, cut into wedges
Zest from 1 lime
1 egg yolk
3 tablespoons ghee, melted and heated up
½ tablespoons olive oil
Pepper
Salt

Season scallops with salt and pepper, put in a bowl, mix with half of the lime juice and half of the zest, and toss to coat. In a bowl, combine the egg yolk with some salt and pepper, the rest of the lime juice, and the rest of the lime zest, and whisk well. Add melted ghee and stir very well. Also, add fennel leaves and stir. Brush fennel wedges with oil, place on heated grill over medium-high heat, cook for 2 minutes, flip and cook for 2 minutes more. Add scallops to the grill, cook for 2 minutes, flip and cook for 2 minutes more. Enjoy! Divide fennel and scallops on plates, drizzle fennel and ghee mix and serve with lime wedges on the side.

Nutrition: Calories: 340 Fat: 24g Carbohydrates: 12g Protein: 25g

Salmon Stuffed with Shrimp

Preparation Time: 10 minutes **Cooking Time:** 25 minutes **Servings:** 2

2 salmon fillets
A drizzle of olive oil
150 grams tiger shrimp, peeled, deveined, and chopped
6 mushrooms, chopped
3 green onions, chopped
250 grams spinach
35 grams macadamia nuts, toasted and chopped
Black pepper and salt to taste
A pinch of nutmeg
30 grams mayonnaise

Heat a pan, add mushrooms, onions, salt, and pepper, stir and cook for 4 minutes. Add macadamia nuts, stir and cook for 2 minutes. Add spinach, stir and cook for 1 minute. Add shrimp, stir and cook for 1 minute. Take off heat, leave aside for a few minutes, add mayo and nutmeg and mix well. Grease the pan with oil over medium-high heat, add stuffed salmon, skin side down, cook for 1 minute, reduce temperature, cover pan and cook for 8 minutes. Make an incision lengthwise in each salmon fillet, sprinkle salt and pepper, divide spinach and shrimp mix into incisions, and place on a working surface. Broil for 3 minutes, divide among plates and serve.
Enjoy!

Nutrition: Calories: 430 Fat: 30g Carbohydrates: 7g Protein: 50g

Pork Casserole

Preparation Time: 10 minutes **Cooking Time:** 40 minutes **Servings:** 4

130 grams of cheddar cheese, grated
2 eggs, whisked
500 grams pork loin, cubed
60 ml. avocado oil
2 shallots, chopped
3 garlic cloves, minced
120 grams red bell peppers
60 grams heavy cream
1 tablespoon chives, chopped
½ teaspoon cumin, ground

Ensure that you heat the pan; add the shallots and the garlic and sauté for 2 minutes. Add the bell peppers and the meat, toss, and cook for 5 minutes. Add the cumin, salt, pepper, toss, and take off the heat. Mix the eggs with the cream and the cheese in a bowl, whisk and pour over the pork mix. Cook with chives on top at 380 degrees F for 30 minutes.
Divide the mix between plates and serve for lunch.

Nutrition: Calories: 455g Fat: 34g Carbohydrates: 13g Protein: 33g

Incredible Salmon Dish

Preparation Time: 10 minutes **Cooking Time:** 15 minutes **Servings:** 4

380 ml. of ice water
2 teaspoons sriracha sauce
4 teaspoons stevia
3 scallions, chopped
Salt
Black Pepper
2 teaspoons flaxseed oil
4 teaspoons apple cider vinegar
3 teaspoons avocado oil
4 medium salmon fillets
250 grams of baby rocket
250 grams cabbage, finely chopped
1 and ½ teaspoon Jamaican jerk seasoning
30 grams pepitas, toasted
250 grams watermelon radish, julienned

Put ice water in a bowl, add scallions, and leave aside. In another bowl, mix sriracha sauce with stevia and stir well. Transfer 2 tablespoons of this mix to a bowl and mix with half of the avocado oil, flaxseed oil, vinegar, salt, pepper, and whisk. Sprinkle jerk seasoning over salmon, rub with sriracha and stevia mix, and season with salt and pepper. Heat a pan with the rest of the avocado oil over medium-high heat, add salmon, flesh side down, cook for 4 minutes, flip and cook for 4 minutes more and divide among plates. In a bowl, mix radishes with cabbage and rocket. Add salt, pepper, sriracha, and vinegar mix and toss well. Add this to salmon fillets, drizzle the remaining sriracha, and stevia sauce all over and top with pepitas and drained scallions. Enjoy!

Nutrition: Calories: 570 Fat: 6g Fiber: 19g Carbohydrates: 1g

Green Chicken Curry

Preparation Time: 15 minutes **Cooking Time:** 30 minutes **Servings:** 4

500 grams of chicken breasts
1 tablespoon olive oil
2 tablespoons green curry paste
130 ml. unsweetened coconut milk
130 ml. chicken broth
130 grams asparagus spears
130 grams green beans
Salt
Black pepper
70 grams basil leaves

Sauté the curry paste for 1–2 minutes. Add the chicken and cook for 8–10 minutes. Add coconut milk and broth, and boil. Cook again to low for 8–10 minutes. Add the asparagus, green beans, salt, and black pepper, and cook for 4–5 minutes. Serve.

Nutrition: Calories 294 Carbohydrates: 4.3 g Fat: 16.2 g Protein 28.6 g

Creamy Pork Stew

Preparation Time: 15 minutes **Cooking Time:** 1 hour 35 minutes **Servings:** 8

120 grams butter
250 grams pounds of boneless pork ribs
1 yellow onion
4 garlic cloves
164 ml. chicken broth
2 cans of sugar-free chopped tomatoes
2 teaspoons dried oregano
1 teaspoon ground cumin
Salt
2 tablespoons lime juice
60 grams of sour cream

Cook the pork, onions, and garlic for 4–5 minutes. Add the broth, tomatoes, oregano, cumin, salt, and mix. Simmer to low. Combine in the sour cream plus lime juice and remove. Serve.

Nutrition: Calories 304 Carbohydrates: 4.7 g Fat: 12.4 g Protein 39.5 g

Salmon & Shrimp Stew

Preparation Time: 20 minutes **Cooking Time:** 25 minutes **Servings:** 6

2 tablespoons coconut oil
70 grams onion
2 garlic cloves
1 Serrano pepper
1 teaspoon smoked paprika
250 grams tomatoes
250 ml. chicken broth
500 grams of salmon fillets
500 grams shrimp
2 tablespoons lime juice
Salt
Ground black pepper
3 tablespoons parsley

Sauté the onion for 5–6 minutes. Add the garlic, Serrano pepper, and paprika. Add the tomatoes and broth, then boil. Simmer for 5 minutes. Add the salmon and simmer again for 3–4 minutes. Put in the shrimp, then cook for 4–5 minutes. Mix in lemon juice, salt, and black pepper, and remove. Serve with parsley.

Nutrition: Calories 247 Carbohydrates: 3.9 g Fat: 17g Protein 32.7 g

Chicken Casserole

Preparation Time: 15 minutes **Cooking Time:** 1 hour 10 minutes **Servings:** 6

Chicken Layer:
6 grass-fed chicken breasts
Salt
Pepper

Bacon Layer:
5 bacon slices
40 grams of yellow onion
40 grams of jalapeno pepper
60 grams mayonnaise
1 package of cream cheese
90 grams of Parmesan cheese
120 grams of cheddar cheese

Topping:
1 package pork skins
30 grams butter
60 grams Parmesan cheese

Warm up the oven to 200° Celsius. Put the chicken breasts in the greased casserole, then salt and black pepper. Bake for 30–40 minutes.

For the bacon layer: Cook the bacon for 8–10 minutes. Sauté the onion for 4–5 minutes. Remove, stir in bacon and remaining fixing. Remove the casserole dish, then put the bacon mixture. Fix all topping fixing. Place the topping over the bacon mixture. Bake for 15 minutes. Serve.

Nutrition: Calories 826 Carbohydrates: 2.5 g Fat: 62.9 g Protein 60.6 g

Creamy Chicken Bake

Preparation Time: 15 minutes **Cooking Time:** 1 hour 10 minutes **Servings:** 6

2 tablespoons
2 onions
3 garlic cloves
1 teaspoon tarragon
250 grams of cream cheese
120 ml. chicken broth
tablespoons lemon juice
70 grams of double cream
160 grams of Herbs de Provence
Salt
Pepper
4 grass-fed chicken breasts

Warm-up oven to 200° Celsius. Cook the onion, garlic, and tarragon for 4–5 minutes. Transfer. Cook the cream cheese, 60 ml. of broth, and lemon juice for 3–4 minutes. Stir in the cream, herbs de Provence, salt, black pepper, and remove. Pour the remaining broth and chicken breast plus the cream mixture. Bake for 45–60 minutes. Serve.

Nutrition: Calories 729 Carbohydrates: 5.6 g Fat: 52.8 g Protein 55.8 g

Beef & Veggie Casserole

Preparation Time: 20 minutes **Cooking Time:** 55 minutes **Servings:** 6

3 tablespoons butter
500 grams of grass-fed ground beef
1 yellow onion
2 garlic cloves
120 grams pumpkin
120 grams broccoli
250 grams of cheddar cheese
1 tablespoon Dijon mustard
6 organic eggs
70 grams of heavy whipping cream
Salt
Black pepper

Cook the beef for 8–10 minutes. Transfer it to a plate. Next, cook the onion and garlic for 10 minutes. Add the pumpkin and cook for additional 6 minutes. Add the broccoli and cook for another 4 minutes. Transfer to the cooked beef, and stir well to combine—warm-up oven to 190° Celsius. Put 2/3 of cheese and mustard in the beef mixture, and mix well. Add cream, eggs, salt, and black pepper to another mixing bowl, and beat. Place the beef mixture and top with egg mixture, plus the remaining cheese, in a baking dish—Bake for 25 minutes. Serve.

Nutrition: Calories 472 Carbohydrates: 5.5 g Fat: 34.6 g Protein 32.6 g

Beef with Bell Peppers

Preparation Time: 15 minutes **Cooking Time:** 10 minutes **Servings:** 4

1 tablespoon Olive oil
500 grams grass-fed flank steak
1 red bell pepper
1 green bell pepper
1 tablespoon ginger
3 tablespoons low-sodium soy sauce
1 ½ tablespoon balsamic vinegar
2 teaspoons Sriracha

Cook the steak slices for 2 minutes. Add the bell peppers and cook for additional 2–3 minutes. Transfer the beef mixture. Boil the remaining fixing for 1 minute. Add the beef mixture and cook for 1–2 minutes. Serve.

Nutrition: Calories 274 Carbohydrates: 3.8 g Fat: 13.1 g Protein 32.9 g

Braised Lamb shanks

Preparation Time: 15 minutes **Cooking Time:** 2 hours 35 minutes **Servings:** 4

4 grass-fed lamb shanks
2 tablespoons butter
Salt
ground black pepper
6 garlic cloves
6 rosemary sprigs
120 ml. chicken broth

Warm up the oven to 220° Celsius. Coat the shanks with butter and put salt and pepper—roast for 20 minutes. Remove the legs and then reduce the heat to 190° Celsius. Place the garlic cloves and rosemary over and around the lamb—roast for 2 hours. Put the broth into a roasting pan. Increase the temperature of the oven to 200° Celsius. Roast 15 minutes more.
Serve.

Nutrition: Calories 1093 Carbohydrates: 2 g Fat: 44.2 g Protein 161.4 g

Shrimp & Bell Pepper Stir-Fry

Preparation Time: 20 minutes **Cooking Time:** 10 minutes **Servings:** 6

70 ml. low-sodium soy sauce
2 tablespoons balsamic vinegar
2 tablespoons Erythritol
1 tablespoon arrowroot starch
1 tablespoon ginger
½ teaspoon red pepper flakes
3 tablespoons olive oil
½ red bell pepper
½ yellow bell pepper
½ green bell pepper
1 onion
1 red chilli
150 grams shrimp
2 scallion greens

Mix soy sauce, vinegar, erythritol, arrowroot starch, ginger, and red pepper flakes. Set aside. Stir-fry the bell peppers, onion, and red chilli for 1–2 minutes. Place the shrimp in the centre of the wok and cook for 1–2 minutes. Stir the shrimp with bell pepper mixture and cook for 2 minutes. Stir in the sauce and cook for 2–3 minutes. Stir in the scallion greens and remove. Serve hot.

Nutrition: Calories 355 Carbohydrates: 6.5 g Fat: 9 g Protein 27.6 g

Veggies & Walnut Loaf

Preparation Time: 15 minutes **Cooking Time:** 1 hour 10 minutes **Servings:** 10

1 tablespoon olive oil
2 yellow onions
2 garlic cloves
1 teaspoon dried rosemary
120 grams walnuts
2 carrots
1 celery stalk
1 green bell pepper
120 grams button mushrooms
5 organic eggs
160 grams of almond flour
Salt
Ground black pepper

Warm up the oven to 190° Celsius. Sauté the onion for 4–5 minutes. Add the garlic and rosemary and sauté for 1 minute. Add the walnuts and vegetables for 3–4 minutes. Beat the eggs, flour, sea salt, and black pepper. Mix the egg mixture with the vegetable mixture. Bake for 50–60 minutes. Serve.

Nutrition: Calories 611 Carbohydrates: 4.6 g Fat: 19.5 g Protein 5.9 g

Keto Sloppy Joes

Preparation Time: 15 minutes **Cooking Time:** 1 hour 10 minutes **Servings:** 3

160 grams of almond flour
5 tablespoons ground psyllium husk powder
1teaspoon sea salt
2 teaspoons baking powder
2 teaspoons cider vinegar
60 ml. boiling water
3 egg whites
Olive oil
500 grams of ground beef
1 yellow onion
4 garlic cloves
250 grams of crushed tomatoes
1tablespoon chilli powder
1tablespoon Dijon powder
1tablespoon red wine vinegar
4 tablespoons tomato paste
2 teaspoons salt
¼ teaspoon ground black pepper
50 grams mayonnaise
6oz. cheese

warm up the oven to 220° Celsius and mix all the dry ingredients. Add some vinegar, egg whites, and boiled water. Whisk for 30 seconds. Form the dough into 5 or 8 pieces of bread. Bake it for 55 minutes—Cook the onion and garlic. Add the ground beef and cook for additional 5 minutes. Add the rest of the ingredients and continue cooking the mixture for 10 minutes. Let it simmer for five more minutes. Serve.

Nutrition: Calories: 456 Carbohydrates: 19g Fat: 10g Protein: 30g

Low Carb Crack Slaw Egg Roll in a Bowl Recipe

Preparation Time: 15 minutes **Cooking Time:** 20 minutes **Servings:** 2

500 ground beef
250 grams shredded coleslaw mix
1 tablespoon avocado oil
Salt
Pepper
4 cloves garlic
3 tablespoons ginger
30 grams coconut amines
2 tablespoons toasted sesame oil
30 grams of green onions

Warm-up avocado oil in a large pan put in the garlic, and cook. Add the ground beef and cook for 10 minutes; put salt and black pepper. Lower the heat and add the coleslaw mix and the coconut amines. Stir to cook for 5 minutes. Remove and put in the green onions and the toasted sesame oil. Serve.

Nutrition: Calories: 336 Carbohydrates: 2g Fat: 13g Protein: 8g

Low Carb Beef Stir Fry

Preparation Time: 15 minutes **Cooking Time:** 20 minutes **Servings:** 4

60 grams courgettes
30 grams organic broccoli florets
1 baby book Choy
2 tablespoons avocado oil
2 teaspoons coconut amines
1 ginger
250 grams skirt steak

Cook the steak on high heat for 10 minutes. Then, adjust to medium heat and put in the broccoli, ginger, ghee, and coconut amines. Add in the book Choy and cook for two to three minutes. Put the courgettes into the mix and cook it for five more minutes. Serve.

Nutrition: Calories: 658 Carbohydrates: 12g Fat: 25g Protein: 40g

One Pan Pesto Chicken and Veggies

Preparation Time: 15 minutes **Cooking Time:** 25 minutes **Servings:** 4

2 tablespoons olive oil
120 grams cherry chopped tomatoes
30 grams basil pesto
43 grams of sun-dried tomatoes
500 grams of chicken thigh
500 grams asparagus

Warm up a large skillet. Put olive oil and the sliced chicken on medium heat. Add salt, stir well and then add the sun-dried tomatoes. Cook for 10 minutes, and then transfer the chicken and tomatoes. Put the asparagus in the skillet and pour it into the pesto. Put the remaining sun-dried tomatoes. Cook for 5 to 10 minutes. Transfer. Turn the chicken back in the skillet and pour it in pesto. Stir for 2 minutes. Serve with the asparagus.

Nutrition: Calories: 540 Carbohydrates: 9g Fat: 24g Protein: 23g

Crispy Peanut Tofu and Cauliflower Rice Stir-Fry

Preparation Time: 15 minutes **Cooking Time:** 1-hour **Servings:** 4

250 grams tofu
1 tablespoon toasted sesame oil
2 cloves minced garlic
1 cauliflower head

Sauce:
1 ½ tablespoon toasted sesame oil
½ teaspoon chilli garlic sauce
2 ½ tablespoons peanut butter
32 ml. low sodium soy sauce
60 grams of light brown sugar

Warm-up oven to 200° Celsius. Cube the tofu—Bake the tofu for 25 minutes and cool. Combine the sauce fixing. Put the tofu in the sauce and stir. Leave for 15 minutes. Cook the veggies with a bit of sesame oil and soy sauce. Set it aside. Grab the tofu and put it on the pan. Stir, then set aside. Steam the cauliflower rice for 5 to 8 minutes. Add some sauce and stir. Add up the rest of the ingredients. Put the cauliflower rice with the veggies and tofu. Serve.

Nutrition: Calories: 524 Carbohydrates: 39g Fat: 34g Protein: 25g

Simple Keto Fried Chicken

Preparation Time: 15 minutes **Cooking Time:** 45 minutes **Servings:** 4

4 boneless chicken thighs
Frying oil
2 eggs
2 tablespoons heavy whipping cream
Breading
150 grams grated parmesan cheese
150 grams blanched almond flour
Salt
½ teaspoon black pepper
½ teaspoon cayenne
½ teaspoon paprika

Beat the eggs and heavy cream. Separately, mix all the breading fixing. Set aside. Cut the chicken thigh into three even pieces.
Dip the chicken in the bread first before dipping it in the egg wash and then finally dipping it in the breading again—Fry, the chicken for 5 minutes. Pat dry the chicken. Serve.

Nutrition: Calories: 455 Carbohydrates: 12g Fat: 15g Protein: 30g

Keto Butter Chicken

Preparation Time: 15 minutes **Cooking Time:** 20 minutes **Servings:** 4

500 grams of chicken breast
1 tablespoon coconut oil
2 teaspoons garam masala
3 teaspoons grated ginger
3 teaspoons garlic
115 grams of plain yoghurt

Sauce:
50 grams butter
1 tablespoon ground coriander
60 grams of double cream
½ tablespoon garam masala
2 teaspoon ginger
2 teaspoon minced garlic
2 teaspoon cumin
1 teaspoon chilli powder
1 onion
250 grams of crushed tomatoes
Salt

Mix chicken pieces, gram masala, minced garlic, and grated ginger. Stir and add the yoghurt. Chill for 30 minutes. Blend the ginger, garlic, onion, tomatoes, and spices for the sauce. Put aside—Cook the chicken pieces. Once cooked, pour in the sauce, and simmer for 5 minutes. Serve.

Nutrition: Calories: 459 Carbohydrates: 7g Fat: 22g Protein: 36g

Keto Shrimp Scampi Recipe

Preparation Time: 15 minutes **Cooking Time:** 25 minutes **Servings:** 2

2 summer squashes
500 grams shrimp
2 tablespoons butter unsalted
2 tablespoons lemon juice
2 tablespoons parsley
120 ml. chicken broth
1/8 teaspoon red chilli flakes
1 clove garlic
Salt
Pepper

Put salt in the squash noodles on top. Set aside for 30 minutes. Pat dry. Fry the garlic. Add some chicken broth, red chilli flakes, and lemon juice. Once it boils, add the shrimp, and cook. Lower the heat. Add salt and pepper, and put the summer squash noodles and parsley into the mix. Serve.

Nutrition: Calories: 366 Carbohydrates: 7g Fat: 15g Protein: 49g

Keto Lasagna

Preparation Time: 15 minutes **Cooking Time:** 1-hour **Servings:** 2

250 grams of cream cheese
3 eggs
Kosher salt
Ground black pepper
250 grams mozzarella
50 grams parmesan
Pinch red pepper flakes
Parsley
Sauce:
100 ml. marinara
1 tablespoon tomato paste
500 grams of ground beef
100 grams parmesan
220 grams mozzarella
Olive oil
1tablespoon extra virgin olive oil
1teaspoon dried oregano
50 grams onion
220 grams ricotta

Warm up the oven to 220° Celsius. Melt in the cream cheese, mozzarella, and parmesan. Put the eggs, salt, and pepper. Bake for 15 to 20 minutes. Cook the onion for 5 minutes, then the garlic. Put the tomato paste. Add the ground beef, and put salt and pepper. Cook, then set aside. Cook marinara sauce, put pepper, red pepper flakes, and ground pepper. Stir. Please cut the noodles half widthwise and then cut them again into three pieces. Put two noodles at the bottom of the dish, then layer the parmesan and mozzarella shreds alternately—Bake for 30 minutes. Garnish and serve.

Nutrition: Calories: 508 Carbohydrates: 8g Fat: 39g Protein: 33g

Creamy Tuscan Garlic Chicken

Preparation Time: 15 minutes **Cooking Time:** 30 minutes **Servings:** 4

500 grams of chicken breast
100 ml. chicken broth
100 grams of parmesan cheese
100 grams of sun-dried tomatoes
130 grams of double cream
150 grams spinach
1 tablespoon olive oil
1 teaspoon garlic powder
1 teaspoon Italian seasoning

Cook the chicken using olive oil, medium heat for 5 minutes, and put aside. Combine the heavy cream, garlic powder, Italian seasoning, parmesan cheese, and chicken broth. Add the sundried tomatoes and spinach and simmer. Add the chicken back and serve.

Nutrition: Calories: 368 Carbohydrates: 7g Fat: 24g Protein: 30g

Ancho Macho Chili

Preparation Time: 20 minutes **Cooking Time:** 1 hour and 30 minutes **Servings:** 4

1 kg. lean sirloin
Salt
Pepper
1,5 tablespoons Olive oil
1 Onion, chopped
10 grams of Chili Powder
200 grams tomato with green chilis
70 ml. chicken broth
2 cloves garlic

Warm-up oven to a temperature of 220° Celsius. Coat beef with pepper and salt. Cook a third of the meat. Cook the onion for a few minutes. Put in the last four ingredients and simmer. Add in the beef with all its juices and cook for 2 hours. Stir and serve.

Nutrition: Calories: 644 Carbohydrates: 6g Fat: 40g Protein: 58g

Chicken Supreme Pizza

Preparation Time: 25 minutes **Cooking Time:** 30 minutes **Servings:** 4-8

150 grams of cooked chicken breast
130 grams of almond flour
1 teaspoon baking powder
Salt
60 ml. water
1 Red Onion
1 Red Pepper
1 Green Pepper
120 grams of Mozzarella Cheese

Warm up the oven to a temperature of 200° Celsius. Blend the flour, both the salt and baking powder. Put the water and the oil added to the flour mixture to make the dough. Flatten the dough. Dump out the dough. Press it out and coat the pan with oil.
Bake for 12 minutes. Remove, sprinkle with cheese, and add chicken, pepper, and onion. Bake again for 15 minutes, slice and serve.

Nutrition: Calories: 654 Carbohydrates: 44g Fiber: 10g Fat: 12g Protein: 16g

Baked Jerked Chicken

Preparation Time: 20 minutes **Cooking Time:** 1 hour and 30 minutes **Servings:** 4

1 kg. chicken thighs
Olive oil
Apple Cider Vinegar
Salt
1 teaspoon powdered onion
½ teaspoon garlic
½ teaspoon nutmeg
½ teaspoon pepper
½ teaspoon powdered ginger
½ teaspoon powdered cayenne
½ teaspoon cinnamon
½ teaspoon dried thyme

Mix all ingredients, excluding the chicken. Leave it for 5 minutes. Then, add in the prepared chicken pieces. Stir well. Marinade for 4 hours. Warm-up oven to a temperature of 220°Celsius. Cook for 1 hour and 25 minutes. Serve

Nutrition: Calories: 459 Carbohydrates: 4g Fat: 12g Protein: 16g

Chicken Schnitzel

Preparation Time: 15 minutes **Cooking Time:** 15 minutes **Servings:** 3

500 grams of chicken breast
60 grams almond flour
1 egg
½ tablespoon garlic powder
½ tablespoon onion powder
Keto-Safe Oil

Combine the garlic powder flour and onion in a bowl. Separately, beat the egg. With a mallet, pound out the chicken. Put the chicken in the egg mixture. Then roll well through the flour. Take a deep-frying pan and warm up the oil to medium-high temperature. Add chicken in batches. Fry. Pat dry and serve.

Nutrition: Calories: 541 Carbohydrates: 32g Fat: 17g Protein: 61g

Broccoli and Chicken Casserole

Preparation Time: 15 minutes **Cooking Time:** 10 minutes **Servings:** 4

500 grams of chicken breast
250 grams softened cream cheese
80 grams of double cream
1 teaspoon garlic powder
1 teaspoon onion powder
Salt
Pepper
250 grams, broccoli florets
120 grams mozzarella
120 grams parmesan

Warm up the oven to a temperature of 200° Celsius. Combine the cream cheese with pepper and salt. Stir in the cubed chicken.
Put in the baking dish. Put the broccoli into the chicken-cheese mixture. Top the dish with cheese, bake for about 26 minutes and remove. Take off the foil and bake again for 10 minutes. Serve.

Nutrition: Calories: 393 Carbohydrates: 20g Fat: 25g Protein: 21g

Baked Fish with Lemon Butter

Preparation Time: 15 minutes **Cooking Time:** 15 minutes **Servings:** 2

250 grams of white fish fillets
Olive oil
Pepper
Salt
1 medium-sized broccoli
60 grams butter
1 teaspoon garlic paste
1 medium-sized lemon

Warm up the oven to a temperature of 220° Celsius. Set the fish out onto the parchment paper and put pepper and salt. Pour over olive oil and lemon slices—Bake for 15 minutes. Steam the broccoli for five minutes. Put aside. Warm-up up the butter, then stir in zest, garlic, remaining lemon slices, and broccoli—Cook for 2 minutes before serving.

Nutrition: Calories: 357 Carbohydrates: 14g Fat: 15g Protein: 34g

Chicken Broccoli

Preparation Time: 15 minutes **Cooking Time:** 10 minutes **Servings:** 4

500 grams of chicken breast
250 grams spinach
120 grams broccoli
1 tablespoon butter
50 ml. Double cream
1 clove garlic
2 tablespoons onion, chopped
Salt
Pepper

Boil broccoli for 10 minutes. Melt the butter with onion and garlic, and put the chicken. Sauté for 5 minutes. Put the spinach and broccoli, then stir in the cream with seasonings. Cook for five more minutes and serve.

Nutrition: Calories: 523 Carbohydrates: 34g Fat: 19g Protein: 34g

Grilled Cheesy Buffalo Chicken

Preparation Time: 15 minutes **Cooking Time:** 10 minutes **Servings:** 2

300 grams of chicken breast
2 garlic cloves
90 grams of mozzarella cheese
1 tablespoon butter
50 grams of hot sauce
1 tablespoon lemon juice
½ teaspoon celery salt
Pepper
Salt

Mix the minced garlic, hot sauce, celery salt, melted butter, lemon juice, pepper, and salt, and then put the chicken into the mixture. Fill each chicken breast with cheese. Roll up, then secure with a toothpick to close the pocket. Grease the grill. Cook for 5 minutes, flipping, and do another 5 minutes. Cooldown and serve.

Nutrition: Calories: 499 Carbohydrates: 22g Fat: 5g Protein: 24g

Middle Eastern Shawarma

Preparation Time: 15 minutes **Cooking Time:** 10 minutes **Servings:** 3

500 grams lamb shoulder
2 tablespoons yoghurt
1 tablespoon water
1 teaspoon white vinegar
2 teaspoons lemon juice
1 teaspoon olive oil
60 grams chopped onion
1 clove garlic
½ teaspoon black pepper
½ teaspoon cumin
½ teaspoon nutmeg
½ teaspoon cloves
½ teaspoon mace
½ teaspoon powdered cayenne

Mix the yoghurt with the garlic, and put everything else except the lamb. Whisk it. Marinade the lamb strips with this mixture full day. Get the large skillet to a high temperature. Put the lamb pieces and cook for 5 minutes. Serve.

Nutrition: Calories: 677 Carbohydrates: 45g Fat: 16g Protein: 32g

Tex Mex Casserole

Preparation Time: 15 minutes **Cooking Time:** 15 minutes **Servings:** 4

120 grams of Sour cream
1 Scallion
120 grams Guacamole
120 grams Leafy greens
1 kg. Ground beef
3 tablespoons tex-mix seasoning
120 grams of Monterey Jack cheese
56 grams of Jalapenos pickled
200 grams of Crushed Tomatoes
56 grams Butter

Warm up the oven to 200° Celsius. Put the meat batter in a greased baking pan—Cook the ground beef entirely in the melted butter. Add in the Tex Mex seasoning and the tomatoes and mix well. Scatter the cheese, and the jalapenos on top, then bake for twenty-five minutes. Chop up the scallion, then mix it with the sour cream. Serve the meat mix with a spoon of sour cream, a scoop of guacamole, and some leafy greens.

Nutrition: Calories: 860 Carbohydrates: 8g Fat: 69g Protein: 49g

Baked Fish Fillets with Vegetables in Foil

Preparation Time: 15 minutes **Cooking Time:** 40 minutes **Servings:** 3

450 grams cod
1 red bell pepper
6 cherry tomatoes
1 leek
60 grams onion
60 grams courgettes
1 clove garlic
2 tablespoons olives
30 grams butter
Olive oil
1 lemon, sliced
Coriander leaves
Salt
Pepper

Warm-up oven to 200° Celsius. Transfer all the vegetables to a baking sheet lined with foil. Cut the fish into bite-sized and add them to the vegetables. Add salt and pepper, olive oil, and add pieces of butter. Bake for 35 – 40 minutes. Serve.

Nutrition: Calories 339 Fat 19g Protein 35g Carbohydrates: 5g

Fish & Chips

Preparation Time: 15 minutes **Cooking Time:** 30 minutes **Servings:** 2

For chips:
½ tablespoons olive oil
1 medium courgette
Salt
Pepper

For fish:
100 grams cod
Oil
70 grams of almond flour
¼ teaspoon onion powder
For Sauce:
2 tablespoons dill pickle relish
1 tablespoon curry powder
10 grams mayonnaise
½ teaspoon paprika powder
10 grams of parmesan cheese
1 egg
Salt
Pepper

Mix all the sauce fixing in a bowl. Set aside. Warm-up oven to 200° Celsius. Make thin courgettes rods, brush with oil, and spread on the baking sheet. Put salt and pepper, then bake for 30 minutes. Beat the egg in a bowl. Combine the parmesan cheese, almond flour, and the remaining spices on a separate plate. Slice the fish into 1 inch by 1-inch pieces. Roll them into the flour mixture. Dip in the beaten egg and then in the flour again. Fry the fish for three minutes. Serve.

Nutrition: Calories 463 Fat 26.2 g Protein 49g Carbohydrates: 6g

Baked Salmon with Almonds and Cream Sauce

Preparation Time: 10 minutes **Cooking Time:** 20 minutes **Servings:** 2

Almond Crumbs Creamy Sauce
3 tablespoons almonds
2 tablespoons almond milk
100 grams of cream cheese
Salt
1 salmon fillet
1 teaspoon coconut oil
2 tablespoons lemon zest
Salt
Pepper

Cut the salmon in half. Rub the salmon with lemon zest, salt, and pepper. Marinade for 20 minutes. Fry the fish on both sides. Top with almond crumbs and bake for 10 to 15 minutes. Remove and put aside. Place the baking dish on fire and add the cream cheese. Combine the fish baking juices and the cheese. Mix, then pour the sauce onto the fish. Serve.

Nutrition: Calories 522 Fat 44g Protein 28g Carbohydrates: 2.4g

Shrimp and Sausage Bake

Preparation Time: 15 minutes **Cooking Time:** 20 minutes **Servings:** 4

2 tablespoons Olive oil
180 grams of chorizo sausage
60 grams pound shrimp
1 small onion, chopped
10 grams of garlic powder
40ml. Herbed Chicken Stock
Pinch red pepper flakes
1 red bell pepper

Sauté the sausage for 6 minutes. Add the shrimp and sauté for 4 minutes. Remove both and set them aside—Cook the red pepper, onion, and garlic in the skillet for 4 minutes. Put the chicken stock along with the cooked sausage and shrimp. Simmer for 3 minutes. Stir in the red pepper flake and serve.

Nutrition: Calories 588 Fat 24g Protein 20g Carbohydrates: 6g

Herb Butter Scallops

Preparation Time: 10 minutes **Cooking Time:** 10 minutes **Servings:** 4

500 grams of sea scallops
Black pepper
Salt
8 teaspoons butter
2 teaspoons garlic
Lemon juice of 1 lemon
2 teaspoons basil
1 teaspoon thyme

Pat dry the scallops, then put pepper. Sear each side for 2 60 grams minutes per side. Remove, then set aside. Sauté the garlic for 3 minutes. Stir in the lemon juice, basil, and thyme and return the scallops to the skillet; mix. Serve.

Nutrition: Calories 512 Fat 24g Protein 19g Carbohydrates: 4g

Pan-Seared Halibut with Citrus Butter Sauce

Preparation Time: 10 minutes **Cooking Time:** 15 minutes **Servings:** 4

4 halibut fillets
Salt
ground pepper
30 grams butter
1 tablespoon garlic
1 shallot
3 tablespoons dry white wine
1 tablespoon orange juice
1 tablespoon lemon juice
2 teaspoons parsley
2 teaspoons olive oil

Panfry the fish for 10 minutes. Pat dry the fish, then put salt and pepper. Set aside. Sauté the garlic and shallot for 3 minutes. Whisk in the white wine, lemon juice, and orange juice and simmer for 2 minutes. Remove the sauce and stir in the parsley; set aside. Serve with sauce.

Nutrition: Calories 741 Fat 26g Protein 22g Carbohydrates: 2g

Baked Coconut Haddock

Preparation Time: 10 minutes **Cooking Time:** 12 minutes **Servings:** 4

4 boneless haddock fillets
Salt
Freshly ground pepper
120 grams shredded unsweetened coconut
60 grams ground hazelnuts
2 tablespoons coconut oil

Warm oven to 200° Celsius. Pat dry fillets and lightly season them with salt and pepper. Stir together the shredded coconut and hazelnut in a small bowl. Dredge the fish fillets in the coconut mixture to be thickly coated on both sides of each piece. Put the fish on the baking sheet and lightly brush both sides of each piece with the coconut oil.

Bake the haddock until the topping is golden, and the fish flakes easily with a fork, about 12 minutes total. Serve.

Nutrition: Calories 447 Fat 24g Protein 20g Carbohydrates: 13g

Spicy Steak Curry

Preparation Time: 15 minutes **Cooking Time:** 40 minutes **Servings:** 6

120 grams of plain yoghurt
½ teaspoon garlic paste
½ teaspoon ginger paste
½ teaspoon ground cloves
½ teaspoon ground cumin
2 teaspoons red pepper flakes
¼ teaspoon ground turmeric Salt
2 pounds grass-fed round steak
Olive oil
1 medium yellow onion
2 tablespoons lemon juice
40 grams cilantro

Mix yoghurt, garlic paste, ginger paste, and spices. Add the steak pieces. Set aside. Sauté the onion for 4-5 minutes. Add the steak pieces with marinade and mix. Simmer for 25 minutes. Stir in the lemon juice and simmer for 10 minutes. Garnish with cilantro and serve.

Nutrition: Calories: 440 Carbohydrates: 47g Fat: 23g Protein: 48.3g

Beef Stew

Preparation Time: 15 minutes **Cooking Time:** 1 hour 40 minutes **Servings:** 4

500 grams grass-fed chuck roast
Salt
Black Pepper
60 grams butter
1 yellow onion
2 garlic cloves
120 ml. beef broth
1 bay leaf
1 teaspoon dried thyme
½ teaspoon dried rosemary
1 carrot
120 grams celery stalks
1 tablespoon lemon juice

Put salt and black pepper in beef cubes. Sear the beef cubes for 4-5 minutes. Add the onion and garlic, then adjust the heat to medium and cook for 4-5 minutes. Add the broth, bay leaf, and dried herbs and boil. Simmer for 45 minutes. Stir in the carrot and celery and simmer for 30-45 minutes. Stir in lemon juice, salt, and black pepper. Serve.

Nutrition: Calories: 413 Carbohydrate: 5.9g Fat: 32g Protein: 52g

Beef & Cabbage Stew

Preparation Time: 15 minutes **Cooking Time:** 2 hours 10 minutes **Servings:** 8

1kg. grass-fed beef stew meat
200 ml. hot chicken broth
2 yellow onions
2 bay leaves
1 teaspoon Greek seasoning
Salt
Black Pepper
3 celery stalks
1 package cabbage
1 can sugar-free tomato sauce
1 can sugar-free whole plum tomatoes

Sear the beef for 4-5 minutes. Stir in the broth, onion, bay leaves, Greek seasoning, salt, and black pepper and boil. Adjust the heat to low and cook for 160 grams hours. Stir in the celery and cabbage and cook for 30 minutes. Stir in the tomato sauce, chopped plum tomatoes, and cook uncovered for 15-20 minutes. Stir in the salt, discard bay leaves and serve.

Nutrition: Calories: 478 Carbohydrate: 7g Fat: 23g Protein: 36.5g

Cheese steak soup

Preparation Time: 15 minutes **Cooking Time**: 20 minutes

3 tablespoons butter
55 grams red onion
140 grams green bell pepper
110 grams mushrooms
Salt
Pepper
950 ml. beef broth
110 grams cream cheese
170 grams shredded white cheddar cheese
85 grams provolone cheese, sliced

In a large saucepan over medium heat, melt the butter. Once hot, add the onions and sauté until tender but not browned, about 5 minutes. Stir in the peppers and mushrooms and sprinkle with salt and pepper. Cook another 3 to 4 minutes, until tender. Add the roast beef and toss to mix well. Stir in the broth and bring to a simmer. Cook 10 minutes. Place the cream cheese in a blender and add about ¼ of the hot broth from the pan. Blend until smooth and the cream cheese is melted. Pour the mixture back into the pan and stir in the shredded cheese until melted.
Preheat the broiler. On a baking sheet, place under the broiler until the cheese is melted and bubbly, 2 to 4 minutes. Ladle the soup into oven-safe bowls or ramekins and top with a piece of provolone.
Serve immediately.

Nutrition: Calories: 567 Carbohydrates: 33g Fat: 25 g Protein: 29 g

Keto Fajitas

Preparation Time: 15 minutes **Cooking Time**: 20 minutes **Servings**: 4

1 tablespoon chili powder
1 tablespoon paprika powder
2 teaspoon dried oregano
2 teaspoons ground cumin
Salt
650 grams chicken breasts
120 grams red bell pepper
110 grams yellow onion
2 garlic cloves
60 ml olive oil
2 tablespoons lime juice
30 grams cilantro

Preheat oven to 200°Celsius. Mix the chili powder, paprika, oregano, cumin, and salt in a small bowl and set aside.
Put the chicken strips, bell peppers, onion, garlic, oil, and lime juice in a large bowl and mix to distribute the oil and lime juice thoroughly. Sprinkle in the spice mixture and toss to coat the chicken and vegetables: Spread the seasoned chicken and veggies on the sheet pan in a single layer. Bake for 20-25 minutes, stirring halfway through the baking time until the chicken is cooked. If you enjoy a little char on your fajitas, you can place the pan under the broiler for three to 5 minutes before serving—Garnish with fresh cilantro and serve.

Nutrition: Calories: 456 Fat: 33g Carbohydrates: 22g Protein: 22g

Keto Salmon with Lemon Sauce

Preparation Time: 10 minutes **Cooking Time**: 30 minutes **Servings**: 2

120 ml vegetable stock
160 ml heavy whipping cream
1 tablespoon fresh chives
2 tablespoon fresh parsley
½ lemon juice
½ teaspoon salt
Black pepper
2 tablespoons olive oil
450 grams salmon
1 tablespoon butter
450 grams spinach

Lemon sauce
1. Pour the vegetable stock into a small saucepan and bring to a boil over high heat. Boil for a few minutes to slightly reduce the stock.
2. Add the cream, chives, parsley, lemon juice, salt, and pepper to the stock, and whisk to combine. Reduce the temperature to low, keep uncovered, and whisk occasionally. The sauce will thicken as the salmon is being prepared.

Salmon
3. In a large, non-stick pan, heat the olive oil over medium-high heat for a couple of minutes. Season the salmon on both sides with salt and pepper. Place the salmon in the pan (skin side down, if applicable) and sear for about 4 minutes until golden and crispy. Gently flip with a spatula and reduce the heat to medium. Cook for another 3-5 minutes, until golden crisp on the outside, and a light pink color inside. Transfer to a serving platter and keep warm.

Serving
4. Melt the butter in a large frying pan or wok, over medium heat—Increase the temperature to medium-high and add the spinach. Toss with tongs for a couple of minutes until wilted. Remove from heat, and season with salt and pepper.
5. To serve, drizzle the lemon sauce over the salmon, with the sautéed spinach on the side.

Nutrition: Calories: 422 Carbohydrates: 23g Fat: 80 g Protein: 56 g

Chicken with parmesan and mushrooms

Preparation Time: 10 minutes **Cooking Time**: 30 minutes **Servings**: 4

2 tablespoons avocado oil
650 grams boneless chicken thighs
230 grams baby bella mushrooms
4 garlic cloves
350 ml heavy whipping cream
40 grams shredded parmesan cheese
1 teaspoon fresh parsley
120 grams red bell pepper
110 grams yellow onion
2 garlic cloves
60 ml olive oil
2 tablespoons lime juice
30 grams cilantro

Over medium heat, in a large skillet, warm the avocado oil. Fry in the skillet until browned or cooked through; remove chicken to a plate with a slotted spoon, reserving juices in the pan. Season the chicken thighs with salt and pepper.
Add garlic to the frying pan and stir-fry until soft; add mushrooms and sauté until softened, for about 5-7 minutes.
On low heat, add heavy cream, stirring well. Allow to simmer for about 10 minutes stirring often. Stir in parmesan cheese until melted. Add additional salt and pepper to taste. Add chicken back into skillet and coat with sauce. Serve garnished with parsley.

Nutrition: Calories: 455 Fat: 34g Carbohydrates: 20g Protein: 14g

Keto Pizza

Preparation Time: 15 minutes **Cooking Time**: 30 minutes **Servings**: 4

Crust
170 grams mozzarella cheese
2 tablespoons cream cheese
85 grams almond flour
1 teaspoon white wine vinegar
1 egg
Olive oil
Topping
230 grams Italian sausage
1 tablespoon butter
120 ml. unsweetened tomato sauce
½ teaspoon dried oregano
170 grams mozzarella cheese

Preheat the oven to 200° Celsius. Heat mozzarella and cream cheese in a non-stick pan on medium heat or in a bowl in the microwave oven. Stir until they melt together. Add the other ingredients and mix well. Tip: use a hand mixer with dough hooks. Moisten your hands with olive oil and flatten the dough on parchment paper, making a circle about 8" (20 cm) in diameter. You can also use a rolling pin to flatten the dough between two sheets of parchment paper. Remove the top parchment sheet (if used). Prick the crust with a fork (all over) and bake in the oven for 10–15 minutes until golden brown. Remove from the oven. While the crust is baking, sautée the ground sausage meat in olive oil or butter. Spread a thin layer of tomato sauce on the crust. Top the pizza with meat and plenty of cheese. Bake for 10–15 minutes or until the cheese has melted. Sprinkle with oregano and enjoy!

Nutrition: Calories: 600 Fat: 23g Protein: 17g Carbohydrates: 22g

Beef & Mushroom Chili

Preparation Time: 15 minutes **Cooking Time:** 3 hours 10 minutes **Servings:** 8

1kg. grass-fed ground beef
1 yellow onion
60 grams green bell pepper
60 grams carrot
120 grams mushrooms
2 garlic cloves
1 can sugar-free tomato paste
60 grams of red chili powder
6 grams ground cumin
6 grams ground cinnamon
6 grams of red pepper flakes
6 grams ground allspice
Salt
Pepper
250 ml. of water
70 grams of sour cream

Cook the beef for 8-10 minutes. Stir in the remaining fixing except for sour cream and boil. Cook on low, covered, for 3 hours. Top with sour cream and serve.

Nutrition: Calories: 333 Carbohydrates: 5.9g Fat: 8.2g Protein: 25.1g

Steak with Cheese Sauce

Preparation Time: 15 minutes **Cooking Time:** 17 minutes **Servings:** 4

500 grams grass-fed filet mignon
Salt
ground black pepper
2 tablespoons butter
65 grams of yellow onion
110 grams of blue cheese
120 grams of double cream
1 garlic clove
ground nutmeg

Cook onion for 5-8 minutes. Add the blue cheese, double cream, garlic, nutmeg, salt, and black pepper and stir well to combine. Cook for about 3-5 minutes. Put salt and black pepper in filet mignon steaks. Cook the steaks for 4 minutes per side. Transfer and set aside. Top with cheese sauce, then serve.

Nutrition: Calories: 521 Carbohydrates: 3g Fat: 33g Protein: 44.7g

Grilled Steak

Preparation Time: 15 minutes **Cooking Time:** 12 minutes **Servings:** 6

1 teaspoon lemon zest
1 garlic clove
1 tablespoon red chili powder
1 tablespoon paprika
1 tablespoon ground coffee
Salt
Pepper
2 grass-fed skirt steaks

Mix all the ingredients except steaks. Marinate the steaks and keep them aside for 30-40 minutes. Grill the steaks for 5-6 minutes per side. Remove, then cool before slicing. Serve.

Nutrition: Calories: 473 Carbohydrate: 17g Fat: 23g Protein: 60.8g

Roasted Tenderloin

Preparation Time: 10 minutes **Cooking Time:** 50 minutes **Servings:** 10

2kg. grass-fed beef tenderloin roast
4 garlic cloves
Salt
Black Pepper
1 tablespoon rosemary

Warm-up oven to 200° Celsius. Place beef meat into the prepared roasting pan. Massage it with garlic, rosemary, salt, and black pepper and oil. Roast the beef for 45-50 minutes. Remove, cool, slice, and serve.

Nutrition: Calories: 669 Carbohydrates: 15g Protein: 39.5g Fat: 13.9g

Garlicky Prime Rib Roast

Preparation Time: 15 minutes **Cooking Time:** 1 hour 35 minutes **Servings:** 15

10 garlic cloves
2 teaspoons dried thyme
2 tablespoons olive oil
Salt
Pepper
1 grass-fed prime rib roast

Preheat the oven to 220° Celsius. Mix the garlic, thyme, oil, salt, and black pepper. Marinate the rib roast with garlic mixture for 1 hour. Roast for 20 minutes. Lower to 220° Celsius and roast for 65-75 minutes. Remove, cool down for 10-15 minutes, slice, and serve.

Nutrition: Calories: 499 Carbohydrates: 12g Protein: 61.5g Fat: 25.9g

Beef Taco Bake

Preparation Time: 15 minutes **Cooking Time:** 1-hour **Servings:** 6

For Crust:
3 organic eggs
120 grams of cream cheese
½ teaspoon taco seasoning
40 ml. heavy cream
200 grams of cheddar cheese
For Topping:
500 grams of grass-fed ground beef
120 grams of green chillies
30 grams sugar-free tomato sauce
3 teaspoons taco seasoning
170 grams of cheddar cheese

Preheat the oven to 220° Celsius. For the crust: beat the eggs, cream cheese, taco seasoning, and heavy cream. Place cheddar cheese in the baking dish. Spread cream cheese mixture over cheese. Remove, then set aside for 5 minutes. Bake for 25-30 minutes.
For topping:
Cook the beef for 8-10 minutes. Stir in the green chilies, tomato sauce, and taco seasoning and transfer. Place the beef mixture over the crust and sprinkle with cheese. Bake for 18-20 minutes. Remove, then slice and serve.

Nutrition: Calories: 569 Carbohydrates: 3.8g Fat: 12g Protein: 38.7g

Meatballs with Curry

Preparation Time: 15 minutes **Cooking Time:** 25 minutes **Servings:** 6

2 garlic cloves
1 red chilly, deseeded
1 thick slice of white bread
small pack mint leaves, reserving some to serve
400 grams lamb mince
1 egg, lightly beaten
1 tbsp vegetable oil
1 large onion, roughly chopped
1 tablespoon masala curry paste
400 grams chopped tomato
400 ml. lamb stock
100 grams baby spinach leaves
cooked basmati rice and cucumber & mint raita, to serve (optional)

Place the garlic, chili, bread and mint in a food processor and pulse until finely chopped. Tip into a bowl and mix with the lamb, egg and seasoning. Using damp hands, shape into 16 small meatballs. Heat half the vegetable oil in a large non-stick frying pan. Fry the meatballs in batches over a high heat until golden, then set aside.

Heat, the remaining oil in the frying pan, add the onion and cook for 3-4 mins until beginning to soften. Add the curry paste and fry for 1 min, then tip in the tomatoes and stock and bring to a simmer. Add the meatballs and simmer for 15 mins until the sauce is thickened. Stir through the spinach until just wilted. Scatter over the reserved mint leaves, and serve with rice and cucumber & mint raita, if you like.

Nutrition: Calories: 444 Carbohydrate: 8.6g Fat: 12g Protein: 17g

Meatballs in Cheese Sauce

Preparation Time: 20 minutes **Cooking Time:** 25 minutes **Servings:** 5

Meatballs:
60 grams panko breadcrumbs
1 large egg
1 teaspoon each: garlic powder and onion powder
½ teaspoon each: red pepper flakes, salt, and black pepper
1 tablespoon low sodium soy sauce
130 grams grated parmesan cheese
2 tablespoons chopped parsley
500 grams ground beef

Sauce:
olive oil, for cooking
60 grams of each: chopped onions, chopped green bell peppers, and chopped mushrooms
2 tablespoons each: all-purpose flour and chopped parsley
1 teaspoon garlic powder
130ml. low sodium beef stock (or chicken)
1 tablespoon low sodium soy sauce
60 grams sour cream
130 grams shredded provolone cheese

In a medium mixing bowl, mix together the breadcrumbs, egg, garlic powder, onion powder, salt, red pepper flakes, black pepper, soy sauce, parmesan, and parsley. The mixture will resemble a coarse breading. Add the ground beef and mix until *just* combined. You don't want to overwork the meat. Roll into 23-27 meatballs. Mine were about 1 ½ tablespoon each.
Heat 1 tablespoon of oil in a large skillet over medium-high heat. Add the meatballs to the skillet but do not overcrowd the pan. Cook in batches if they don't all fit. Sear the meatballs for 5-6 minutes, flipping to brown all sides evenly and cook the meatballs all the way through. Remove the meatballs to a plate. Repeat until all the meatballs are cooked.

Depending on how much oil is left in your skillet, you'll want to have 2 tablespoons worth before adding the onions and sautéing for 2 minutes or until the onions begin to turn translucent. Add the peppers and mushrooms and continue to cook until everything softens a bit, about 2-3 minutes. Sprinkle the flour and garlic powder over the veggies and push the veggies around the pan to coat evenly and cook for about 1 minute to cook out the raw taste of flour. Gradually whisk in the stock and cook. Add 60ml. of water and soy sauce, and continue to whisk.

You want to whisk continuously so you don't have lumps, about 2-3 minutes. When the sauce begins to thicken just a bit, add the sour cream, whisking it in if necessary. Add in the cheese and stir continuously using a wooden spoon until it melts. Allow the sauce to start bubbling and allow for it to thicken; about 3-5 minutes. Remove from the stove, add the meatballs and cover them in the sauce. Sprinkle with parsley and serve in baguettes, over pasta, mashed potatoes, or rice.

Nutrition: Calories: 555 Carbohydrate: 6.6g   Protein: 38.6g Fat: 24.8g

Chocolate Chili

Preparation Time: 15 minutes **Cooking Time:** 260 grams hours **Servings:** 8

Olive oil
1 small onion
1 green bell pepper
4 garlic cloves
1 jalapeño pepper
1 teaspoon dried thyme
2 tablespoons red chilli powder
1 tablespoon ground cumin
1kg. lean ground pork
250 grams of fresh tomatoes
120 grams of sugar-free tomato paste
1½ tablespoons cacao powder
250 ml. chicken broth
120 ml. of water
Salt
Black pepper
110 grams of cheddar cheese

Sauté the onion and bell pepper for 5-7 minutes. Add the garlic, jalapeño pepper, thyme, and spices and sauté for 1 minute. Add the pork and cook for 4-5 minutes. Stir in the tomatoes, tomato paste, and cacao powder and cook for 2 minutes. Add the broth and water, and boil. Simmer, covered for 2 hours. Stir in the salt and black pepper. Remove, then top with cheddar cheese and serve.

Nutrition: Calories: 369 Carbohydrate: 9.1g Protein: 23.3g Fat: 22.9g

Pork Stew

Preparation Time: 15 minutes **Cooking Time:** 45 minutes **Servings:** 6

1kg. boneless pork roast
60 grams all-purpose flour
2 1/2 teaspoons salt
1 1/2 teaspoons black pepper
3 tablespoons extra virgin olive oil
2 small leeks, white and green part thinly sliced
130 grams chopped shallots
4 large garlic cloves, minced
220 ml. white wine
5 medium carrots, peeled and cut into 3/4 inch pieces
4 medium Yukon Gold potatoes, peeled and sliced into 1-inch cubes
220 ml. chicken stock
1 can chopped tomatoes
2 tablespoons balsamic vinegar
2 bay leave
1 teaspoon dried basil
1 teaspoon dried organo
1 teaspoon dried thyme
100 grams cremini mushrooms, cut in half
Chopped parsley for garnish

In medium bowl, toss pork cubes in flour, 1/2 teaspoon salt, and 1/2 teaspoon black pepper. Heat olive oil in a large dutch oven over medium-high heat. Place one half on the pork in an·even layer in the dutch oven. Do not overcrowd. Brown for two to three minutes. Turn each piece and brown for two to three minutes—transfer browned pork to a plate. Repeat with remaining pork, transferring to plate when browned. Add leeks, shallots, and garlic to dutch oven and saute for two to three minutes until the leeks are wilted. Add wine and stir to deglaze the pan, scraping the bottom of the pot to remove browned bits.

Add carrots, potatoes, chicken stock, tomatoes, vinegar, bay leaves, basil, oregano, thyme, two teaspoons salt, and one teaspoon pepper to Dutch oven. Bring to a boil, mixing well. Reduce heat to low and simmer for five minutes.

5. Add pork to the stew, cover, and simmer for 30 to 40 minutes. Add mushrooms and continue simmering for ten to 15 minutes or until vegetables are tender. Adjust seasoning with salt and pepper to taste. Serve immediately garnished with chopped parsley.

Nutrition: Calories: 777   Carbohydrates: 22g   Fiber: 12g Protein: 41g Fat: 10.4g

Pork & Chiles Stew

Preparation Time: 15 minutes **Cooking Time:** 2 hours & 10 minutes **Servings:** 8

3 tablespoons unsalted butter
250 grams pounds of boneless pork ribs
1 large yellow onion
4 garlic cloves
160 ml. chicken broth
2 cans of sugar-free tomatoes
120 grams canned roasted poblano chilies
2 teaspoons dried oregano
1 teaspoon ground cumin
Salt
30 grams cilantro
2 tablespoons lime juice

Cook the pork, onions, and garlic for 5 minutes. Add the broth, tomatoes, poblano chilies, oregano, cumin, and salt and boil. Simmer, covered for 2 hours. Mix with the fresh cilantro and lime juice and remove it. Serve.

Nutrition: Calories: 369 Carbohydrates: 36g   Fat: 21g Protein: 39.6g

SNACK

Chips

Preparation Time: 10 Minutes **Cooking Time:** 20 Minutes **Servings:** 4

Oil spray (make sure its avocado)

What you need for the coating:
1 tablespoon of paprika
½ of a tablespoon of cayenne pepper for a little bit of a kick
½ of a tablespoon of onion powder
¼ teaspoon nutritional yeast
½ tablespoon of garlic powder

What you need for the chip:
A bag of pork belly skin (take note that whatever bag you choose will change the nutrition information at the end of the recipe)

Spray your pork rinds with oil to make the coating stick better. Transfer the skins to a plastic bag and pour the toppings in before you begin to shake them. Add the coating ingredients to a spice grinder and blend until everything becomes smooth.

Nutrition: Calories: 124 **Fat:** 2.7g **Carbohydrates:** 2g

Pickle

Preparation Time: 20 Minutes **Cooking Time:** 20 Minutes **Servings:** 3

1 can of tuna (go for a version that is light flaked)
30 grams of mayo (it needs to be sugar-free if you can get it and a light version)
1 tablespoon dill
5 or 6 pickles depending on what you need

Cut your pickles in half so that they are lengthwise. Seed your pickles. Drain the tuna, and then mix the dill, mayo, and tuna in a bowl before mixing. Spoon the tuna mixture onto the pickle. It will only take you five minutes. You can get up to four servings from this.

Nutrition: Calories: 133 **Protein:** 6g **Carbohydrates:** 3.6g **Fat:** 0.6g

Cucumber Sushi

Preparation Time: 15 minutes **Cooking Time:** 20 minutes **Servings**: 10

2 medium cucumbers, halved
1/4 avocado, thinly sliced
1/2 red bell pepper, thinly sliced
1/2 yellow bell pepper, thinly sliced
2 small carrots, thinly sliced
FOR THE DIPPING SAUCE
90 grams mayonnaise
1 tablespoon sriracha
1 teaspoon. soy sauce

Using a small spoon, remove seeds from the center of cucumbers until they are utterly hollow. Press avocado into the center of the cucumber, using a butter knife to press inside the cucumber. Next, slide in bell peppers and carrots until the cucumber is full of veggies. Make dipping sauce: combine mayo, sriracha, and soy sauce in a small bowl. Whisk to combine. Slice cucumber rounds into 1" thick pieces and serve with sauce on the side.

Nutrition: Calories: 190 Carbohydrates 5g Fat: 15 g Protein: 3g

Chips from Brussels Sprout

Preparation Time: 5 minutes **Cooking Time**: 10 minutes **Servings**: 2

500 grams broccoli
1 tablespoon olive oil
2 tablespoons parmesan cheese, grated
1 teaspoon garlic powder
Black pepper
Salt
Caesar dressing, optional

Preheat oven to 200°Celsius. In a large bowl, toss brussels sprouts with oil, Parmesan, and garlic powder and season with salt and pepper. Spread in an even layer on a medium baking sheet. Bake 10 minutes, toss, and bake 8 to 10 minutes more, until crisp and golden. Garnish with more Parmesan and serve with caesar dressing for dipping.

Nutrition: Calories 220 Fat: 25 g Carbohydrates 4g Protein: 3g

Keto Taquitos

Preparation Time: 15 minutes **Cooking Time**: 45 minutes **Servings**: 12

2 tablespoons extra-virgin olive oil
1/2 onion, finely chopped
4 cloves garlic, minced
1 teaspoon ground cumin
1 teaspoon chili powder
160 grams shredded chicken
3 tablespoons red enchilada sauce
4 tablespoons freshly chopped cilantro, plus more for garnish
Kosher salt
220 grams shredded cheddar
220 grams shredded Monterey jack
Sour cream, for serving (optional)

Preheat oven to 375° and line two baking sheets with parchment paper. In a medium skillet over medium heat, heat oil. Add onion and cook until slightly soft, 3 minutes. Add garlic and spices and cook until fragrant, 1 to 2 minutes more. Add chicken and enchilada sauce, then bring mixture to a simmer. Stir in cilantro, season with salt, and remove from heat.

Make taquito shells: In a medium bowl, mix cheeses. Divide mixture into twelve 3 ½" piles on prepared baking sheet. Bake until cheese is melty and slightly golden around the edges, about 10 minutes. Let excellent 2 to 4 minutes, then peel shells off parchment. Add a small pile of chicken to each and roll tightly. Repeat until all taquitos are made.

Garnish with cilantro and serve with sour cream for dipping.

Nutrition: Calories: 330 Fat: 4g Protein 3g Carbohydrates 11g

Bacon Asparagus Bites

Preparation Time: 10 minutes **Cooking Time**: 30 minutes **Servings**: 6

6 slices bacon, cut into thirds
220 grams cream cheese, softened to room temperature
1 garlic clove, minced
Freshly ground black pepper
Kosher salt
9 asparagus spears, blanched

Preheat oven to 200°Celsius and line 1 medium baking sheet with parchment paper. Cook bacon: In a large skillet over medium heat, cook bacon until most of the fat is cooked out but is not crisp. Remove from pan and drain on a paper towel-lined plate. In a small bowl, combine cream cheese with garlic and season with salt and pepper. Stir until combined.

Assemble bites:

Spread about 1/2 tablespoon cream cheese onto each strip of bacon. Place asparagus in the center and roll bacon until bacon ends meet. Once all bites are made, place on prepared baking sheet and bake 5 minutes until bacon is crisp and cream cheese is warmed through. Serve.

Nutrition: Calories: 234 Fat: 5g Protein: 5g Carbohydrates: 3g

Avocado Boats with Crab

Preparation Time: 5 minutes **Cooking Time**: 10 minutes **Servings**: 4

500 grams lump crab meat
220 grams Greek yoghurt
1/2 red onion, minced
2 tablespoons Chopped chives
3 tablespoons lemon juice
1/2 tsp. cayenne pepper
kosher salt
130 grams shredded Cheddar
2 avocados, halved and pitted

In a medium bowl, stir together lump crab meat, yogurt, red onion, chives, lemon juice, and cayenne and season with salt. Scoop out avocados to create bowls, leaving a small border. Dice scooped out avocado and fold into crab mixture—Preheat broiler. Fill avocado bowls with crab mixture and top with cheddar. Broil until cheese is just melted, about 1 minute. Serve immediately.

Nutrition: Calories: 350 Fat: 11 g Protein: 5 g

Pinwheel Delight

Preparation Time: 5 Minutes **Cooking Time:** 5 Minutes

1 block of cream cheese
10 slices of salami (genoa) and pepperoni
5 tablespoons pickles
(make sure they are finely chopped)

Have your cream cheese brought to room temperature. Whip the cream cheese until it becomes fluffy. Spread your cream cheese in a rectangle that is a quarter-inch thick. Make sure to use an appropriately sized plastic wrap. Put pickles on top of the cream cheese Place the salami over the cream cheese in overlapping layers so that each cream cheese layer is covered. Place another layer of the wrap over the layer of salami and press down. Be gentle. Flip your whole rectangle over so that the bottom cream cheese layer is now facing the top instead. Peel back your plastic wrap very carefully from the top cream cheese layer. It would help if you began rolling this into a log shape, slowly removing the bottom layer of your plastic wrap as you go along. Place the pinwheel in a tight plastic wrap. Place in the fridge overnight or wait at least four hours. Slice, whatever thick you want it.

Nutrition: Calories: 133 Fat: 4.2g Carbohydrates: 0.8g Protein: 1g

Zesty olives

Preparation Time: 5 Minutes **Cooking Time:** 5 Minutes **Servings:** 6

30 grams of oil (make sure that it is extra virgin olive oil)
¼ teaspoon pepper flakes
1 thinly sliced garlic clove
1 tablespoon lemon juice
1 strip of zest from a lemon
120 grams of olives
2 sprigs of thyme
1 tablespoon orange juice
1 strip of zest from an orange

Get a saucepan. Heat your oil over medium-high heat. Add zest, thyme, garlic, and zest in and cook it. Be sure that you stir occasionally. Cook for a few minutes, and you will notice that the garlic is golden. You will then need to mix in the olives and cook them. Stir them as they cook but only cook for 2 minutes. You want them to be warmed. Turn off your heat. Stir in your juice—place in a dish.

Nutrition: Calories: 180 Fat: 20g Carbohydrates: 2g Protein: 4g

Deviled Eggs Keto Style!

Preparation Time: 5 Minutes **Cooking Time:** 5 Minutes **Servings:** 6

3 large eggs (hardboiled)
1/2 avocado (make sure it is ripe)
1/2 lemon (you will need to juice this)
1/2 tablespoon mustard (use Dijon)
Paprika (use smoked)

Slice your eggs in half and take out the yolks. Combine your yolks, avocado, and lemon juice in a bowl and stir thoroughly. Spoon the mixture into the egg halves. Sprinkle the top with paprika.

Nutrition: Calories: 250 Fat: 4g Carbohydrates: 6g Protein: 3g

Cucumber

Preparation Time: 5 Minutes **Cooking Time:** 0 Minutes **Servings:** 1

120 grams of cucumbers (make sure they are sliced)
10 olives (Kalamata olives. Use large ones)

Mix them in a bowl, and there you go!

Nutrition: Calories: 71 Fat: 4.8g Carbohydrates: 5g Protein: 1.29g

Nutty Yoghurt

Preparation Time: 5 Minutes **Cooking Time:** 0 Minute **Servings:** 1

56 grams of yoghurt (use whole milk Greek yoghurt)
½ teaspoon cinnamon
1 tablespoon walnuts

Place the yoghurt in a dish. Add the walnuts. Add the cinnamon.

Nutrition: Calories: 160 Fat: 12.5g Protein: 8g Carbohydrates: 6g

Creamy Celery

Preparation Time: 5 Minutes **Cooking Time:** 0 Minutes **Servings:** 4

2 stalks of celery
2 tablespoons cream cheese

Clean the celery and cut it into pieces. Place the pieces on a plate before adding cream cheese to them. Repeat this process if necessary.

Nutrition: Calories: 113 Fat: 10.1g Carbohydrates: 4g Protein: 2.3g

Parmesan Cheese Strips

Preparation Time: 15 minutes **Cooking Time:** 30 minutes **Servings:** 12 (You can store it for several days)

120 grams of parmesan cheese
1 teaspoon dried basil

Heat the oven to 190° Celsius. Form small piles of parmesan cheese on the baking sheet. Flatten and sprinkle dried basil on top of the cheese—Bake for 5 to 7 minutes. Serve.

Nutrition: Calories: 455 Fat: 2g Protein: 2g Carbohydrates: 6.21g

Peanut Butter Power Granola

Preparation Time: 15 minutes **Cooking Time:** 40 minutes **Servings:** 12 (You can store it for several days)

120 grams shredded coconut
160 grams almonds
150 grams pecans
10 grams swerve sweetener
10 grams of vanilla whey protein powder
10 grams of peanut butter
10 grams of sunflower seeds
10 grams butter
20 ml. water

Heat the oven to 220° Celsius. Process the almonds and pecans using a food processor. Transfer and add the sunflower seeds, shredded coconut, vanilla, sweetener, and protein powder. Dissolve the peanut butter and butter in the microwave. Mix the melted butter into the nut mixture. Put in the water to create a lumpy mixture. Scoop out the batter and place it on the baking sheet—Bake for 30 minutes. Serve!

Nutrition: Calories: 338 Fat: 30g Carbohydrates: 5g Protein: 9.6g

Homemade Graham Crackers

Preparation Time: 15 minutes **Cooking Time:** 1 hour 10 minutes **Servings:** 10 (You can store it for several days)

1 egg
250 grams of almond flour
43 grams swerve brown
6 grams cinnamon
5 grams of baking powder
2 teaspoons melted butter
1 teaspoon vanilla extract
Salt

Heat the oven to 220° Celsius. Mix the almond flour, cinnamon, sweetener, baking powder, and salt. Put in the egg, molasses, melted butter, and vanilla extract. Mix to form a dough. Roll out the dough evenly. Cut the dough into the shapes. Bake for 20 to 30 minutes. Cool for 30 minutes and then put back in for another 30 minutes, 200 Fahrenheit. Serve.

Nutrition: Calories: 156 Fat: 13.35g Carbohydrates: 6.21g Protein: 5.21g

Keto No-Bake Cookies

Preparation Time: 15 minutes **Cooking Time:** 2 minutes **Servings:** 18 (You can store it for several days)

83 grams of natural peanut butter
120 grams coconut, unsweetened
1 tablespoon real butter
4 drops of vanilla lakanto

Dissolve the butter in the microwave. Remove and put in the peanut butter. Stir. Add the sweetener and coconut. Mix. Spoon it onto a pan lined with parchment paper Freeze for 10 minutes. Cut and serve.

Nutrition: Calories: 98 Fat: 1g Carbohydrates: 12g Protein: 5g

Swiss Cheese Crunchy Nachos

Preparation Time: 15 minutes **Cooking Time:** 20 minutes **Servings:** 2

70 grams of Swiss cheese
70 grams of cheddar cheese
220 grams of cooked bacon

Heat the oven to 220° Celsius. Spread the Swiss cheese on the parchment. Sprinkle it with bacon and top it with the cheese. Bake for 10 minutes. Cool and cut into triangle strips. Broil for 2 to 3 minutes. Serve.

Nutrition: Calories: 280 Fat: 21.8g Protein: 18.6g Carbohydrates: 2.44g

Homemade Thin Mints

Preparation Time: 15 minutes **Cooking Time:** 60 minutes **Servings:** 20 (You can store it for several days)

1 egg
250 grams of almond flour
43 grams of cocoa powder
43 grams swerve sweetener
2 tablespoons butter, melted
1 teaspoon Baking powder
½ teaspoon Vanilla extract
¼ teaspoon Salt
1 tablespoon coconut oil
50 grams of sugar-free dark chocolate
1 teaspoon peppermint extract

Heat up the oven to 220° Celsius. Mix the cacao powder, sweetener, almond flour, salt, and baking powder. Then put the beaten egg, vanilla extract, and butter. Knead the dough and roll it on the parchment paper. Cut into a cookie. Bake the cookies for 20 to 30 minutes. For the coating, dissolve the oil and chocolate. Stir in the peppermint extract. Dip the cookie in the coating, chill, and serve.

Nutrition: Calories: 116 Fat: 10.41g Carbohydrates: 6.99g Protein: 8g

Mozzarella Cheese Pockets

Preparation Time: 15 minutes **Cooking Time:** 25 minutes **Servings:** 8

1 egg
8 mozzarella cheese sticks
250 grams of mozzarella cheese
90 grams of almond flour
30 grams cream cheese
60 grams crushed pork belly skin

Grate the mozzarella cheese. Mix the almond flour, mozzarella, and cream cheese—microwave for 30 seconds.
Put in the egg and mix to form a dough. Put the dough between 2 wax papers and roll it into a semi-rectangular shape. Cut them into smaller rectangle pieces and wrap them around the cheese sticks. Roll the stick onto crushed pork rinds—Bake for 20 to 25 minutes at 200° Celsius. Serve.

Nutrition: Calories: 272 Fat: 22g Carbohydrates: 2.4g Protein: 17g

No-Bake Coconut Cookies

Preparation Time: 15 minutes **Cooking Time:** 10 minutes **Servings:** 8 (You can store it for several days)

400 grams of unsweetened shredded coconut
60 grams sweetener
Coconut oil
Salt
2 teaspoons Vanilla
Topping: coconut shreds

Process all the fixing in a food processor. Form into shape. Put the topping. Chill and serve.

Nutrition: Calories: 329 Carbohydrates: 4.1g Protein: 2.1g Fat: 30g

Cheesy Cauliflower Breadsticks

Preparation Time: 15 minutes **Cooking Time:** 45 minutes **Servings:** 8

4 eggs
250 grams cauliflower, riced
250 grams of mozzarella cheese
4 cloves minced garlic
3 teaspoons oregano
Salt
Pepper

Warm-up oven to 200° Celsius. Process cauliflower in a food processor. Microwave for 10 minutes. Cool and drain; put the eggs, oregano, garlic, salt, pepper, and mozzarella. Mix. Separate the mixture into individual sticks—Bake for 25 minutes. Remove and sprinkle mozzarella on top. Bake again for 5 minutes. Serve.

Nutrition: Calories: 121 Carbohydrates: 4g Protein: 13g Fat: 11g

Easy Peanut Butter Cups

Preparation Time: 15 minutes **Cooking Time:** 1 hour 35 minutes **Servings:** 12 (You can store it for several days)

60 grams of peanut butter
30 grams butter
30 grams cacao butter
43 grams powdered swerve sweetener
½ teaspoon vanilla extract
120 grams of sugar-free dark chocolate

Dissolve the peanut butter, butter, and cacao butter in low heat. Add the vanilla and sweetener. Put the mixture in the muffin cups. Chill. Put the chocolate in a bowl and steam. Take out the muffin and drizzle the chocolate on top. Chill again for 15 minutes. Serve.

Nutrition: Calories: 200 Fat: 19g Carbohydrates: 6g Protein: 2.9g

Fried Green Beans Rosemary

Preparation Time: 10 minutes **Cooking Time:** 5 minutes **Servings:** 2

150 grams of green beans
2 teaspoons minced garlic
2 tablespoons rosemary
Salt
1 tablespoon butter

Preheat an Air Fryer to 220° Celsius. Put the chopped green beans, then brush with butter. Sprinkle salt, minced garlic, and rosemary, then cook for 5 minutes. Serve.

Nutrition: Calories: 277 Fat: 6.3g Protein: 0.7g Carbohydrates: 4.5g

Crispy Broccoli Popcorn

Preparation Time: 15 minutes **Cooking Time:** 10 minutes **Servings:** 4

220 grams of broccoli florets
220 grams of coconut flour
4 egg yolks
Salt
Pepper
1 stick butter

Dissolve butter, then let it cool. Break the eggs in it. Put coconut flour into the liquid, then put salt and pepper. Mix.
Preheat an Air Fryer to 200°Celsius. Dip a broccoli floret in the coconut flour mixture, then place it in the Air Fryer.
Cook the broccoli florets for 6 minutes. Serve.

Nutrition: Calories: 202 Fat: 17.5g Protein: 5.1g Carbohydrates: 7.8g

Cheesy Cauliflower Croquettes

Preparation Time: 10 minutes **Cooking Time:** 16 minutes **Servings:** 4

220 grams cauliflower florets
2 tablespoons garlic
60 grams onion
¾ teaspoon Mustard
½ teaspoon Salt
½ teaspoon pepper
2 tablespoon butter
100 grams of cheddar cheese

Microwave the butter. Let it cool. Process the cauliflower florets using a processor. Transfer to a bowl, then put chopped onion and cheese. Put minced garlic, mustard, salt, and pepper, then pour melted butter. Shape the cauliflower batter into medium balls. Warm up an Air Fryer to 200° Celsius and cook for 14 minutes. Serve.

Nutrition: Calories: 160 Fat: 13g Protein: 6.8g Carbohydrates: 5.1g

Spinach in Cheese Envelopes

Preparation Time: 15 minutes **Cooking Time:** 30 minutes **Servings:** 8

220 grams of cheddar cheese
164-gram coconut flour
3 egg yolks
2 eggs
60 grams cheese
120 grams of steamed spinach
Salt
Pepper
Onion powder

Whisk cream cheese, and put egg yolks. Stir in coconut flour until becoming a soft dough. Put the dough on a flat surface, then roll until thin. Cut the thin dough into eight squares. Beat the eggs, then place them in a bowl. Put salt, pepper, and grated cheese. Put chopped spinach and onion into the egg batter. Put spinach filling on a square dough, then fold until becoming an envelope. Glue with water—Cook for 12 minutes. Remove and serve! Warm-up an Air Fryer to 200° Celsius.

Nutrition: Calories: 365 Fat: 34.6g Protein: 10.4g Carbohydrates: 4.4g

Cheesy Mushroom Slices

Preparation Time: 8-10 minutes **Cooking Time:** 15 minutes **Servings:** 8

220 grams mushrooms
2 eggs
100 grams of almond flour
70 grams of cheddar cheese
2 tablespoons Butter
Salt
Pepper

Process chopped mushrooms in a food processor, then add eggs, almond flour, and cheddar cheese. Put salt and pepper, then pour melted butter into the food processor. Transfer. Warm-up an Air Fryer to 190° Celsius. Put the loaf pan on the Air Fryer's rack, then cook for 15 minutes. Slice and serve.

Nutrition: Calories: 365 Fat: 34.6g Protein: 10.4g Carbohydrates: 4.4g

Asparagus Fries

Preparation Time: 10 minutes **Cooking Time:** 10 minutes **Servings:** 4

10 organic asparagus spears
1 roasted red pepper
1 tablespoon Organic roasted red pepper
¼ Almond flour
½ teaspoon Garlic powder
½ teaspoon Smoked paprika
2 tablespoons parsley
60 grams Parmesan cheese, full fat
2 organic eggs
3 tablespoons mayonnaise, full fat

Preheat the oven to 200° Celsius. Process cheese in a food processor, add garlic and parsley and pulse for 1 minute.
Add almond flour, pulse for 30 seconds, transfer, and put paprika. Whisk eggs into a shallow dish. Dip asparagus spears into the egg batter, coat with parmesan mixture, and place them on a baking sheet. Bake in the oven for 10 minutes. Put the mayonnaise in a bowl, add red pepper, whisk, and chill. Serve with prepared dip.

Nutrition: Calories: 453 Fat: 33.4 g Protein: 19.1g Carbohydrates: 5.5g

Kale Chips

Preparation Time: 5 minutes **Cooking Time:** 12 minutes **Servings:** 4

1 organic kale
Salt
Olive oil

Warm-up oven to 220° Celsius. Put kale leaves into a large plastic bag and add oil. Shake and then spread on a large baking sheet—Bake for 12 minutes. Serve with salt.

Nutrition: Calories: 163 Fat: 10 g Protein: 2 g Carbohydrates: 14 g

Guacamole

Preparation Time: 10 minutes **Cooking Time:** 0 minutes **Servings:** 4

2 organic avocados pitted
1/3 organic red onion
1 organic jalapeño
½ teaspoon salt
½ teaspoon ground pepper
2 tablespoons tomato salsa
1 tablespoon lime juice
½ organic cilantro

Slice the avocado flesh horizontally and vertically. Mix in onion, jalapeno, and lime juice in a bowl. Put salt and black pepper, add salsa and mix. Fold in cilantro and serve.

Nutrition: Calories: 16.5 Fat: 1.4 g Protein: 0.23 g Carbohydrates: 0.5 g

Courgette Noodles

Preparation Time: 5 minutes **Cooking Time:** 6 minutes **Servings:** 2

2 courgettes, spiralised into noodles
2 tablespoons butter, unsalted
1 ½ tablespoon garlic
90 grams of Parmesan cheese
Salt
¼ teaspoon ground black pepper
¼ teaspoon red chilli flakes

Sauté butter and garlic for 1 minute. Put courgettes noodles, cook for 5 minutes, then put salt and black pepper. Transfer then top with cheese and sprinkle with red chilli flakes. Serve.

Nutrition: Calories: 298 Fat: 26.1 g Protein: 5 g Carbohydrates: 2.3 g

Cauliflower Souffle

Preparation Time: 10 minutes **Cooking Time:** 12 minutes **Servings:** 6

1 cauliflower, florets
2 eggs
2 tablespoons double cream
60 grams of cream Cheese
60 grams of sour cream
60 grams of Asiago cheese
120 grams of cheddar cheese
30 grams Chives
2 tablespoons butter, unsalted
6 bacon slices, sugar-free
120 ml. of water
½ organic cilantro

Pulse eggs, double cream, sour cream, cream cheese, and all cheeses in a food processor. Put cauliflower florets, pulse for 2 seconds, add butter and chives and pulse for 2 seconds. Put water in a pot and insert a trivet. Put the cauliflower batter in a greased round casserole dish, then put the plate on the trivet—Cook for 12 minutes. Remove, top with bacon and cilantro, and serve.

Nutrition: Calories: 342 Fat: 28 g Protein: 17g Carbohydrates: 5 g

No-Churn Ice Cream

Preparation Time: 10 minutes **Cooking Time:** 0 minutes **Servings:** 3

Pinch salt
120 grams of heavy whipping cream
¼ teaspoon xanthan gum
2 tablespoon zero-calorie sweetener powder
1 teaspoon vanilla extract
1 tablespoon vodka

Put the xanthan gum, heavy cream, vanilla extract, sweetener, vodka, and salt into a jar and mix. Blend the batter into the immersion blender for 2 minutes. Put the batter back in the pot, cover it, and chill for 4 hours. Stir the cream batter at 40 minutes intervals. Serve.

Nutrition: Calories: 291 Carbohydrates: 3.2g Protein: 1.6g Fat: 29.4g

Cheesecake Cupcakes

Preparation Time: 10 minutes **Cooking Time:** 15 minutes **Servings:** 12 (You can store it for days)

1 teaspoon vanilla extract
60 grams almonds
50 grams granulated no-calorie sucralose sweetener
30 grams melted butter
2 eggs
250 grams pack of softened cream cheese

Preheat the oven to 220° Celsius. Mix butter and almond meal put into the bottom of the muffin cup. Mix vanilla extract, cream cheese, sucralose sweetener, and egg in an electric mixer. Put this batter on the top of the muffin cups. Bake for 17 minutes. Cool and serve.

Nutrition: Calories: 209 Carbohydrates: 3.5g Protein: 4.9g Fat: 20g

Chocolate Peanut Butter Cups

Preparation Time: 15 minutes **Cooking Time:** 3 minutes **Servings:** 12 (You can store it for several days)

30 grams peanuts, salted
120 ml. coconut oil
Salt
60 grams of natural peanut butter
¼ teaspoon vanilla extract
2 tablespoons double cream
1 teaspoon liquid stevia
1 tablespoon cocoa powder

Dissolve coconut oil for 5 minutes, then put peanut butter, salt, double cream, cocoa powder, vanilla extract, and liquid stevia into the pan. Stir. Put the batter into muffin molds. Put the salted peanuts on top. Chill for an hour. Serve.

Nutrition: Calories: 246 Carbohydrates: 3.3g Protein: 3.4g Fat: 26g

Peanut Butter Cookies

Preparation Time: 15 minutes **Cooking Time:** 15 minutes **Servings:** 12 (You can store it for several days)

1 teaspoon vanilla extract, sugar-free
120 grams of peanut butter
1 egg
60 grams natural sweetener, low-calorie

Heat up the oven to 220° Celsius. Mix peanut butter, vanilla extract, sweetener, and egg to form a dough. Mold the dough into balls. Bake for 15 minutes. Cool and serve.

Nutrition: Calories: 133 Carbohydrates: 12.4g Protein: 5.9g Fat: 11.2g

Low-Carb Almond Coconut Sandies

Preparation Time: 15 minutes **Cooking Time:** 12 minutes **Servings:** 18 (You can store it for several days)

1 teaspoon stevia powder
120 grams coconut, unsweetened
5 grams Himalayan Sea salt
120 grams almond meal
1 tablespoon vanilla extract
80 ml. melted coconut oil
2 tablespoons water
1 egg white

Warm-up oven to 220° Celsius. Mix Himalayan Sea salt, unsweetened coconut, stevia powder, almond meal, vanilla extract, coconut oil, water, and egg white. Put aside for 10 minutes. Mold into little balls. Press down on the balls. Bake for 15 minutes. Cool and serve.

Nutrition: Calories: 107 Carbohydrates: 2.7g Protein: 1.9g Fat: 10.5g

Creme Brûleé

Preparation Time: 15 minutes **Cooking Time:** 34 minutes **Servings:** 4

5 tablespoons natural sweetener, low calorie
4 egg yolks
250 grams of heavy whipping cream
1 teaspoon vanilla extract

Heat up the oven to 220° Celsius. Mix the vanilla extract and egg yolks in it. Simmer 15 grams. of natural sweetener and heavy cream to the pan and mix. Put the ramekins with batter in a glass baking dish and add hot water. Bake for 30 minutes. Put 15 grams. natural sweetener on top. Serve.

Nutrition: Calorie: 466 Carbohydrates: 16.9g Protein: 5.1g Fat: 48.4g

Chocolate Fat Bomb

Preparation Time: 15 minutes **Cooking Time:** 0 minutes **Servings:** 10   (You can store it for several days)

220 grams chocolate pudding mix, sugar-free
250 grams of cream cheese
Coconut oil

Mix the chocolate pudding mix, cream cheese, and coconut oil using an electric mixer. Put this batter into a mold to form mounds. Cover and chill for 30 minutes. Serve.

Nutrition: Calories: 231 Carbohydrates: 3.5g Protein: 1.9g Fat: 24.3g

Cocoa Mug Cake

Preparation Time: 15 minutes **Cooking Time:** 5 minutes **Servings:** 2

2 tablespoons coconut oil, melted
6 tablespoons almond flour
2 eggs
3 tablespoons cocoa powder, unsweetened
Salt
2 teaspoons natural sweetener, low-calorie
½ teaspoon baking powder

Mix salt, almond flour, baking powder, cocoa powder, and natural sweetener. Beat the eggs using an electric mixer. Put the coconut oil and stir. Put this egg batter into the bowl containing baking powder. Whisk. Put the batter into mugs. Microwave to high for 1 minute. Serve.

Nutrition: Calories: 338 Carbohydrates: 8.6g Protein: 12.3g Fat: 30.9g

Dark Chocolate Espresso Paleo and Keto Mug Cake

Preparation Time: 15 minutes **Cooking Time:** 5 minutes **Servings:** 2

1 tablespoon brewed espresso
120 grams of dark chocolate chips
1 egg
1 tablespoon coconut oil
Baking soda
2 tablespoons water
1 tablespoon coconut flour
1 tablespoon almond flour

Put both the coconut oil and chocolate chips in a mug. Put baking soda, water, coconut flour, and almond flour. Microwave and cook for 1 minute and 30 seconds. Cool and serve.

Nutrition: Calories: 793 Carbohydrates: 83.7g Protein: 14g Fat: 52.2g

Keto Matcha Mint Bars

Preparation Time: 15 minutes **Cooking Time:** 0 minutes **Servings:** 12 (You can store it for several days)

6 drops stevia
120 grams almond flour
3 tablespoon melted butter
1 tablespoon cocoa powder, unsweetened
3 tablespoon warmed coconut oil
130 grams of coconut butter
1 teaspoon peppermint extract
1 teaspoon vanilla extract
120 grams of coconut butter
2 ripe avocados
1 tablespoon matcha
3 tablespoons stevia powder

Mix almond flour, stevia powder, cocoa powder, and butter. Press down on it till a crust is formed. Let it chill for 15 minutes.
For the filling:
Mix stevia powder, coconut butter, vanilla extract, matcha, avocados, and peppermint extract using an electric mixer. Put this on the crust. Let it chill. Mix liquid stevia, coconut oil, cocoa powder, and peppermint extract into the crust. Chill for 30 minutes.

Nutrition: Calories: 276 Carbohydrates: 12.6g Protein: 4.3g Fat: 26.1g

Keto No-Churn Blueberry Maple Ice Cream

Preparation Time: 15 minutes **Cooking Time:** 0 minutes **Servings:** 2

Salt
120 grams of heavy whipping cream
¼ teaspoon xanthan gum
250 grams of blueberries, frozen
½ teaspoon maple extract
2 tablespoons natural sweetener, low calorie
1 tablespoon vodka

Put heavy cream, salt, blueberries, xanthan gum, natural sweetener, maple extract, and vodka in a jar. Process this mixture for 75 seconds with an immersion blender. Chill for 35 minutes, stirring occasionally. Serve.

Nutrition: Calories: 304 Carbohydrates: 13.4g Protein: 1.8g Fat: 29.6g

Keto Raspberry Cake and White Chocolate Sauce

Preparation Time: 15 minutes **Cooking Time:** 45 minutes **Servings:** 4

5 ounces cacao butter
4 teaspoons vanilla extract
4 eggs
300 grams raspberries
260 grams of grass-fed ghee
1 teaspoon baking powder
1 teaspoon apple cider vinegar
120 grams of green banana flour
90 grams of coconut cream
90 grams granulated sweetener
120 grams cacao butter
2 tablespoons pure vanilla extract
90 grams of coconut cream
Salt

Mix the butter and the sweetener. Pour the grass-fed ghee into the mix, and blend. Beat the eggs in a different bowl.

Warm-up oven to 220° Celsius. Grease a baking pan. Put the mixed eggs into the butter and sweetener mixture. Mix well. Pour in the banana flour and mix. Then the vanilla extract, apple cider, coconut cream, and baking powder, and mix again. Spoon around the sliced raspberries. Then, sprinkle flour in the baking pan. Put the mixture into the pan, then bake for 45 minutes. Cool down.

For the sauce:

Mix cacao butter with two tablespoons of pure vanilla extract. Add coconut cream and beat. Put salt and beat. Chop the remaining berries and throw them in the mix. Pour the mixture onto the cake. Serve cold.

Nutrition: Calories: 325 Fat: 12g Carbohydrates:: 3g Protein: 40g

Keto Chocolate Chip Cookies

Preparation Time: 15 minutes **Cooking Time:** 10 minutes **Servings:** 4

90 grams of unsweetened coconut powder
7 tablespoons Keto chocolate chips
5 tablespoons butter
2 tablespoons baking powder
2 eggs
90 grams confectioner's swerve
200 grams of almond flour
1 teaspoon vanilla extract

Warm-up oven to 220° Celsius. Melt half chocolate chips, then the butter. Mix. Mix the eggs in the chocolate and butter mixture. Mix vanilla extract, coconut powder, confectioners swerve, and almond flour. Mix well. Add chocolate chip cookies. Then, add baking powder, and mix until dough forms. Spread out and cut out cookies, top with chocolate chips. Bake for 8 to 10 minutes. Serve.

Nutrition: Calories: 287 Fat: 19g Carbohydrates:: 6.5g Protein: 6.8g

Keto Beef and Sausage Balls

Preparation Time: 15 minutes **Cooking Time:** 20 minutes **Servings:** 3

For the meat:
1 kg. ground beef
1 kg. ground sausage
2 eggs
60 grams of Keto mayonnaise
50 grams of ground pork rinds
60 grams Parmesan cheese
Salt
Pepper
60 grams butter
50 ml. oil
For the sauce:
3 chopped onions
2 pounds mushrooms
5 cloves garlic
380 grams of beef broth
120 grams of sour cream
60 grams mustard
Worcestershire sauce
Salt
Pepper
Parsley
15 grams Arrowroot powder

Put meat, egg, and onions in a bowl, and mix. Put beef, parmesan, egg, mayonnaise, sausage, and pork rind in a bowl. Add salt and pepper—warm-up oil in a skillet. Mould the beef mixture into balls, and fry for 7-10 minutes. Put aside. Fry the chopped onions, then the garlic and mushrooms, and cook for 3 minutes. Then, add the broth. Mix in mustard, sour cream, and Worcestershire sauce. Boil for 2 minutes, then adds in the meatballs. Add salt and pepper, and simmer. Serve.

Nutrition: Calories: 592 Fat: 53.9g Carbohydrates: 1.3g Protein: 25.4g

Keto Coconut Flake Balls

Preparation Time: 15 minutes **Cooking Time:** 0 minutes **Servings:** 2

1 Vanilla Shortbread Collagen Protein Bar
1 tablespoon lemon juice
¼ teaspoon ground ginger
60 grams of unsweetened coconut flakes
½ teaspoon ground turmeric

Process protein bar, ginger, turmeric, and ¾ of the total flakes into a food processor. Remove and add a spoon of water and roll till dough forms. Roll into balls and sprinkle the rest of the flakes on it. Serve.

Nutrition: Calories: 204 Fat: 11g Carbohydrates:: 4.2g Protein: 1.5g

Keto Chocolate Greek Yoghurt Cookies

Preparation Time: 15 minutes **Cooking Time:** 30 minutes **Servings:** 3

3 eggs
1/8 teaspoon tartar
5 tablespoons softened Greek yoghurt

Beat the egg whites and the tartar, and mix. In the yolk, put in the Greek yoghurt, and mix. Combine both egg whites and yolk batter into a bowl. Bake for 25-30 minutes. Serve.

Nutrition: Calories: 287 Fat: 19g Carbohydrates: 6.5g Protein: 6.8g

Keto Coconut Flavored Ice Cream

Preparation Time: 15 minutes **Cooking Time:** 0 minutes **Servings:** 4

250 ml. coconut milk
30 grams xylitol
¼ teaspoon salt
2 teaspoons vanilla extract
1 teaspoon coconut extract

Add the coconut milk to a bowl with the sweetener, extracts, and salt. Mix well to combine. Pour this mixture into the ice cube trays and put it in the freezer. Serve.

Nutrition: Calories: 244 Fat: 48g Carbohydrates: 6g Protein: 15g

Chocolate-Coconut Cookies

Preparation Time: 15 minutes **Cooking Time:** 20 minutes **Servings:** 4

2 eggs
60 grams of cocoa powder
60 grams flour
60 grams of coconut oil
30 grams grated coconut
Stevia

Warm-up oven to 200° Celsius. Crack eggs and separate whites and yolks, mix separately. Put salt to the yolks. Warm-up oil in a skillet, add cocoa, and egg whites, and mix. Add in the salted yolks; then, add stevia. Add in coconut flour and mix until dough forms. On a flat surface, sprinkle grated coconut. Roll the dough around in the coconut, and mix. Mold into cookies. Bake for 15 minutes, and serve.

Nutrition: Calories: 260 Fat: 26g Carbohydrates: 4.5g Protein: 1g

Keto Buffalo Chicken Meatballs

Preparation Time: 15 minutes **Cooking Time:** 20 minutes **Servings:** 3

500 grams of ground chicken
1 large
2 tablespoons hot sauce
60 grams almond flour
Salt
10 grams pepper
60 grams melted butter
1 large onion
1 teaspoon garlic

Combine meat, egg, and onions in a bowl. Pour in almond flour, garlic, salt, and pepper. Warm up the oven to 220° Celsius and grease a baking tray. Mold the egg mixture into balls. Bake for 18-20 minutes. Melt butter in the microwave for a few seconds; mix it with hot sauce. Put the sauce into meatballs. Serve.

Nutrition: Calories: 360 Fat: 26g Carbohydrates: 4.5g Protein: 1g

Aubergine and Chickpea Bites

Preparation Time: 15 minutes **Cooking Time:** 90 minutes **Servings:** 6

3 large auberges
Spray oil
2 large cloves of garlic
2 tablespoons coriander powder
2 tablespoons cumin seeds
400 grams canned chickpeas
2 tablespoons chickpea flour
Lemon zest and lemon juice of 1 lemon
3 tablespoons polenta

Warm-up oven to 200ºC. Grease the aubergine halves and place them on the meat side up on a baking sheet. Sprinkle with coriander and cumin seeds, and then place the cloves of garlic on the plate. Roast for 40 minutes, put aside.
Add chickpeas, chickpea flour, zest, and lemon juice. Crush roughly and mix well. Form about twenty pellets and place them on a baking sheet. Fridge for 30 minutes. Warm-up oven to 180ºC. Remove the meatballs from the fridge and coat them in the polenta. Roast for 20 minutes. Serve with lemon wedges.

Nutrition: Calories: 70 Carbohydrates: 4g Fat: 5g Protein: 2g

Baba Ganouj

Preparation Time: 15 minutes **Cooking Time:** 20 minutes **Servings:** 3

1 large aubergine
1 head of garlic
30 ml of olive oil
Lemon juice

Warm-up oven to 200° Celsius. Place the aubergine on the plate, skin side up. Roast, about 1 hour. Place the garlic cloves in a square of aluminum foil. Fold the edges of the sheet. Roast with the aubergine, for about 20 minutes. Let cool. Purée the pods with a garlic press. Puree the flesh of the aubergine. Add the garlic puree, the oil, and the lemon juice.
Serve.

Nutrition: Calories: 99 Carbohydrates: 6g Fat: 6g Protein: 2g

Spicy Crab Dip

Preparation Time: 15 minutes **Cooking Time:** 20 minutes **Servings:** 3

250 grams of cream cheese
2 onions, chopped
1 tablespoon lemon juice
2 tablespoons Worcestershire sauce
Black pepper
Cayenne pepper
2 tablespoons milk
180 grams crabmeat

Warm-up oven to 220° Celsius. Pour the cream cheese into a bowl. Add the onions, lemon juice, Worcestershire sauce, black pepper, and cayenne pepper. Mix. Stir in the milk and crab meat. Cook uncovered for 15 minutes. Serve.

Nutrition: Calories: 134 Carbohydrates: 4g Fat: 12g Protein: 4g

Parmesan Cheese "Potatoes"

Preparation Time: 15 minutes **Cooking Time:** 10 minutes **Servings:** 3

75 grams Parmesan cheese
1 tablespoon Chia seeds
2 tablespoons whole flaxseeds
2 ½ tablespoons pumpkin seeds

Warm-up oven to 180°Celsius. Combine both the cheese and seeds in a bowl. Put small piles of the mixture on the baking paper, bake for 8 to 10 minutes Remove and serve.

Nutrition: Calories: 165 Carbohydrates: 18g Fat: 9g Protein: 3g

Chili Cheese Chicken with Crispy and Delicious Cabbage

Preparation Time: 15 minutes **Cooking Time:** 70 minutes **Servings:** 5

Chili Cheese Chicken:
200 grams of chicken
200 grams tomatoes
100 grams of cream cheese
125 grams cheddar
40 grams jalapenos
60 grams of bacon
Crispy Cabbage Salad:
0.5 pcs casserole
200 grams of Brussels sprouts
2 grams of almonds
3 tangerines
11 teaspoon olive oil
1 teaspoon apple cider vinegar
Salt
10 grams pepper
11 teaspoon lemon

Warm-up oven to 200°Celsius. Put tomatoes half in the bottom of a baking dish. Put chicken fillets and half cream cheese on each chicken fillet, sprinkle with cheddar—spread jalapenos and bake for 25 minutes. Place bacon on a baking sheet with baking paper and bake for 10 minutes.
For cabbage salad:
Blend the Brussels sprouts and cumin in a food processor. Make the juice dressing from one tangerine, olive oil, apple cider vinegar, salt, pepper, and lemon juice. Put the cabbage in a dish and spread the dressing over it. Chop almonds, cut the tangerine into slices and place it on the salad. Sprinkle the bacon over the chicken dish. Serve.

Nutrition: Calories: 515 Carbohydrates: 35g Fat: 23g Protein: 42g

Keto Pumpkin Pie Sweet and Spicy

Preparation Time: 15 minutes **Cooking Time:** 60 minutes **Servings:** 5

Pie Bottom:
110 grams of almond flour
50 grams sucrine
Salt
1 scoop of protein powder
1 egg
80 grams butter
The Filling:
1 pcs Hokkaido
3 egg yolks
60 grams of coconut fat
5 grams vanilla powder
15 grams of protein powder
¼ teaspoon ground cinnamon
2 grams sucrine
½ teaspoon black cardamom
½ teaspoon cloves

Warm-up oven to 175°Celsius. Combine all the dry fixing and add the wet ones. Mix and shape it into a dough lump. Put in a baking paper, then flatten the dough. Prick holes, then bake for 8-10 minutes.
For filling:
Cut the meat of Hokkaido and cook for 15-20 minutes. Process it with the other fixing. Pour the stuffing into the baked pie and bake again for 25-30 minutes. Cool and serve.

Nutrition: Calories: 229 Carbohydrates: 4g Fat: 22g Protein: 8g

Blackened Tilapia with Courgettes Noodles

Preparation Time: 15 minutes **Cooking Time:** 10 minutes **Servings:** 5

2 Courgettes
Salt
2 garlic cloves
120 grams Pico de Gallo
200 grams pounds of fish
2 teaspoons olive oil
½ teaspoon cumin
¼ teaspoon garlic powder
10 grams paprika
Pepper

Mix half salt, pepper, cumin, paprika, and garlic powder, and thoroughly rub the fish. Cook for 3 minutes on each side and remove it. Cook courgettes and garlic, remaining salt for 2 minutes. Serve.

Nutrition: Calories: 220 Carbohydrates: 27g Fat: 2g Protein: 24g

Bell Pepper Nachos

Preparation Time: 15 minutes **Cooking Time:** 10 minutes **Servings:** 2

2 bell peppers
120 grams of beef ground
¼ teaspoon cumin
30 grams guacamole
Salt
120 grams cheese
¼ teaspoon chilli powder
1 tablespoon vegetable oil
2 tablespoons sour cream
30 grams Pico de Gallo

Put the bell peppers in a microwave dish, sprinkle salt and splash water on it and microwave for 4 minutes and cut it into four pieces. Toast the chili powder and cumin in the pan for 30 seconds. Put the salted beef, stir, and cook for 4 minutes. Put on all the pieces of pepper. Add cheese and cook for 1 minute. Serve with Pico de Gallo, guacamole, and cream.

Nutrition: Calories: 475 Carbohydrates: 19g Fat: 24g Protein: 50g

Radish, Carrot & Cilantro Salad

Preparation Time: 15 minutes **Cooking Time:** 0 minutes **Servings:** 2

400 grams carrots
30 grams cilantro
60 grams radish
½ teaspoon salt
6 onions
¼ teaspoon black pepper
3 tablespoons lemon juice
3 tablespoons orange juice
2 tablespoons olive oil

Mix all the ingredients until they merged properly. Chill and serve.

Nutrition: Calories: 123 Carbohydrates: 7g Fat: 3g Protein: 3g

Asparagus-Mushroom Frittata

Preparation Time: 15 minutes **Cooking Time:** 25 minutes **Servings:** 2

1 tablespoon olive oil
1 garlic clove
30 grams onion
250 grams button mushrooms
1 asparagus
1 tablespoon thyme
6 eggs
60 grams feta cheese
Salt
Black pepper

Cook onions for 5 minutes. Put mushroom plus garlic, then cook for 5 minutes. Mix thyme, salt, pepper, and asparagus and cook for 3 minutes. Beat eggs and cheese in a bowl, pour it into the pan and cook for 2 to 3 minutes. Bake for 10 minutes.

Nutrition: Calories: 129 Carbohydrates: 2g Fat: 7g Protein: 9g

Shrimp Avocado Salad

Preparation Time: 15 minutes **Cooking Time:** 0 minutes **Servings:** 1

2 onions
1 tomato
2 limes juice
1 avocado
Salt
Pepper
1 jalapeno
500 grams shrimp
1 tablespoon cilantro

Mix onion, lime juice, salt, and pepper, and let it stand 5 minutes. Add chopped shrimp, avocado, tomato, jalapeno, and onion mixture to another bowl. Put salt and pepper, toss and serve.

Nutrition: Calories: 365 Carbohydrates: 15g Fat: 17g Protein: 25g

Smoky Cauliflower Bites

Preparation Time: 15 minutes **Cooking Time:** 25 minutes **Servings:** 2

1 cauliflower
2 garlic cloves
2 tablespoon olive oil
2 tablespoons parsley
1 teaspoon Paprika
Salt

Warm-up oven at 450. Mix cauliflower, olive oil, paprika, and salt. Bake for 10 minutes. Put garlic and bake for 10 to 15 minutes. Serve with parsley.

Nutrition: Calories: 69 Carbohydrates: 8g Fat: 3g Protein: 1g

Avocado Crab Boats

Preparation Time: 15 minutes **Cooking Time:** 2 minutes **Servings:** 2

12oz lump crab meat
3 tablespoons lemon juice
60 grams of Greek yoghurt
Pepper
1/2 onion
Salt
2 tablespoons chives
130 grams of cheddar cheese
2 avocados

Mix meat, yoghurt, onion, chives, lemon juice, cayenne, and salt. Scoop the avocado flesh, fill the avocado bowl with meat mixture, and top with cheddar cheese. Microwave for 2 minutes and serve.

Nutrition: Calories: 325 Carbohydrates: 8g Fat: 28g Protein: 0g

Coconut Curry Cauliflower Soup

Preparation Time: 15 minutes **Cooking Time:** 40 minutes **Servings:** 2

Olive oil
2 to 3 teaspoons curry powder
1 onion
2 teaspoons ground cumin
3 garlic cloves
½ teaspoon turmeric powder
1 teaspoon ginger
30 ml. coconut milk
220 grams tomatoes
120 grams of vegetable broth
1 cauliflower
Salt
Pepper

Mix olive oil and onion in a pot, and sauté for 3 minutes. Put garlic, ginger, curry powder, cumin, turmeric powder and sauté for 5 minutes. Put coconut milk, tomatoes, vegetable broth, and cauliflower. Cook on low for 20 minutes, blend the mixture through a blender and warm up the soup for 5 minutes. Put salt and pepper. Serve.

Nutrition: Calories: 112 Carbohydrates: 4g Fat: 3g Protein: 0g

Parmesan Asparagus

Preparation Time: 15 minutes **Cooking Time:** 15 minutes **Servings:** 4

2 kg. asparagus
Salt
200 grams butter
220 grams parmesan cheese shredded
Pepper

Boil asparagus for 3 minutes. Drain and put aside—Preheat the oven to 220°Celsius. Arrange asparagus into the pan and pour butter, sprinkle pepper, salt, and parmesan cheese—Bake for 10 to 15 minutes. Serve.

Nutrition: Calories: 166 Carbohydrates: 5g Fat: 5g Protein: 6g

Cream Cheese Pancakes

Preparation Time: 15 minutes   **Cooking Time:** 10 minutes   **Servings:** 12 (You can store it for several days)

220 grams of cream cheese
Vanilla extract
4 eggs
Butter

Blend cream cheese and eggs in a blender, and put them aside. Grease skillet with butter. Cook the butter for 2 minutes. Serve with sprinkled cinnamon.

Nutrition: Calories: 344 Carbohydrates: 3g Fat: 29g Protein: 17g

Sugar-Free Mexican Spiced Dark Chocolate

Preparation Time: 15 minutes **Cooking Time:** 0 minutes **Servings:** 1

20 grams of cocoa powder
¼ teaspoon ground cinnamon
½ teaspoon chilli powder
1/8 teaspoon nutmeg
Black pepper
Salt
40 grams melted butter
¼ teaspoon vanilla extract
25 drops of liquid stevia

Mix cocoa powder, cinnamon, chilli powder, nutmeg, black pepper, and salt. Put aside. Stir melted butter with vanilla extract and stevia and mix the butter mixture with dry ingredients. Put the mixture in chocolate moulds. Chill and serve.

Nutrition: Calories: 163 Carbohydrates: 8g Fat: 5g Protein: 1g

Tuna in Cucumber Cups

Preparation Time: 15 minutes **Cooking Time:** 0 minutes **Servings:** 10 (You can store it for more days)

150 grams Mayonnaise
Dill
Black pepper
1 can tuna
1 cucumber
Black pepper
Salt
1 Cucumber

Mix the cucumber flesh with the remainder of the fixing and then fill the holes in the cucumber slices. Garnish with fresh dill. Serve.

Nutrition: Calories 187 Protein: 3g Fat: 2g Carbohydrates: 2g

Parmesan Crisps

Preparation Time: 15 minutes **Cooking Time:** 10 minutes **Servings:** 2

150 grams Provolone cheese
Jalapeno pepper
90 grams of Parmesan cheese

Preheat the oven to 200° Celsius. Grease a baking sheet then set the 8tablespoons of parmesan cheese. Lay the slices of jalapeno over the parmesan cheese mounds. Put one square provolone over the parmesan mounds. Bake for nine minutes and serve.

Nutrition: Calories 160 Protein: 15g Fat: 9g Carbohydrates: 2g

Onion Rings

Preparation Time: 15 minutes **Cooking Time:** 15 minutes **Servings:** 2

2 Eggs
120 grams Parmesan cheese
1 tablespoon Heavy whipping cream
220 grams of Coconut flour
500 grams of Pork rinds
1 white Onion

Warm-up oven to 200° C. Arranges the first bowl with the coconut flour, the second bowl with mixed whipping cream and beaten egg, and the third bowl with crushed pork rinds and grated parmesan cheese. Dip the rings into the coconut flour, then into the egg-cream mixture, and lastly, into the cheese and pork rinds—Bake for fifteen minutes. Serve.

Nutrition: Calories: 205 Fat: 18g Protein: 12g Carbohydrates: 4g

Cold Crab Dip

Preparation Time: 15 minutes **Cooking Time:** 0 minutes **Servings:** Up to you

1 teaspoon lemon juice
2 tablespoons chives
½ teaspoon Old Bay seasoning
45 grams of sour cream
250 grams Crabmeat
150 grams of Cream cheese

Mix the cream cheese, lemon juice, seasoning, and sour cream. Fold the crab meat, then the chives, stirring. Serve.

Nutrition: Calories: 244 Fat: 4g Carbohydrates: 4g Protein: 5g

Baked Coconut Shrimp

Preparation Time: 15 minutes **Cooking Time:** 20 minutes **Servings:** 4

500 grams shrimp
Black pepper
220 grams of Coconut flakes
Salt
¼ teaspoon Garlic powder
3 Eggs
¼ teaspoon paprika
3 tablespoons Coconut flour

Warm-up oven to 200° Celsius. In the first bowl, put the beaten eggs. In the second bowl, place the coconut flakes, and in the last bowl, put a mix of garlic powder, salt, paprika, pepper, and coconut flour. Dip each shrimp into the flour mixture first, then into the egg wash, and then roll them in the coconut flakes— Bake for ten minutes. Serve.

Nutrition: Calories: 440 Protein: 3g Fat: 32g Carbohydrates: 5g

Spicy Deviled Eggs

Preparation Time: 15 minutes **Cooking Time:** 0 minutes **Servings:** 24

1 tablespoon sriracha sauce
1 tablespoon chilli powder
1 tablespoon chives
1 tablespoon Dijon mustard
80 grams mayonnaise
Black pepper
12 eggs
Salt

Mash the yolks into a paste—mix salt, mayonnaise, chili powder, sriracha sauce, pepper, and mustard. Refill the egg whites with this mixture. Serve with chopped chives on top.

Nutrition: Calories: 173 Protein: 3g Carbohydrates: 1g Fat: 5g

Bacon-Wrapped Scallops

Preparation Time: 15 minutes **Cooking Time:** 20 minutes **Servings:** 4

16 Toothpicks, 16
Salt
2 tablespoons olive oil
Black pepper
150 grams of sea scallops
Bacon

Warm-up oven to 200° Celsius. Grease a baking sheet. Use 1/2 of a bacon slice to wrap around each scallop and stick in the toothpick. Brush on the olive oil and put the salt and pepper—Bake for fifteen minutes. Serve.

Nutrition: Calories 225 Protein: 13g Fat: 16g Carbohydrates: 2g

Buffalo Chicken Jalapeno Poppers

Preparation Time: 15 minutes **Cooking Time:** 30 minutes **Servings:** 5

Ranch dressing
Green onions
4 slices of bacon
10 Jalapeno peppers
2 tablespoons Garlic powder
220 grams of Cream cheese
350 grams Chicken
11 teaspoons buffalo wing sauce
½ tablespoon Onion powder
250 grams of blue cheese
200 grams of Mozzarella cheese
Salt

Warm-up oven to 220°Celsius. Lay the half pieces of the jalapeno peppers on the cookie sheet. Fry the onion powder, ground chicken, garlic, and salt for fifteen minutes. Blend in the mozzarella cheese, wing sauce, and one-quarter of the crumbled blue cheese. Combine into the pepper halves, then top with bacon and blue cheese. Bake for thirty minutes, then serve.

Nutrition: Calories 250 Protein: 15g Fat: 20g Carbohydrates: 4g

Baked Garlic Parmesan Wings

Preparation Time: 15 minutes **Cooking Time:** 60 minutes **Servings:** 6

10 grams parsley
Salt
1 teaspoon onion powder
1kg. chicken wings
50 grams butter
220 grams of parmesan cheese
2 tablespoons garlic powder
2 tablespoons baking powder
Pepper

Warm-up oven to 250°Celsius. Sprinkle the pepper and salt on the wings and let them sit for ten minutes. Put baking powder over the wings, and toss. Bake the wings for thirty minutes. Adjust to 200° Celsius and then bake again for thirty minutes. Meanwhile, mix the minced garlic, parmesan cheese, onion powder, parsley, and melted butter—Toss wings in the sauce. Serve.

Nutrition: Calories 459 Protein: 32g Fat:40g Carbohydrates: 2g

Sausage Stuffed Mushrooms

Preparation Time: 15 minutes **Cooking Time:** 30 minutes **Servings:** 20

Salt
2 tablespoons butter
2 sausages
2 tablespoons garlic powder
Black pepper
1 onion, chopped
20 baby Bella mushrooms
130 grams of cheddar cheese

Warm-up oven to 220°Celsius. Fry sausage meat with butter, remove and put aside. Cook the mushroom stalks, garlic, and chopped onion in the pan with the leftover liquid for five minutes. Mix with the salt, cheddar cheese, pepper, and sausage. Fill all of the mushroom caps with this mixture—Bake for twenty minutes. Serve.

Nutrition: Calories 187 Protein: 5g Fat: 4g Carbohydrates: 2g

DESSERT

Egg Custard

Preparation Time: 15 minutes **Cooking Time:** 55 minutes **Servings:** 8

6 organic eggs
60 ml. yacon syrup
500 ml. of unsweetened almond milk
¼ teaspoon of ground ginger
¼ teaspoon of ground cinnamon
¼ teaspoon of ground nutmeg
¼ teaspoon of ground cardamom
1/8 teaspoon of ground cloves
1/8 teaspoon of ground allspice

Preheat your oven to 190° Celsius. Grease 8 small ramekins. In a bowl, add the eggs and salt and beat well. Arrange a sieve over a medium bowl. Through a sieve, strain the egg mixture into a bowl. Add the Yacon syrup to eggs and stir to combine. Add the almond milk and spices and beat until well combined. Transfer the mixture to prepared ramekins. Now, place ramekins in a large baking dish. Add hot water to the baking dish about 2-inch high around the ramekins. Place the baking dish in the oven and bake for about 30–40 minutes or until a toothpick inserted in the centre comes out clean. Remove ramekins from the oven and set them aside to cool. Refrigerate to chill before serving.

Nutrition: Calories: 104 **Fat:** 3.8g **Carbohydrates:** 6g **Protein:** 3.8g

Mocha Ice Cream

Preparation Time: 15 minutes **Cooking Time:** 15 minutes **Servings:** 2

120 grams of unsweetened coconut milk
30 grams of double cream
2 tablespoons of granulated erythritol
15 drops of liquid stevia
2 tablespoons of cacao powder
1 tablespoon of instant coffee
¼ teaspoon of xanthan gum

In a container, add the ingredients (except xanthan gum), and with an immersion blender, blend until well combined.
Slowly add the xanthan gum and blend until a slightly thicker mixture is formed. Transfer the mixture to the ice cream maker and process it according to the manufacturer's instructions. Transfer the ice cream into an airtight container and freeze for at least 4–5 hours before serving.

Nutrition: Calories: 246 **Carbohydrates:** 6.2g **Fat:** 23.1g **Protein:** 2.8g

Vanilla Crème Brûlée

Preparation Time: 20 minutes **Cooking Time:** 1 hour 20 minutes **Servings:** 4

250 grams of double cream
1 vanilla bean (halved with seeds scraped out)
4 organic egg yolks
1/3 teaspoon stevia powder
1 teaspoon vanilla extract
Salt
4 tablespoons granulated erythritol

Preheat your oven to 190° Celsius. Add double cream over medium heat and cook until heated in a pan. Stir in the vanilla bean seeds and bring to a gentle boil. Reduce the heat to very low and cook, covered for about 20 minutes.
Meanwhile, add the remaining ingredients (except erythritol) to a bowl and beat until thick and pale mixture forms.
Remove the double cream from heat, and through a fine-mesh strainer, strain into a heat-proof bowl.
Slowly add the cream to the egg yolk mixture beating continuously until well combined. Divide the mixture into four ramekins evenly.
Arrange the ramekins into a large baking dish. In the baking dish, add hot water and about half of the ramekins. Bake for about 30–35 minutes. Remove the pan from the oven, and then let it cool slightly. Refrigerate the ramekins for at least 4 hours.
Just before serving, sprinkle the ramekins with erythritol evenly. Holding a kitchen torch about 4–5-inches from the top, caramelize the erythritol for about 2 minutes.
Set aside for 5 minutes before serving.

Nutrition: Calories: 264 **Fat:** 26.7g **Carbohydrates:** 2.4g **Protein:** 3.9g

Lemon Soufflé

Preparation Time: 15 minutes **Cooking Time:** 35 minutes **Servings:** 4

2 large organic eggs (whites and yolks separated)
60 grams of granulated erythritol (divided)
120 grams of ricotta cheese
1 tablespoon of fresh lemon juice
2 teaspoons of lemon zest (grated)
1 teaspoon of poppy seeds
1 teaspoon of organic vanilla extract

Preheat your oven to 220°Celsius—grease 4 ramekins. Add egg whites and beat in a clean glass bowl until it has a foam-like texture. Add 2 tablespoons of erythritol and beat the mixture until it is stiff. Add ricotta cheese, egg yolks, and the remaining erythritol in another bowl until mixed thoroughly. Put the lemon juice and lemon zest in the bowl and mix well. Add the poppy seeds and vanilla extract and mix again. Add the whipped egg whites into the ricotta mixture and gently stir. Place the mixture into the prepared ramekins evenly—Bake for about 20 minutes. Remove from the oven and serve immediately.

Nutrition: Calories: 130 **Fat:** 7.7g **Carbohydrates:** 4g **Protein:** 10.4g

Cottage Cheese Pudding

Preparation Time: 10 minutes **Cooking Time:** 45 minutes **Servings:** 6

Pudding
120 grams of cottage cheese
120 ml. double cream
3 organic eggs
90 ml. of water
60 grams of granulated erythritol
1 teaspoon organic vanilla extract

Topping
43 grams of heavy whipping cream
43 grams of fresh raspberries

Preheat your oven to 190° Celsius. Grease the ramekins. Add all the ingredients (except cinnamon) and pulse in a blender until smooth. Transfer the mixture into prepared ramekins evenly. Now, place ramekins in a large baking dish. Add hot water to the baking dish and about 1-inch sides of the ramekins—Bake for about 35 minutes. Serve warm with the topping o heavy whipping cream and raspberries.

Nutrition: **Calories:** 226   **Fat:** 19.6g   **Carbohydrates:** 3.7g
Protein: 9g

Cream Cake

Preparation Time: 15 minutes **Cooking Time:** 1 hour and 5 minutes **Servings:** 12

250 grams of almond flour
2 teaspoons organic baking powder
60 grams of butter (chopped)
56 grams of cream cheese (softened)
120 grams of sour cream
120 grams of granulated erythritol
1 teaspoon organic vanilla extract
4 large organic eggs

Preheat your oven to 190° Celsius. Generously grease a 9-inch Bundt pan. Add almond flour and baking powder to a large bowl and mix well. Set aside. Add butter and cream cheese and microwave for about 30 seconds in a microwave-safe bowl.
Remove from microwave and stir well. Add sour cream, erythritol, and vanilla extract and mix until well combined.
Add the cream mixture into the bowl of the flour mixture and mix until well combined. Add eggs and mix until well combined.
Transfer the mixture into the prepared pan evenly. Bake for about 50 minutes or until a toothpick inserted in the centre comes out clean. Remove from the oven and put onto a wire rack to cool for about 10 minutes. Carefully invert the cake onto a wire rack to cool completely. Just before serving, dust the cake with powdered erythritol.
Cut into 12 equal-sized slices and serve.

Nutrition: **Calories:** 258   **Fat:** 24.3g   **Carbohydrates:** 5.5g
Protein: 7.2g

Sugar-Free Lemon Bars

Preparation Time: 15 minutes **Cooking Time:** 45 minutes **Servings:** 8

60 grams butter, melted
200 grams almond flour, divided
120 grams powdered erythritol, divided
3 medium-size lemons
3 large eggs

Prepare the parchment paper and baking tray. Combine butter, 120 grams of almond flour, 30 grams of erythritol, and salt. Stir well—Bake for about 20 minutes. Then set it aside to let it cool—zest one lemon and juice all of the lemons in a bowl. Add the eggs, 90 grams of erythritol, 90 grams of almond flour, and salt. Stir together to create the filling. Please put it on top, then cook for 25 minutes. Cut into small pieces and serve with lemon slices.

Nutrition: Calories: 272 Carbohydrates: 4 g Fat: 26 g Protein: 8 g

Creamy Hot Chocolate

Preparation Time: 5 minutes **Cooking Time:** 5 minutes **Servings:** 4

90 grams dark chocolate, chopped
64 ml. unsweetened almond milk
70 grams double cream
1 tablespoon erythritol
60 grams vanilla extract

Combine the almond milk, erythritol, and cream in a small saucepan. Heat it (choose medium heat and cook for 1-2 minutes). Add vanilla extract and chocolate. Stir continuously until the chocolate melts. Pour into cups and serve.

Nutrition: Calories: 193 Carbohydrates: 4g Fat: 18g Protein: 2g

Delicious Coffee Ice Cream

Preparation Time: 10 minutes **Cooking Time:** 5 minutes **Servings:** 1

180 grams coconut cream, frozen into ice cubes
1 ripe avocado, chopped and frozen
60 grams coffee expresso
2 tablespoons sweetener
1 teaspoon vanilla extract
1 tablespoon water
Coffee beans

Take out the frozen coconut cubes and avocado from the fridge. Slightly melt them for 5-10 minutes. Add the sweetener, coffee expresso, and vanilla extract to the coconut-avocado mix and whisk with an immersion blender until it becomes creamy (for about 1 minute). Pour in the water and blend for 30 seconds. Top with coffee beans and enjoy!

Nutrition: Calories: 596 Carbohydrates: 20.5 g Fat: 61 g Protein: 6.3 g

Fatty Bombs with Cinnamon and Cardamom

Preparation Time: 10 minutes **Cooking Time:** 35 minutes **Servings:** 10

120 grams unsweetened coconut, shredded
90 grams of unsalted butter
¼ teaspoon green cinnamon
¼ ground cardamom
½ teaspoon vanilla extract

Roast the unsweetened coconut (choose medium-high heat) until it turns light brown. Combine the room-temperature butter, half of the shredded coconut, cinnamon, cardamom, and vanilla extract in a separate dish. Cool the mix in the fridge for about 5-10 minutes. Form small balls and cover them with the remaining shredded coconut.
Cool the balls in the fridge for about 10-15 minutes.

Nutrition: Calories: 258 Carbohydrates: 15g Fat: 10g Protein: 3g

Fudgy Brownie

Preparation Time: 10 minutes **Cooking Time:** 4 hours **Servings:** 8

60 grams Butter
220 grams Unsweetened baking chocolate
130 grams Almond Flour
90 grams powdered erythritol
2 tablespoon Cocoa powder
2 large Eggs (at room temperature)
1 teaspoon Vanilla extract (optional)
1/4 teaspoon Sea salt (only if using unsalted butter)
120 grams Walnuts (optional, chopped)

Preheat the oven to 177 degrees C. Line an 8x8 in (20x20 cm) pan with parchment paper, with the edges of the paper over the sides. Melt the butter and chocolate together in a double boiler, stirring occasionally, until smooth—remove from heat. Stir in the vanilla extract—Add the almond flour, powdered sweetener, cocoa powder, sea salt, and eggs. Stir together until uniform. The batter will be a little grainy looking. Transfer the batter to the lined pan. Smooth the top with a spatula or the back of a spoon. If desired, sprinkle with chopped walnuts and press into the top. Bake for about 13-18 minutes, until an inserted toothpick comes out almost clean with just a little batter on it that balls up between your fingers. (Do NOT wait for it to come out totally clean, and don't worry about any butter pooled on top - just watch the actual brownie part to be super soft but not fluid.) Cool completely before moving or cutting. There may be some butter pooled on top - do not drain it, it will absorb back in after cooling.

Nutrition: Calories: 174 Carbohydrates:4g Fat: 16 g Protein: 3g

Chocolate Spread with Hazelnuts

Preparation Time: 5 minutes **Cooking Time:** 5 minutes **Servings:** 6

2 tablespoons cocoa powder
150 grams hazelnuts, roasted and without shells
30 grams of unsalted butter
32 ml. of coconut oil

Whisk all the spread ingredients with a blender. Serve.

Nutrition: Calories: 271 Carbohydrates: 2 g Fat: 28 g Protein: 4 g

Quick and Simple Brownie

Preparation Time: 20 minutes **Cooking Time:** 5 minutes **Servings:** 2

3 tablespoons Keto chocolate chips
1 tablespoon unsweetened cacao powder
2 tablespoons salted butter
2 ¼ tablespoon powdered sugar

Combine the chocolate chips with the butter, and melt them in a microwave for 10-15 minutes. Remove, and let it cool aside. Add the cacao powder and powdered sugar to the sauce and whisk well until you have a dough.
Preheat the oven to 220° Celsius. Put the butter inside the range and bake for 10 minutes. Place the dough on a baking sheet, and form the Brownie.

Nutrition: Calories: 100 Carbohydrates: 9 g Fat: 30 g Protein: 13 g

Cute Peanut Balls

Preparation Time: 20 minutes **Cooking Time:** 20 minutes **Servings:** 18

120 grams salted peanuts, chopped
120 grams of peanut butter
120 grams powdered sweetener
250 grams keto chocolate chips

Combine the chopped peanuts, peanut butter, and sweetener in a separate dish. Stir well and make a dough. Divide it into 18 pieces and form small balls. Put them in the fridge for 10-15 minutes. Use a microwave to melt your chocolate chips. Plunge each ball into the melted chocolate. Return your balls to the fridge. Cool for about 20 minutes.

Nutrition: Calories: 194 Carbohydrates: 7g Fat: 17g Protein: 7g

Chocolate Mug Muffins

Preparation Time: 5 minutes **Cooking Time:** 2 minutes **Servings:** 4

4 tablespoon almond flour
1 teaspoon baking powder
4 tablespoon granulated erythritol
2 tablespoons cocoa powder
½ teaspoon vanilla extract
Salt
2 eggs beaten
3 tablespoon butter, melted
1 teaspoon coconut oil, for greasing the mug
60 grams sugar-free dark chocolate, chopped

Mix the dry ingredients in a separate bowl. Add the melted butter, beaten eggs, and chocolate to the bowl. Stir thoroughly. Divide your dough into 4 pieces. Put these pieces in the greased mugs and put them in the microwave. Cook for 1-1.5 minutes (700 watts). Let them cool for 1 minute and serve.

Nutrition: Calories: 208 Carbohydrates: 2 g Fat: 19 g Protein: 5 g

Keto Peanut Butter Cup Style Fudge

Preparation Time: 10 minutes **Cooking Time:** 30 minutes **Servings:** 36

60 grams of natural peanut butter
30 grams butter
120 grams powdered swerve sweetener
1 teaspoon vanilla extract
Salt
3 tablespoons peanuts, chopped
Salt

Line a baking sheet with parchment pepper for easy removal. Add peanut butter, vanilla, and butter to a pan and heat over medium heat until melted and smooth. Turn off the heat, stir in sweetener and salt, and mix well. Spread the mixture on the prepared baking sheet in an even layered. Chill for 20-30 minutes, cut into 36 slices.
Sprinkle with sea salt or other toppings, and keep in an airtight container.

L

Nutrition: Calories: 247 Fat: 10g Carbohydrates: 22g Protein: 41g

Keto and Dairy-Free Vanilla Custard

Preparation Time: 11 minutes **Cooking Time:** 5 minutes **Servings:** 4

6 egg yolks
64 ml. unsweetened almond milk
1 teaspoon vanilla extract
32 ml. melted coconut oil

Mix egg yolks, almond milk, and vanilla in a metal bowl. Gradually stir in the melted coconut oil. Boil water in a saucepan, and place the mixing bowl over the saucepan. Whisk the mixture constantly and vigorously until thickened for about 5 minutes. Remove from the saucepan, and serve hot or chill in the fridge.

Nutrition: Calories: 222 Fat: 24g Carbohydrates: 11g Protein: 3g

Keto Triple Chocolate Mug Cake

Preparation Time: 3 minutes **Cooking Time:** 1 minute **Servings:** 3

1 ½ tablespoon coconut flour
½ teaspoon baking powder
2 tablespoons cacao powder
2 tablespoons powdered sweetener
1 medium egg
5 tablespoons double/heavy cream
2 tablespoons sugar-free chocolate chips
¼ teaspoon vanilla extract optional

Mix all dry fixing- coconut flour, baking powder, cacao powder, and a bowl. Whisk together the egg, cream, and vanilla extract, and pour the mixture into the dry ingredients. Add the chocolate chips to the mixture and let the batter rest for a minute. Grease the ramekins with melted butter, and pour the batter into the ramekins. Place in the microwave and microwave for 1 minute until cooked through.

Nutrition: Calories: 250 Carbohydrates: 9.7g Protein: 6g Fat: 22g

Keto Cheesecake Stuffed Brownies

Preparation Time: 11 minutes **Cooking Time:** 30 minutes **Servings:** 16

For the Filling:
250 grams of cream cheese
30 grams sweetener
1 large egg

For the Brownie:
85 grams low carb milk chocolate
5 tablespoons butte
3 large eggs
60 grams sweetener
30 grams cocoa powder
60 grams almond flour

Heat-up oven to 200° Celsius, line a brownie pan with parchment. In a mixing bowl, whisk cream cheese, egg, and sweetener until smooth. Set aside. Place chocolate and butter in a microwave-safe bowl and microwave for 30 seconds. Whisk frequently until smooth, and allow to cool for a few minutes. Whisk together the remaining eggs and sweetener until fluffy. Mix in the almond flour plus cocoa powder until soft peaks form. Mix in the chocolate and butter mixture and beat with a hand mixer for a few seconds. Fill the prepared pan with ¾ of the batter, then top with the cream cheese and the brownie batter. Bake the cheesecake brownie until mostly set for about 25-30 minutes. The jiggling parts of the cake will firm when you remove it from the oven.

Nutrition: Calories: 177 Fat: 13g Carbohydrates: 12g Protein: 5g

Keto Raspberry Ice Cream

Preparation Time: 45 minutes **Cooking Time:** 0 minutes **Servings:** 8

250 grams of heavy whipping cream
120 grams raspberries
60 grams powdered erythritol
1 pasteurized egg yolk

Process all the ice cream ingredients in a food processor. Add the blended mixture into the ice cream maker. Turn on the ice cream machine and churn according to the manufacturer's directions.

Nutrition: Calories: 120 Fat: 23g Carbohydrates: 4g Protein: 0g

Chocolate Macadamia Nut Fat Bombs

Preparation Time: 11 minutes **Cooking Time:** 30 minutes **Servings:** 4

40 grams sugar-free dark chocolate
1 tablespoon
Salt
40 grams raw macadamia nuts,halves

Put three macadamia nut halves in each of the eight wells of the mini muffin pan. Microwave the chocolate chips for about a few seconds. Whisk until smooth, add coconut oil and salt, and mix until well combined. Fill the mini muffin pan with the chocolate mixture to cover the nuts completely. Refrigerate the muffin pan until chilled and firm for about 30 minutes.

Nutrition: Calories: 153 Fat: 1g Carbohydrates: 2g Protein: 4g

Keto Peanut Butter Chocolate Bars

Preparation Time: 11 minutes **Cooking Time:** 10 minutes **Servings:** 8

For the Bars:
85 grams Superfine Almond Flour
60 grams Butter
45 grams Swerve, Icing sugar style
60 grams of Peanut Butter
1 teaspoon Vanilla extract
For the Topping:
90 grams of Sugar-Free Chocolate Chips

Microwave the chocolate in the microwave oven for 30 seconds and whisk it until smooth. Pour the melted chocolate over the bar's ingredients. Combine all the ingredients for the bars and spread into a small 6-inch pan. Refrigerate for at least an hour or 2 until the bars are firmed. Keep in an airtight container.

Nutrition: Calories: 246 Fat: 23g Carbohydrates: 7g Protein: 7g

Salted Toffee Nut Cups

Preparation Time: 11 minutes **Cooking Time:** 10 minutes **Servings:** 5

140 grams of low-carb milk chocolate
3 tablespoons plus 2 tablespoons sweetener
2 tablespoons cold butter
15 grams, walnuts, chopped
Sea salt to taste

Microwave the chocolate in 45 seconds intervals and continue to whisk until the chocolate melts. Line the cupcake pan with five paper liners and add chocolate to the bottom of the cupcake. Spread the chocolate to coat the bottom of the cupcake evenly, and freeze to harden. Heat the cold butter and sweetener on power 8 for three minutes in a heat-proof bowl. Stir the butter every 20 seconds to prevent burning. Mix in the 28 grams of sweetener and whisk to thicken. Fold in the walnuts. Fill the chocolate cups with the toffee mixture quickly. Remove from the cups and sprinkle with sea salt! Top the cupcakes with the remaining chocolate and refrigerate to firm for 20-30 minutes.

Nutrition: Calories: 194 Fat: 18g Carbohydrates: 2g Protein: 2.5g

Crisp Meringue Cookies

Preparation Time: 10 minutes **Cooking Time:** 40 minutes **Servings:** 8

4 large egg whites
¼ teaspoon cream of tartar
½ teaspoon almond extract
6 tablespoons Swerve Confectioners
Pinch of salt

Preheat the oven to 100 °Celsius. Whip egg whites and cream of tartar in a mixing bowl on medium speed until foamy. While whipping, gradually add the swerve confectioners 60 grams tsp at a time. Turn the mixer up to high speed and whip when all the shift is added. Add in the almond extract and whip until very stiff. Pour the batter into a piping bag with a French star tip and pipe the batter onto the lined baking sheet. Bake the meringue for 40 minutes. Enjoy! Serve immediately.

Nutrition: Calories: 234 Fat: 14g Carbohydrates: 12g Protein: 4g

Instant Pot Matcha Cheesecake

Preparation Time: 11 minutes **Cooking Time:** 55 minutes **Servings:** 6

Cheesecake:
450 grams cream cheese, room temperature
60 grams sweetener
2 teaspoons coconut flour
½ teaspoon vanilla extract
2 tablespoons heavy whipping cream
1 tablespoon matcha powder
2 large eggs, room temperature

In a mixing bowl, combine cream cheese, Swerve, coconut flour, vanilla extract, whipping cream, and matcha powder until well combined. Stir in the eggs one at a time. Add the cheesecake batter into the prepared springform pan. Pour 60 ml. of water into the bottom of the Instant Pot. Put the trivet in the instant pot. Place the springform on the top of the trivet, sealing, and securing the instant pot's lid. Set the instant pot on high pressure, and set the timing for 35 minutes. Once the cooking time is up, release the pressure naturally. Transfer the cheesecake to a cooling rack and allow it to cool the cake for 30 minutes. Top with your favourite toppings, enjoy!

Nutrition: Calories: 350 Fat: 33.2g Carbohydrates: 5.8g Protein: 8.4g

Matcha Skillet Souffle

Preparation Time: 5 minutes **Cooking Time:** 5 minutes **Servings:** 1

3 large eggs
2 tablespoons sweetener
1 teaspoon vanilla extract
1 tablespoon matcha powder
1 tablespoon butter
7 whole raspberries
1 tablespoon coconut oil
1 tablespoon unsweetened cocoa powder
30 grams whipped cream

Broil, then heat a heavy-bottom pan over medium heat. Whip the egg whites with one tablespoon of Swerve confectioners. Once the peaks form, add in the matcha powder, and whisk again. With a fork, break up the yolks. Mix in the vanilla, then adds a tiny amount of the whipped whites. Carefully fold the remaining whites into the yolk mixture. Dissolve the butter in a pan, and put the souffle mixture in the pan. Reduce the heat to low and top with raspberries. Cook until the eggs double in size and set. Transfer the pan to the oven and keep an eye on it. Cook until golden browned. Melt the coconut oil and combine with cocoa powder and the remaining Swerve. Drizzle the chocolate mixture across the top.

Nutrition: Calories 578 Fat: 44g Carbohydrates: 5. g Protein: 19g

Instant Pot Matcha Cheesecake

Preparation Time: 11 minutes **Cooking Time:** 55 minutes **Servings:** 6

Cheesecake:
450 grams cream cheese, room temperature
60 grams sweetener
2 teaspoons coconut flour
½ teaspoon vanilla extract
2 tablespoons heavy whipping cream
1 tablespoon matcha powder
2 large eggs, room temperature

In a mixing bowl, combine cream cheese, Swerve, coconut flour, vanilla extract, whipping cream, and matcha powder until well combined. Stir in the eggs one at a time. Add the cheesecake batter into the prepared springform pan. Pour 60 ml. of water into the bottom of the Instant Pot. Put the trivet in the instant pot. Place the springform on the top of the trivet, sealing, and securing the instant pot's lid. Set the instant pot on high pressure, and set the timing for 35 minutes. Once the cooking time is up, release the pressure naturally. Transfer the cheesecake to a cooling rack and allow it to cool the cake for 30 minutes. Top with your favourite toppings, enjoy!

Nutrition: Calories: 350 Fat: 33.2g Carbohydrates: 5.8g Protein: 8.4g

Flourless Keto Brownies

Preparation Time: 10 minutes **Cooking Time:** 25 minutes **Servings:** 4

141 grams of low-carb milk chocolate
4 tablespoons butter
3 large eggs
F60 grams Swerve
30 grams mascarpone cheese
30 grams unsweetened cocoa powder, divided
Salt

Heat oven to 190 °Celsius. And line a baking sheet with parchment. In a glass bowl over medium heat, melt the 5 oz. Chocolate for 30 seconds, stirring until smooth. Stir in the butter and microwave the bowl for another ten seconds. Repeat the process until smooth. Put aside. Beat the eggs and sweetener in a large mixing bowl until the eggs become pale and the mixture fluffy. Stir in the mascarpone cheese and whisk until smooth. Gently sift in the half cocoa powder and salt, combine. Sift the remaining cocoa powder and whisk until combined and form the mixture into a batter. Heat the chocolate again if firmed, and whisk in the mixture until creamy. Add the mixture to the prepared baking pan and bake until it no longer jiggles for about 25 minutes. Allow to cool before serving; enjoy!

Nutrition: Calories: 130 Fat: 8g Carbohydrates: 2.9g Protein: 2.18g

Tropical Chocolate Mousse Bites

Preparation Time: 5 minutes **Cooking Time:** 2 minutes **Servings:** 1

300 sugar-free dark chocolate
30 ml. coconut oil
60 grams of heavy whipping cream
1 tablespoon shredded coconut
1 tablespoon lemon zest

Chill the moulds in the freezer. Microwave the chocolate and coconut oil in 10-second intervals, stirring continuously until smooth. In a separate mixing bowl, whip the cream until medium-stiff peaks form. Stir in the lemon zest and shredded coconut and fold into the cream. Gradually stir 1/3 of the melted chocolate into the cream until well combined, reserving 2/3 for the moulds. Place the mousse in the fridge to cool. Pour the remaining melted chocolate into the chilled moulds to form a thick layer on the sides. Refrigerate the moulds for 10-15 minutes. Fill the cooled ice moulds with the mousse batter, leaving some space for the chocolate topping. Pour the remaining melted chocolate over the mousse, refrigerate, and mould for 10-15 minutes. Keep in the airtight container in the fridge.

Nutrition: Calories: 175 Fat: 13.75g Carbohydrates: 1.02g Protein: 1.98g

Coconut Raspberry Slice

Preparation Time: 11 minutes **Cooking Time:** 20 minutes **Servings:** 12 (You can store it for several days)

110 grams of butter melted
50g coconut flour
4 tablespoons granulated sweetener
2 teaspoons vanilla
1 teaspoon baking powder
8 eggs - medium
120 grams of frozen raspberries

Mix the melted butter, coconut flour, sweetener, vanilla, and baking powder until smooth. Put the eggs, and whisk in between each one. Add the mixture to a rectangle baking dish lined with baking parchment. Top each frozen raspberry evenly onto the cake. Bake the raspberry fingers at 180°/220° Celsius for 20-25 minutes until cooked through in the centre. Allow cooling for raspberry fingers, cut down in the centre, then cut across.

Nutrition: Calories: 146 Fat: 11.5g Carbohydrates: 6g Protein: 4.7g

White Chocolate Bark

Preparation Time: 11 minutes **Cooking Time:** 1 0 minutes **Servings:** 12 (You can store it for several days)

60 grams cacao butter
43 grams sweetener
1 teaspoon vanilla powder
½ teaspoon hemp seed powder
Pinch of Salt
1 teaspoon toasted pumpkin seeds

Finely chop, measure cacao butter and melt in a double boiler over a pan of boiling water. Mix the remaining ingredients in a bowl. Grease a plate or bowl With coconut oil, mix the melted butter into the remaining ingredients and combine well. Pour the mixture into the greased plate or bowl, and freeze until firm for 15 minutes. Remove the dish from the freezer and break the frozen mix into 12 even pieces. Chill and serve.

Nutrition: Calories: 258 Fat: 33g Carbohydrates: 24g Protein: 3g

Keto Hot Chocolate

Preparation Time: 5 minutes **Cooking Time:** 10 minutes **Servings:** 1

60 grams of heavy cream, divided
½ teaspoon vanilla extract, divided
40 ml. water
2 tablespoons cocoa powder, unsweetened
4 teaspoons erythritol or comparable measure
of preferred sweetener, divided

Mix half of the heavy cream, half of the erythritol, and half of the vanilla extract in a bowl. Using a hand mixer, beat the mixture until it becomes light and fluffy. Set to chill in the refrigerator while you prepare the cocoa. Warm a medium saucepan over medium-low heat and combine 60 ml. of water, the cocoa powder, and the remainder of the erythritol. Stir. Kick the heat back up to medium. Once smooth, add the remaining heavy cream and water. Stir continuously to combine. Stir the vanilla into the mixture and allow it to get nice and hot, to your preference. Pour the mixture into your favourite mug and serve topped with about 60 ml. of your whipped cream in the refrigerator.

Nutrition: Calories: 320 Carbohydrates: 9g Fat: 31g Protein: 1g

Carrot Cake Chia Pudding

Preparation Time: 15 minutes **Cooking Time:** 0 minutes **Servings:** 4

60 grams of chia seeds
½ teaspoon erythritol or comparable measure of preferred sweetener
1 ½ teaspoon Cinnamon, ground
¼ teaspoon Nutmeg, ground
¼ teaspoon ginger, ground
130 grams carrot, grated
1 teaspoon vanilla extract
130 grams Greek yoghurt, plain
60 grams pecans, toasted
220 ml. almond milk, unsweetened

Mix chia seeds with seasonings, carrot, and almond milk in a bowl. Stir to combine thoroughly. Let chill for 30 minutes so the chia seeds can swell. The mixture will become very thick, like a pudding. Remove the mixture from the refrigerator and stir the yoghurt into it. Serve chilled! Top with toasted pecans.

Nutrition: Calories: 123   Carbohydrates: 6g Fat: 15g Protein: 9g

Carrot Cake Energy Balls

Preparation Time: 15 minutes **Cooking Time:** 0 minutes **Servings:** 8

60 grams coconut, shredded & unsweetened
64 ml. sugar-free maple syrup
60 grams carrot, grated
½ teaspoon cinnamon, ground
130 grams of almond flour
40 grams of coconut flour
1/8 teaspoon ginger, grated
1/8 teaspoon nutmeg
3 tablespoons erythritol or comparable measure
of preferred sweetener

Combine all fixing except for the shredded coconut and pulse until a thick dough is formed. If the dough is too wet, add a little extra flour and pulse. If the dough is too dry, add more water and pulse. Once the dough has reached the desired consistency, take about a tablespoon of dough at a time and roll it into a smooth ball. Roll each ball through the shredded coconut to coat thoroughly and set it on the baking sheet in an even layer. Once you've rolled out all your balls, put them in the refrigerator for 30 minutes to become firm. Keep stored in the fridge, in an airtight container for a snack, or serve chilled to guests!

Nutrition: Calories: 158 Carbohydrates: 22g Fat: 9g Protein: 2g

Caramel Pecan Muffins

Preparation Time: 10 minutes **Cooking Time:** 20 minutes **Servings:** 8

For the Muffins:
60 grams of coconut flour
64 ml. coconut milk, canned & unsweetened
60 grams almond flour
60 grams scoops vanilla protein powder of choice
1 ½ tablespoons coconut oil, melted
1 egg, beaten
1 teaspoon baking powder
Sea salt
2 tablespoons erythritol or comparable measure
of preferred sweetener
For the Filling:
64 ml. water
60 grams erythritol
1 egg, yolk only
2 tablespoons Coconut oil
½ teaspoon Vanilla extract
¼ teaspoon Yacon syrup
¼ teaspoon Sea salt
¼ teaspoon Cinnamon, ground
60 grams pecans, chopped

Heat the oven to 190° Celsius. In a large sauté pan, combine all the filling ingredients (except the pecans). Warm them over medium heat, continually stirring until it begins to bubble. Allow the filling to bubble for about 30 seconds, kill the heat, and set the pan on a cold burner or trivet. The mixture should have a slight thickness but will be a little thinner than the traditional caramel. Stir the pecans into the filling until thoroughly incorporated and set aside. In a large mixing bowl, combine all dry ingredients for the muffins, whisking to combine. In a smaller bowl, combine the wet ingredients for the muffins and whisk to combine. Mix the wet and the dry fixing. Beat. Once the mixture is smooth, scoop a little batter into each cup to cover the bottoms. Spoon a teaspoon of the filling into each muffin liner, then top each with the bowl's remaining batter. Add small dollops of caramel to each muffin's top and, using a toothpick, give each a quick swirl to give the muffin a swirled and delicious top. Bake for 18 to 22 minutes, then cool for about 10 minutes before removing from the tin. Serve warm!

Nutrition: Calories: 369   Carbohydrates: 12g Fat: 10g Protein: 5g

Cinnamon Roll Cookies

Preparation Time: 25 minutes **Cooking Time:** 6 minutes **Servings:** 16

For the Cookies:
60 grams of coconut flour
60 grams erythritol or comparable measure of preferred sweetener
¼ teaspoon xanthan gum
½ teaspoon vanilla extract
100 grams of almond flour
1 tablespoon egg whites
1/8 teaspoon baking soda
1/8 teaspoon sea salt
3 tablespoons butter, cubed

For the Filling:
½ tablespoon butter, melted
½ teaspoon cinnamon, ground
2 teaspoon erythritol or comparable measure of preferred sweetener

For the Frosting:
1 tablespoon coconut oil
1 teaspoon erythritol or comparable measure of preferred sweetener
1/8 teaspoon vanilla extract
3 tablespoons cream cheese

Mix all the dry ingredients for the cookie dough in a bowl. Drop the butter cubes into the dough and use your hands to crumble it into the mixture of dry ingredients. Stir the wet ingredients into the dough mix and combine until a smooth dough begins to form. You may need to let it stand for about five minutes once it's soft to allow it to firm up.
On a baking sheet, place a piece of parchment paper.
Turn your cookie dough onto the parchment paper and shape it into a long rectangular sheet. You may need to place parchment paper on the dough to make it easier to roll out. Try to ensure that it is of even thickness (about half an inch) all the way through.

Chill the baking sheet, then allow the dough to chill and firm up for about 20 minutes.
Grease the dough with melted butter, then put the filling ingredients over it, spreading them evenly.
Take hold of one of the short sides of the dough and roll it up tightly. Cut the dough into disks about a quarter of an inch thick and place onto a baking sheet lined with parchment paper. Chill the baking sheet for another 20 minutes and set the oven to preheat to 190° Celsius. Bake the cookies for 7 minutes or until an inserted toothpick comes out clean. Mix all the fixing for the frosting, dip, and drizzle into the cookies. Serve and enjoy!

Nutrition: Calories: 358 Carbohydrates: 14g Fat: 5g Protein: 2g

Courgettes Cookies

Preparation Time: 10 minutes **Cooking Time:** 12 minutes
Servings: 10

1 egg, beaten
1 teaspoon vanilla extract
60 grams courgettes, grated & drained
130 grams of almond flour
¼ teaspoon Psyllium husk powder or xanthan gum
½ teaspoon baking powder
1 teaspoon Cinnamon, ground
60 grams of sugar-free chocolate chips
Sea salt
¼ teaspoon nutmeg, ground
40 grams butter softened
85 grams erythritol or comparable measure of preferred sweetener

Heat the oven to 190° Celsius and line a baking sheet with parchment paper. Combine sweetener, eggs, vanilla, and butter in a medium mixing bowl. Mix until thoroughly combined. Add courgettes to the bowl and mix once more. Stir the psyllium husk powder (or xanthan gum), cinnamon, nutmeg, salt, and baking powder into the bowl and form a smooth batter. Fold the sugar-free chocolate chips into the batter using your spoon or spatula. Make ten evenly sized blobs of dough on your cookie sheet, taking care to space them evenly. Flatten each chunk just a little bit so the dough is more cookie shaped. Bake for 11 to 12 minutes or until the edges begin to crisp up. Let stand for about 10 minutes, then move to a cooling rack.
Serve and enjoy!

Nutrition: Calories: 120 Carbohydrates: 2 g Fat: 10 g Protein: 2 g

Mint Chocolate Pie

Preparation Time: 15 minutes **Cooking Time:** 0 minutes **Servings:** 10

60 grams almond flour
60 grams erythritol or comparable measure of preferred sweetener, powdered
60 grams mint, fresh & chopped
2 drops of green food colouring
250 grams of heavy cream, divided
2 teaspoons gelatin powder, unflavored
3 tablespoons water
4 eggs, yolks only
4 tablespoons butter, melted
5 tablespoons erythritol or comparable measure of preferred sweetener, granulated
6 tablespoons cocoa powder, unsweetened

Mix almond flour, granulated erythritol, and cocoa powder in a bowl. Whisk to combine thoroughly.
Stir butter into the mixture until nice and crumbly. Press the mixture into a pie plate, pushing it up the dish's sides. Set the crust to chill in the refrigerator until you're ready for it.
Warm 60 grams of the cream cheese and the mint in medium heat, stirring thoroughly to keep smooth. When the mixture is hot, kill the heat, cover the pan, and let it stand on a cold burner or trivet for 30 minutes. Pour the cream cheese mixture into a mixing bowl through a strainer. Use a plastic or silicone spatula to push the cream through the filter without the leaves. Set the cream aside.
Whisk the water and gelatin until it's fully dissolved in medium heat. Slowly stir the cream mixture into the water and continue to whisk until the mixture is entirely smooth and hot all the way through.
In another bowl, beat the egg yolks and powdered erythritol. Beat until smooth.
Take 200 grams of the cream mixture and slowly stir it into the egg yolks, constantly whisking so they don't seize.
Once the cream's cup is thoroughly mixed in, mix the egg mixture into the remainder of the cream. Overheat and whisk until it thickens to a puddling-like consistency.
Stir the food colouring (optional) into the mix and beat until peaks form in the cream.
Fill the pie crust with the creamy mixture and use your spoon or spatula to smooth the top.
Chill for about three hours, then slice and serve chilled!

Nutrition: Calories: 161 Carbohydrates: 2g Fat: 14g Protein: 5g

Truffle Balls

Preparation Time: 15 minutes **Cooking Time:** 0 minutes **Servings:** 12

60 grams butter, melted
60 grams erythritol or comparable measure of preferred sweetener
140 grams of almond flour
1 ½ teaspoon vanilla extract
1 pinch salt
1 tablespoon coconut oil
150 grams sugar-free chocolate, chopped
6 tablespoons cocoa powder

In a medium mixing bowl, combine the erythritol, almond flour, salt, and cocoa powder. Whisk to combine Stir the butter and vanilla into the mixture and allow the dough to form.

Mix until the desired consistency is reached. Use a spoon, take enough dough out of the bowl to form one-inch balls, roll them in your palms, and lay them in one layer on the parchment paper.

Chill the balls for about an hour to allow them to be firm enough to stand up to chocolate dipping.

In a double boiler or a heat-resistant glass bowl over boiling water, warm the chocolate and the coconut oil, continually stirring to make a coating. Once the mixture is smooth, remove it from the boiler and place it on a trivet. Gently dip and roll each ball in the coating (using two forks is a great way to move the balls and pull them out without burning your fingers), then place back on the parchment. Once all the balls are coated, place all the truffles into the refrigerator for about an hour to stiffen. If you have chocolate coating left over, set it to cool until the truffles are done chilling.

Put back the batter into the double boiler to melt again, then drizzle the remaining chocolate on top of the truffle balls.

Chill and serve.

Nutrition: Calories: 240 Carbohydrates: 14g Fat: 8g Protein: 2g

Peanut Butter Chocolate Cupcakes

Preparation Time: 15 minutes **Cooking Time:** 20 minutes **Servings:** 12

130 grams of peanut flour
100 grams cocoa powder, unsweetened
2 teaspoons baking powder
Salt
4 egg whites
100 grams erythritol or comparable measure
of preferred sweetener, powdered
½ teaspoon stevia powdered
½ tablespoons vanilla extract
12 tablespoons butter, melted
100 ml. almond milk, unsweetened
120 grams of sugar-free peanut butter

Heat the oven to 190° Celsius, then line a muffin tin with paper liners. Mix the flour, baking powder, cocoa powder, and salt in a bowl. Whisk to combine. In another bowl, mix eggs, sweeteners, and vanilla. Whisk the melted butter and almond milk with the other wet ingredients. Mix all the dry ingredients into the wet and create a smooth batter with no lumps. Spoon the batter into the cups (they won't rise too much). Bake for 18 to 20 minutes or until an inserted toothpick comes out clean.

Let cool for about five minutes in the muffin tin, then set them out on wire racks to cool completely.

Using 60 grams for each cupcake, frost with peanut butter. Serve and enjoy!

Nutrition: Calories: 340 Carbohydrates: 6.5g Fat: 30.5g Protein: 12.5g

Keto Cheesecakes

Preparation Time: 15 minutes **Cooking Time:** 10 minutes **Servings:** 9

2 tablespoons butter
1 tablespoon caramel syrup; sugar-free
3 tablespoons coffee
250 grams of cream cheese
43 grams swerve
3 eggs
For the frosting:
250 grams mascarpone cheese
50 ml. caramel syrup
60 grams swerve
50 grams butter

Pulse cream cheese with eggs, 60 grams butter, coffee, 11 teaspoon caramel syrup, and 43 grams twist in a processor. Scoop into a cupcakes pan and bake for 15 minutes. Chill for 3 hours. Combine 50 grams butter, 50 grams caramel syrup, 60 grams swerve, and mascarpone cheese. Top over cheesecakes and serve.

Nutrition: Calories: 254 Fat: 23 Carbohydrates: 3g Protein: 5g

Keto Coco Walnuts Brownies

Preparation Time: 15 minutes **Cooking Time:** 35 minutes **Servings:** 4

43 grams of cocoa powder
43 grams erythritol
1 egg
30 grams almond flour
30 grams walnuts
½ teaspoon baking powder
7 tablespoons ghee
½ teaspoon vanilla extract
1 tablespoon peanut butter
Salt

Warm-up 84 grams of ghee and the erythritol, and cook for 5 minutes. Transfer, mix with salt, vanilla extract, and cocoa powder. Put egg, beat. Add baking powder, walnuts, and almond flour; stir and pour into a skillet—mix 11 teaspoon ghee with peanut butter, and warm up in the microwave for a second. Drizzle over brownies mix in the skillet, and bake for 30 minutes. Slice and serve.

Nutrition: Calories: 223   Fat: 32g Carbohydrates: 21g Protein: 4g

Keto Brownies

Preparation Time: 15 minutes **Cooking Time**: 20 minutes **Servings:** 9

180 grams of coconut oil
120 grams of cream cheese
5 tablespoons swerve
6 eggs
2 tablespoons vanilla extract
90 grams of cocoa powder
½ teaspoon baking powder

Blend eggs with coconut oil, cocoa powder, baking powder, vanilla, and cream cheese, and swerve using a mixer. Put into a lined baking dish at 220° Celsius, and bake for 20 minutes. Chill and serve.

Nutrition: Calories: 178 Fat: 14g Carbohydrates: 3g Protein: 5g

Raspberry and Coconut

Preparation Time: 15 minutes **Cooking Time:** 5 minutes **Servings:** 12

30 grams swerve
64 ml. coconut oil
60 grams raspberries; dried
60 grams coconut
60 grams of coconut butter

Blend dried berries using a processor. Warm up the butter over medium heat. Add oil, coconut, and swerve; cook for 5 minutes. Pour half into a baking pan. Add raspberry powder. Put the rest of the butter mixture, chill and serve.

Nutrition: Calories: 234 Fat: 22g Carbohydrates: 4g Protein: 2g

Chocolate Pudding Delight

Preparation Time: 60 minutes **Cooking Time:** 10 minutes **Servings:** 2

1/2 teaspoon stevia powder
2 tablespoons cocoa powder
2 tablespoons water
1 tablespoon gelatin
120 ml. coconut milk
2 tablespoons maple syrup

War-up the coconut milk over medium heat; add stevia and cocoa powder and mix. Mix gelatin with water, then adds to the pan. Mix, add maple syrup and chill for 45 minutes. Serve.

Nutrition: Calories: 140 Fat: 2g Carbohydrates: 4g Protein: 4g

Special Keto Pudding

Preparation Time: 4 hours & 15 minutes **Cooking Time:** 10 minutes **Servings:** 2

120 grams of coconut milk
4 teaspoons gelatin
1/4 teaspoon ginger
1/4 teaspoon liquid stevia
A pinch of nutmeg
A pinch of cardamom

In a bowl, mix 32 ml. milk with gelatin. Add gelatin mix, cold, and chill for 4 hours. Transfer to a food processor, add stevia, cardamom, nutmeg, and ginger and blend. Put the remaining coconut milk in a pot and warm up.
Serve cold.

Nutrition: Calories: 150 Fat: 1g Carbohydrates: 2g Protein: 6g

Peanut Butter Fudge

Preparation Time: 2 hours & 15 minutes **Cooking Time:** 10 minutes **Servings:** 12

120 grams of peanut butter
120 ml. of coconut oil
32 ml. almond milk
2 teaspoons vanilla stevia
A pinch of salt
Topping:
2 tablespoons swerve
30 grams cocoa powder
2 tablespoons melted coconut oil

Mix peanut butter with 120 grams of coconut oil; microwave until it melts. Add a pinch of salt, almond milk, and stevia; mix and pour into a lined loaf pan. Chill for 2 hours and slice. Mix 60 ml. melted coconut with cocoa powder and swerve. Drizzle the sauce on top and serve.

Nutrition: Calories: 265 Fat: 23g Carbohydrates: 14g Protein: 6g

Coconut Pear Cream

Preparation Time: 5 minutes **Cooking Time:** 4 hours **Servings:** 4

1 tablespoon lime juice
2 tablespoons coconut cream
4 pears
60 grams of date sugar

Mix all the ingredients and cook on low for 4 hours. Blend using an immersion blender and serve.

Nutrition: Calories: 208 Fat 4g Carbohydrates: 45g Protein: 15g

Lemony Coconut Cream

Preparation Time: 5 minutes **Cooking Time:** 3 hours **Servings:** 4

250 ml. of coconut milk
120 grams of coconut sugar
Lemon juice of 1 lemon
2 tablespoons ground cinnamon
60 grams coconut

Mix all the ingredients in a bowl—Preheat the oven to 170 degrees Celsius. Put the mixture inside the range and bake for 3 hours. Serve cold.

Nutrition: Calories: 345 Fat: 27g Carbohydrates: 70 Protein: 6

Blackberry Stew

Preparation Time: 5 minutes **Cooking Time:** 4 hours **Servings:** 4

250 grams blackberries
2 tablespoons coconut oil
43 ml. rose water
83 grams of coconut sugar

Mix all the ingredients in a bowl. Transfer the mixture into a saucepan and cook it on medium-low for 4 hours.

Nutrition: Calories: 246 Fat: 8g Carbohydrates: 39g Protein: 14g

Peach Jam

Preparation Time: 5 minutes **Cooking Time:** 6 hours **Servings:** 8

3 pounds peaches
120 ml. of water
1 teaspoon vanilla extract
120 grams of date sugar

Mix all the ingredients in a bowl. Transfer the mixture into a saucepan and cook it on medium-low for 6 hours.

Nutrition: Calories: 117 Fat: 18g Carbohydrates: 12g Protein: 4g

Strawberry Bowls

Preparation Time: 5 minutes **Cooking Time:** 3 hours **Servings:** 4

2 kg. strawberries
60 grams honey
2 tablespoons lemon zest
120 ml. of coconut water

Mix all the ingredients in a bowl. Transfer the mixture into a saucepan and cook it on medium-low for 3 hours.

Nutrition: Calories: 215 Fat: 4g Carbohydrates: 32g Protein: 2g

Pineapple Stew

Preparation Time: 5 minutes **Cooking Time:** 3 hours **Servings:** 4

Half a pineapple
250 ml. apple juice
30 grams of coconut sugar

Mix all the ingredients in a bowl. Transfer the mixture into a saucepan and cook it on medium-low for 2 hours.

Nutrition: Calories: 165 Fat: 12g Carbohydrates:16g Protein: 3g

Rhubarb Compote

Preparation Time: 5 minutes **Cooking Time:** 4 hours **Servings:** 6

1 kg. rhubarb
120 ml. of water
4 tablespoons honey
1 teaspoon vanilla extract

Mix all the ingredients in a bowl. Transfer the mixture into a saucepan and cook it on medium-low for 2 hours.

Nutrition: Calories: 188   Fat 12g   Carbohydrates: 15g Protein: 2g

Banana Bowls

Preparation Time: 5 minutes **Cooking Time:** 2 hours **Servings:** 4

1 tablespoon coconut sugar
4 bananas
64 ml. coconut oil

Mix all the ingredients and cook on low for 2 hours. Serve.

Nutrition: Calories: 346 Fat: 27g   Carbohydrates: 28g Protein: 1g

Grapes Compote

Preparation Time: 10 minutes **Cooking Time:** 2 hours **Servings:** 4

100 ml. grape juice
1 kg. green grapes
2 tablespoons coconut sugar

Mix all the ingredients and cook on low for 2 hours. Serve.

Nutrition: Calories: 131 Fat: 12g Carbohydrates: 33g Protein: 2g

Apricot Pudding

Preparation Time: 5 minutes **Cooking Time:** 4 hours **Servings:** 6

3 eggs
250 grams apricots
120 ml. of coconut milk
½ tablespoon baking soda
2 tablespoons lemon juice
150 grams coconut flour
2 tablespoons coconut sugar
43 grams coconut oil
1 teaspoon vanilla extract
Olive oil

Mix all the ingredients together in a bowl. Transfer the mixture into a slow cooker and cook it on medium-low for 4 hours.

Nutrition: Calories: 298 Fat: 27g Carbohydrates: 12g Protein: 4g

Blueberries and Cream

Preparation Time: 5 minutes **Cooking Time:** 3 hours **Servings:** 4

250 grams blueberries
60 grams coconut cream
60 grams of coconut sugar

Mix all the ingredients in a bowl. Transfer them into a saucepan and cook on medium-low heat for 3 hours. Leave aside to cool, and once cooled, use a blender to blend the mixture. Serve

Nutrition: Calories: 384 Fat: 22g Carbohydrates: 51g Protein: 3g

Pumpkin Cream

Preparation Time: 10 minutes **Cooking Time:** 2 hours **Servings:** 2

120 grams of pumpkin puree
64 ml. almond milk
1 teaspoon ground cinnamon
2 tablespoons coconut sugar
1 teaspoon vanilla extract

Mix all the ingredients in a bowl. Transfer them into a saucepan and cook on medium-low heat for 2 hours. Serve.

Nutrition: Calories 211 Fat: 14g Carbohydrates: 20g Protein: 2g

Maple Pumpkin Dessert

Preparation Time: 5 minutes **Cooking Time:** 3 hours **Servings:** 6

1 ½ teaspoon ground cinnamon
½ teaspoon baking soda
2 tablespoons lemon juice
43 ml. pure maple syrup
120 grams of pumpkin puree
380 ml. coconut milk
1 teaspoon grated ginger
2 teaspoons vanilla extract
120 grams walnuts

Mix all the ingredients in a bowl. Transfer them into a saucepan and cook on medium-low heat for 3 hours. Serve.

Nutrition: Calories: 472 Fat: 33g Carbohydrates: 24g Protein: 8g

Coconut Pineapple Bowls

Preparation Time: 5 minutes Cooking time: 3 hours Servings: 2

120 grams of pineapple chunks
2 tablespoons coconut flakes
120 ml. of coconut milk
1 tablespoon ground cinnamon

Mix all the ingredients in a bowl. Transfer them into a saucepan and cook on medium-low heat for 3 hours. Serve.

Nutrition: Calories: 343 Fat: 30g Carbohydrates: 21g Protein: 3g

Almond Papaya Mix

Preparation Time: 10 minutes **Cooking Time:** 2 hours **Servings**: 8

120 ml. of coconut milk
120 grams papaya
1 tablespoon almonds

Mix all the fixing and cook on low for 2 hours. Serve cold.

Nutrition: Calories: 334 Fat: 23g Carbohydrates: 13g Protein: 22g

Cinnamon Crunch Cereal

Preparation Time: 10 minutes **Cooking Time:** 20 minutes **Servings:** 5

For the Cereal
120 grams of Almond Flour
2 teaspoons Cinnamon
150 grams Coconut
1 tablespoon Erythritol sweetener
6 tablespoons Butter

For sugar topping
1 tablespoons erythritol sweetener
½ teaspoon ground cinnamon

Warm-up to a temperature of 200° Celsius. Put the flour, coconut, sweetener, and cinnamon in a processor. Pulse.
Put the butter pieces and pulse. Put the mixture in the pan and cover it with another sheet of parchment. Flatten out the ingredients. Bake for 20-30 minutes. Combine the topping. Sprinkle over the cereal. Cooldown and serve.

Nutrition: Calories: 236 Carbohydrates: 6g Fat: 20g Protein: 9g

Cinnamon Rolls

Preparation Time: 10 minutes **Cooking time:** 20 minutes **Servings:** 8

150 grams Mozzarella
80 grams of Almond Flour
2 tablespoons Cream Cheese
1 Egg
½ teaspoon baking powder
Filling
2 tablespoons water
2 tablespoons Sweetener
2 teaspoons cinnamon
Frosting
2 tablespoons cream cheese
1 tablespoon Greek yoghurt
2 drops of vanilla extract

Warm up the oven to heat at 220° Celsius. Dissolve the shredded mozzarella and cream cheese in a microwave. Remove. Stir in the egg. Mix in the flour and baking powder. Make a ball of smooth dough, divided into four pieces.

Form long rolls, flatten thin. For the cinnamon filling:
Boil water, then put in the sweetener and cinnamon. Put the cinnamon paste over the flattened dough rolls. Roll into a bun and cut sideways in half. Place the buns on a nonstick pie dish. Bake for 18 minutes. Prepare the frosting by thoroughly mixing yoghurt, sweetener, and cream cheese. Serve.

Nutrition: Calories: 321 Carbohydrates: 10g Fat: 9g Protein: 4g

Chocolate Ice Cream

Preparation Time: 10 minutes **Cooking Time:** 15 minutes **Servings:** 8

250 grams of heavy whipping cream
4 egg yolks
10 packet no-calorie sweetener
10 grams of Dry Cocoa Powder
2 tablespoons Chocolate Sweetener
1 teaspoon Vanilla Extract

Warm up the cream to heat over low. Stir in the egg yolks on low heat for 7 minutes. Remove and combine the sweetener, chocolate powder, syrup, and vanilla. Add the mixture to the ice cream maker. Freeze and serve.

Nutrition: Calories: 234 Carbohydrates: 2g Fat: 11g Protein: 7g

Strawberry Ice Cream

Preparation Time: 10 minutes **Cooking Time:** 0 minutes **Servings:** 3

120 grams strawberries
1 ½ tablespoon of vanilla whey protein powder
1 tablespoon Almond Butter
2 tablespoons Coconut Oil
60 ml. heavy cream
2 tablespoons Sweetener

Mix all the ingredients in a bowl. Transfer the ingredients into a blender and pulse. Freeze for 4 hours and serve.

Nutrition: Calories 221 Carbohydrates: 36g Fat: 11g Protein: 5g

Lava Cake

Preparation Time: 10 minutes **Cooking Time:** 10 minutes **Servings:** 2

4 tablespoons Cocoa Powder
½ teaspoon Baking Powder
1 Egg
2 tablespoons Heavy cream
3 tablespoons Stevia
1 teaspoonVanilla Extract
Salt

Warm up the oven to heat at 220° Celsius. Combine the stevia and cocoa powder, and mix with eggs. Stir in baking powder, cream, and vanilla. Add salt. Dump out the batter evenly into cups and bake for 10 minutes. Serve.

Nutrition: Calories: 660 Carbohydrates: 66g Fat: 41g Protein: 5g

Lemon Mousse

Preparation Time: 5 hours & 15 minutes **Cooking Time:** 0 minutes **Servings:** 4

120 grams Heavy cream
1 pack Jell-O with Lemon Flavor
1 tablespoon Lemon Juice
1 teaspoon Erythritol
Sweetener

Whisk the cream until points start to form. Prepare the Jell-O and chill for 12 minutes. Combine the Jell-O and cream mixture for 3 minutes. Flavour it with sweetener and lemon juice. Chill up to 5 hours and serve.

Nutrition: Calories: 250 Carbohydrates: 3g Fat: 27g Protein: 5g

Chocolate Almond Butter Fat Bombs

Preparation Time: 60 minutes **Cooking Time:** 5 minutes **Servings:** 4

60 grams of unsweetened chocolate
2 tablespoons Butter
60 grams of Almond Butter
1 tablespoon Peanut Butter
1 tablespoon coconut oil
1 teaspoon Stevia

Melt the chocolate, and put it into a silicone mould. Let it chill for 15 minutes. Put everything into a mixer. Put stevia, then process. Pour the mixture into the silicone mould. Chill for 45 minutes, and serve.

Nutrition: Calories 123 Carbohydrates: 12g Fat: 60g Protein: 10g

White Chocolate

Preparation Time: 15 minutes **Cooking Time:** 5 minutes **Servings:** 10

250 grams of raw cacao butter
60 grams erythritol
15 grams of Vanilla Protein Powder
2 tablespoons Vanilla Extract
A pinch of salt

Melt the cacao butter on low heat; whisk in Swerve. Cool down for 15 minutes, then put it into a blender. Stir in the remaining ingredients and process in the blender. Pour the mixture onto the chocolate bar moulds. Chill, serve.

Nutrition: Calories: 432 Carbohydrates: 2g Fat: 52g Protein: 5g

Coconut Peanut Butter Balls

Preparation Time: overnight & 1 hour **Cooking Time:** 0 minutes **Servings:** 10

3 tablespoons peanut butter
3 teaspoons cocoa powder
2 ½ teaspoons Erythritol
2 teaspoons almond flour
120 grams of coconut flakes

Mix everything except for the coconut flakes. Chill for an hour. Scoop the mixture and roll it in the coconut. Chill overnight, and serve.

Nutrition: Calories: 260 Carbohydrates: 4g Fat: 12 g Protein: 3 g

Meal Plan 1

DAYS	BREAKFAST	LUNCH/DINNER	SNACKS
1	Blueberry Nutty Oatmeal, 19	Baked Salmon, 46	Pickle, 110
2	Avocados Stuffed with Crab Salad, 20	Buttered Cod, 46	Deviled Eggs Keto Style, 112
3	Keto Goat Cheese Salmon Fat Bomb, 19	Shrimp Scampi with Garlic, 70	Nutty Yoghurt, 113
4	Salmon Cakes with Fried Pork Rind, 19	Roasted Lemon Chicken Sandwich, 45	Chips, 109
5	Bacon Hash, 21	Cabbage Soup with Beef, 71	Pinwheel Delight, 112
6	Bagels with Cheese, 22	Baked Salmon, 46	Zesty olives, 112
7	Baked Apples, 22	Buttered Cod, 46	Crisp Meringue Cookies 140
8	Avocados Stuffed with Crab Salad, 20	Chinese Pork Bowl, 70	Creme Brulee, 120

9	Banana Pancakes, 22	Roasted Lemon Chicken Sandwich, 45	Pickle, 110
10	Salmon Cakes with Fried Pork Rind, 19	Shrimp Scampi with Garlic, 70	Chocolate Ice Cream 153
11	Brunch BLT Wrap, 23	Quick Pumpkin Soup, 69	Strawberry Ice Cream 154
12	Keto Goat Cheese Salmon Fat Bomb, 19	Roasted Lemon Chicken Sandwich, 45	Nutty Yoghurt, 113
13	Coconut Keto Porridge, 23	Chinese Pork Bowl, 70	Almond Papaya Mix 152
14	Avocados Stuffed with Crab Salad, 20	Baked Salmon, 46	Zesty olives, 112
15	Creamy Basil, Baked Sausage, 24	Cabbage Soup with Beef, 71	Creme Brulee, 120
16	Almond, Coconut, Egg Wraps, 24	Baked Salmon, 46	Pickle, 110
17	Salmon Cakes with Fried Pork Rind, 19	Buttered Cod, 46	Flourless Keto Brownies 141
18	Bacon and Cheese Frittata,	Quick Pumpkin Soup, 69	Deviled Eggs Keto Style, 112

	21		
19	Blueberry Nutty Oatmeal, 19	Roasted Lemon Chicken Sandwich, 45	Chips, 109
20	Bacon Hash, 21	Trout and Chili Nuts, 47	Lemon Mousse 154
21	Bagels with Cheese, 22	Buttered Cod, 46	Pinwheel Delight, 112
22	Keto Goat Cheese Salmon Fat Bomb, 19	Chinese Pork Bowl, 70	Creme Brulee, 120
23	Bagels with Cheese 22	Baked Salmon, 46	Nutty Yogurt, 113
24	Salmon Cakes with Fried Pork Rind, 19	Shrimp Scampi with Garlic, 70	Mocha Ice Cream 133
25	Keto Goat Cheese Salmon Fat Bomb, 19	Quick Pumpkin Soup, 69	Pickle, 110
26	Blueberry Nutty Oatmeal, 19	Roasted Lemon Chicken Sandwich, 45	Keto Strawberry Ice Cream 139
27	Cheesy Bacon and Egg Cups, 23	Cabbage Soup with Beef, 71	Deviled Eggs Keto Style, 112
28	Blueberry Nutty	Buttered Cod, 46	Instant Pot

	Oatmeal, 19		Matcha Cheesecake 141
29	Salmon Cakes with Fried Pork Rind, 19	Tuna Salad, 46	Chips, 109
30	Avocados Stuffed with Crab Salad, 20	Fresh Avocado Soup, 69	Pickle, 110

Meal Plan 2

Day	Breakfast	Lunch	Snack	Dinner	Dessert
1	Almond Coconut Egg Wraps, 24	Turkey & Cream Cheese Sauce, 48	Parmesan Cheese Strips, 113	Baked Courgettes Noodles with Feta, 71	Sugar–Free Lemon Bars, 135
2	Bacon & Avocado Omelet, 20	Baked Salmon & Pesto, 48	Peanut Butter Power Granola, 113	Brussels Sprouts with Bacon, 72	Creamy Hot Chocolate, 135
3	Bacon & Cheese Frittata, 21	Keto Chicken with Butter & Lemon, 48	Homemade Graham Crackers, 114	Burger – Keto Style, 72	Delicious Coffee Ice Cream, 135
4	Bacon & Egg Breakfast Muffins, 21	Garlic Chicken, 49	Keto no Bake Cookies, 114	Coffee BBQ Pork Belly, 72	Fatty Bombs with Cinnamon and Cardamom, 136
5	Bacon Hash,21	Salmon Skewers & Wrapped with Prosciutto, 49	Swiss Cheese Crunchy Nachos, 114	Garlic & Thyme Lamb Chops, 72	Keto Cheesecakes 147
6	Bagel with Cheese, 22	Buffalo Drumsticks & Chili Aioli, 49	Homemade Thin Mints, 114	Jamaican Jerk Pork Roast, 73	Quick & Simple Brownie, 137
7	Baked Apples, 22	Slow Cooked Roasted Pork & Creamy Gravy, 49	Mozzarella Cheese Pockets, 115	Keto Meatballs, 73	Cute Peanut Balls, 137

8	Bacon & Avocado Omelet 20	Bacon–Wrapped Meatloaf, 50	No–Bake Coconut Cookies, 115	Mixed Vegetable Patties – Instant Pot, 73	Chocolate Mug Muffins, 137
9	Banana Pancakes, 22	Lamb Chops & Herb Butter, 50	Cheesy Cauliflower Breadsticks, 115	Roasted Leg of Lamb, 73	Chocolate Spreads with Hazelnuts, 136
10	Green Veggies Quiche 32	Crispy Cuban Pork Roast, 50	Easy Peanut Butter Cups, 116	Salmon Pasta, 74	Keto Peanut Butter Cup Style Fudge, 137
11	Brunch BLT Wrap, 23	Keto Barbecued Ribs, 51	Fried Green Beans Rosemary, 116	Skillet Fried Cod, 74	Keto and Dairy–Free Vanilla Custard, 138
12	Cheesy Bacon & Egg Cups, 23	Turkey Burgers & Tomato Butter, 51	Crispy Broccoli Popcorn, 116	Slow–Cooked Kalua Pork & Cabbage, 74	Keto Triple Chocolate Mug Cake, 138
13	Coconut Keto Porridge, 23	Keto Hamburger, 51	Cheesy Cauliflower Croquettes, 116	Steak Pinwheels, 74	Keto Cheesecake Stuffed Brownies, 138
14	Cream Cheese Eggs, 23	Chicken Wings & Blue Cheese Dressing, 52	Spinach in Cheese Envelopes, 117	Tangy Shrimp, 75	Keto Raspberry Ice Cream, 139
15	Creamy Basil Baked	Salmon Burgers with Lemon Butter	Cheesy Mushroom	Chicken Salad with Champagne	Chocolate Macadamia Nut Fat

	Sausage, 24	& Mash, 50	Slices, 117	Vinegar, 75	Bombs, 139
16	Banana Waffles, 24	Egg Salad Recipe, 52	Asparagus Fries, 117	Mexican Beef Salad, 75	Keto Peanut Butter Chocolate Bars, 139
17	Quick Keto Toast 36	Taco Stuffed Avocados, 53	Kale Chips, 118	Cherry Tomatoes Tilapia Salad, 76	Salted Toffee Nut Cups, 140
18	Keto Waffles & Blueberries, 24	Buffalo Shrimp Lettuce Wraps, 53	Guacamole, 118	Crunchy Chicken Milanese, 76	Crisp Meringue Cookies, 140
19	Cream Cheese Eggs 23	Broccoli Bacon Salad, 53	Courgette Noodles, 118	Parmesan Baked Chicken, 76	Instant Pot Matcha Cheesecake, 141
20	Mushroom Omelet, 25	Keto Egg Salad, 54	Cauliflower Souffle, 118	Cheesy Bacon and Broccoli Chicken, 77	Matcha Skillet Souffle, 141
21	Chocolate Sea Salt Smoothie, 25	Loaded Cauliflower Salad, 54	No–Churn Ice Cream, 119	Buttery Garlic Chicken, 77	Flourless Keto Brownies, 141
22	Crustless Broccoli & Cheddar Quiche 36	Caprese Zoodles, 54	Cheesecake Cupcakes, 119	Creamy Slow Cooker Chicken, 77	Tropical Chocolate Mousse Bites, 142

23	Vegan Keto Scramble, 25	Courgettes Sushi, 54	Chocolate Peanut Butter Cups, 119	Braised Chicken Thighs with Kalamata Olives, 78	Coconut Raspberry Slice, 142
24	Bavarian Cream with Vanilla and Hazelnuts, 26	Asian Chicken Lettuce Wraps, 55	Low–Carb Almond Coconut Sandies, 120	Baked Garlic and Paprika Chicken Legs, 78	White Chocolate Bark, 142
25	Vanilla Mousse, 26	California Burger Bowls, 55	Crème Brulee, 120	Chicken Curry with Masala, 78	Keto Hot Chocolate, 143
26	Turkey Hash 35	Parmesan Brussels Sprouts Salad, 55	Chocolate Fat Bomb, 120	Chicken Quesadilla, 79	Carrot Cake Chia Pudding, 143
27	Strawberry Bavarian, 26	Chicken Taco Avocados, 56	Cocoa Mug Cake, 120	Slow Cooker BBQ Ribs, 79	Carrot Cake Energy Balls, 143
28	Almond Mousse, 27	Keto Quesadillas, 56	Dark Chocolate Espresso Paleo & Keto Mug Cake, 121	Barbacoa Beef Roast, 79	Caramel Pecan Muffins, 144
29	Nougat, 27	No–Bread Italian Subs, 56	Keto Matcha Mint Bars, 121	Beef & Broccoli Roast, 80	Cinnamon Roll Cookies, 144
30	Chocolate Crepes, 29	Basil Avocado frail Salad Wraps &	Keto No–Churn Blueberry	Cauliflower and Pumpkin Casserole, 80	Keto Peanut Butter Chocolate

		Sweet Potato Chips, 57	Maple Ice cream, 121		Bars 139

Meal Plan 3

Day	Breakfast	Lunch	Snack	Dinner	Dessert
1	Rusk with Walnut Cream, 28	Cauliflower Leek Soup, 57	Chocolate Fat Bomb, 120	Thai Beef Salad, 80	Mint Chocolate Pie, 145
2	Bavarian Coffee with Hazelnuts, 28	Sugar–free Blueberry Cottage Cheese Parfaits, 57	Cocoa Mug Cake, 120	Stuffed Apples with Shrimp, 81	Truffle Balls, 146
3	Strawberry Butter Bavarian, 28	Low–Calorie Broccoli Leek Soup, 58	Dark Chocolate Espresso Paleo & Keto Mug Cake, 121	Grilled Chicken Salad with Oranges, 81	Peanut Butter Chocolate Cupcakes, 147
4	Cheese Platters, 28	Low Carb Chicken Taco Soup, 58	Keto Matcha Mint Bars, 121	Red Curry with Vegetables, 82	Caramel Pecan Muffins, 147
5	Hazelnut Bavarian with Hot Coffee Drink, 29	Keto Chicken & Veggies Soup, 58	Keto No–Churn Blueberry Maple Ice Cream, 121	Baked Turkey Breast with Cranberry Sauce, 82	Cinnamon Roll Cookies, 144
6	Keto Goat Cheese Salmon Fat Bombs	Low Carb Seafood Soup with Mayo, 58	Keto No–Bake Cookies 114	Italian Keto Casserole, 83	Chocolate Spread with Hazelnuts 136

	19				
7	French toast with Coffee Drink, 29	Keto Tortilla Chips, 59	Parmesan Cheese Strips, 113	Salmon Keto Cutlets, 83	Sugar–Free Lemon Bars, 135
8	Almond Coconut Egg Wraps, 24	Chicken Zucchini Alfredo, 59	Peanut Butter Power Granola, 113	Baked Cauliflower, 83	Creamy Hot Chocolate, 135
9	Bacon & Avocado Omelet, 20	Low Carb Chicken Cheese, 59	Homemade Graham Crackers, 114	Risotto with Mushrooms, 84	Delicious Coffee Ice Cream, 135
10	Bacon & Cheese Frittata, 21	Lemon Chicken Spaghetti Squash Boats, 60	Keto no Bake Cookies, 114	Low Carb Green Bean Casserole, 84	Fatty Bombs with Cinnamon and Cardamom, 136
11	Bacon & Egg Breakfast Muffins, 21	Stuffed Portobello Mushrooms, 60	Swiss Cheese Crunchy Nachos, 114	Avocado Low Carb Burger, 84	Tropical Chocolate Mousse Bites 142
12	Bacon Hash, 21	Low Carb Mexican Stuffed Bell Peppers, 60	Homemade Thin Mints, 114	Protein Gnocchi with Basil Pesto, 85	Quick & Simple Brownie, 137
13	Bagel with Cheese, 22	Low Carb Broccoli Mash, 60	Mozzarella Cheese Pockets, 115	Summery Bowls with Fresh Vegetables and Protein Quark, 85	Cute Peanut Balls, 137
14	Baked	Roasted Tri–	No–Bake	Beef and Kale	Chocolate

	Apples, 22	Color Vegetables, 61	Coconut Cookies, 115	Pan, 85	Mug Muffins, 137
15	Bacon & Avocado Omelet 20	Low Carb Broccoli Leek Soup, 58	Cheesy Cauliflower Breadsticks, 115	Salmon and Lemon Relish, 86	Chocolate Spreads with Hazelnuts, 136
16	Banana Pancakes, 22	Turkey & Cream Cheese Sauce, 48	Easy Peanut Butter Cups, 116	Mustard Glazed Salmon, 86	Keto Peanut Butter Cup Style Fudge, 137
17	Bacon & Cheese Frittata 21	Baked Salmon & Pesto, 48	Fried Green Beans Rosemary, 116	Turkey and Tomatoes, 86	Keto and Dairy–Free Vanilla Custard, 138
18	Brunch BLT Wrap, 23	Keto Chicken with Butter & Lemon, 48	Crispy Broccoli Popcorn, 116	Skillet Fried Cod 74	Keto Triple Chocolate Mug Cake, 138
19	Cheesy Bacon & Egg Cups, 23	Garlic Chicken, 49	Cheesy Cauliflower Croquettes, 116	Salmon Bowls, 87	Keto Cheesecake Stuffed Brownies, 138
20	Coconut Keto Porridge, 23	Salmon Skewers & Wrapped with Prosciutto, 49	Spinach in Cheese Envelopes, 117	Shrimp & Cauliflower Delight, 87	Keto Raspberry Ice Cream, 139
21	Cream Cheese Eggs, 23	Buffalo Drumsticks & Chili Aioli, 49	Cheesy Mushroom Slices, 117	Scallops and Fennel Sauce, 87	Chocolate Macadamia Nut Fat Bombs, 139

22	Creamy Basil Baked Sausage, 24	Slow Cooked Roasted Pork & Creamy Gravy, 49	Asparagus Fries, 117	Salmon Stuffed with Shrimp, 88	Keto Peanut Butter Chocolate Bars, 139
23	Banana Waffles, 24	Bacon–Wrapped Meatloaf, 50	Kale Chips, 118	Crunchy Chicken Milanese 76	Salted Toffee Nut Cups, 140
24	Bacon Hash 21	Lamb Chops & Herb Butter, 50	Guacamole, 118	Incredible Salmon Dish, 88	Crisp Meringue Cookies, 140
25	Keto Waffles & Blueberries, 24	Crispy Cuban Pork Roast, 50	Courgette Noodles, 118	Thai beef Salad, 80	Egg Custard 132
26	Turkey Scrabmle 23	Keto Barbecued Ribs, 51	Cauliflower Souffle, 118	Stuffed Apples with Shrimp, 81	Matcha Skillet Souffle, 141
27	Mushroom Omelet, 25	Turkey Burgers & Tomato Butter, 51	No–Churn Ice Cream, 119	Grilled Chicken Salad with Oranges, 81	Flourless Keto Brownies, 141
28	Chocolate Sea Salt Smoothie, 25	Keto Hamburger, 51	Cheesecake Cupcakes, 119	Red Curry with Vegetables, 82	Tropical Chocolate Mousse Bites, 142
29	Tomato Eggs 25	Chicken wings & Blue Cheese Dressing, 52	Chocolate Peanut Butter Cups, 119	Baked Turkey Breast with Cranberry Sauce, 82	Coconut Raspberry Slice, 142

| 30 | Vegan Keto Scramble, 25 | Salmon Burgers with Lemon Butter & Mash, 50 | Low–Carb Almond Coconut Sandies, 120 | Italian Keto Casserole, 83 | White Chocolate Bark, 142 |

Meal Plan 4

Day	Breakfast	Lunch	Snack	Dinner	Dessert
1	Cheese Crepes, 29	Keto Smoked Salmon Lunch Bowl, 61	Keto Raspberry Cake & White Chocolate Sauce, 122	Green Chicken Curry, 89	Keto Cheesecakes, 147
2	Ricotta Pancakes, 30	Easy one–pan ground beef & green beans, 61	Keto Chocolate Chips Cookies, 122	Creamy Pork Stew, 89	Coconut Raspberry Slice 142
3	Yogurt Waffles, 30	Easy Spinach & Bacon Salad, 61	Keto beef & Sausage balls, 122	Salmon & Shrimp Stew, 89	Keto Brownies, 148
4	Broccoli Muffins, 30	Easy Keto Italian Plate, 62	Keto Coconut Flake Balls, 123	Chicken Casserole, 89	Raspberry & Coconut, 148
5	Pumpkin Bread, 31	Fresh broccoli & Dill Keto Salad, 62	Keto Chocolate Greek Yoghurt	Creamy Chicken Bake, 89	Chocolate Pudding Delight, 148

			Cookies, 123		
6	Eggs in Avocado cups, 31	Keto Smoked Salmon filled Avocados, 62	Keto coconut flavored ice cream, 123	Beef & Veggie Casserole, 89	Special Keto Pudding, 148
7	Cheddar Scramble, 31	Low-carb Broccoli Lemon Parmesan Soup, 62	Chocolate-coconut Cookies, 123	Beef with Bell Peppers, 91	Peanut Butter Fudge, 149
8	Cheese Crepes 29	Prosciutto & Mozzarella Bomb, 63	Keto Buffalo Chicken Meatballs, 124	Braised Lamb Shanks, 91	Coconut Pear Cream, 149
9	Green Veggies Quiche, 32	Summer Tuna Avocado Salad, 63	Eggplant & Chickpea Bites, 124	Shrimp & Bell Pepper Stir-Fry, 91	Blackberry Stew, 149
10	Chicken & Asparagus Frittata, 32	Mushrooms & Goat Cheese Salad, 63	Baba Ganouj, 124	Veggies & Walnut Loaf, 92	Peach Jam, 150
11	Ricotta Pancakes 30	Keto Bacon Sushi, 63	Spicy Crab dip, 125	Keto Sloppy Joes, 92	Strawberry Bowls, 150
12	Bacon Egg Bites, 33	Cole Slaw Keto Wrap, 64	Potatoes" of Parmesan Cheese, 125	Low Carb Crack Slaw Egg Roll in a Bowl Recipe, 92	Pineapple Stew, 150
13	Yogurt Waffles 30	Keto Chicken Club Lettuce Wrap, 64	Chili cheese Chicken with crispy & delicious	Low Carb Beef Stir Fry, 93	Rhubarb Compote, 150

		cabbage salad, 125		
14	Cheddar & Bacon Egg Bites, 33	Keto Broccoli Salad, 64	Keto Pumpkin Pie sweet & spicy, 126	One Pan Pesto Chicken & Veggies, 93	Banana Bowls, 151
15	Avocado Pico Egg Bites, 33	Keto Sheet Pan Chicken & Rainbow Veggies, 64	Blackened Tilapia with Zucchini Noodles, 126	Crispy Peanut Tofu & Cauliflower Rice Stir–Fry, 93	Grapes Compote, 151
16	Salmon Scramble, 34	Skinny Bang– Bang Courgette Noodles, 65	Bell Pepper Nachos, 126	Simple Keto Fried Chicken, 94	Apricot Pudding, 151
17	Mexican Scrambled Eggs, 34	Keto Caesar Salad, 65	Radish, Carrot & Cilantro Salad, 127	Keto Butter Chicken, 94	Blueberries & Cream, 151
18	Caprese Omelet, 34	Keto Buffalo Chicken Empanadas, 65	Asparagus– Mushroom Frittata, 127	Keto Shrimp Scampi Recipe, 94	Pumpkin Cream, 152
19	Sausage Omelet, 34	Pepperoni & Cheddar Stromboli, 65	Shrimp Avocado Salad, 127	Keto Lasagna, 95	Maple Pumpkin Dessert, 152
20	Broccoli Muffins 30	Tuna Casserole, 66	Smoky Cauliflower Bites, 127	Creamy Tuscan Garlic Chicken, 95	Coconut Pineapple Bowls, 152
21	Keto Pizza Wraps	Brussels Sprout & Hamburger	Avocado Crab Boats, 128	Ancho Macho Chili, 95	Cinnamon Crunch Cereals, 153

	32	Gratin, 66			
22	Fennel Quiche, 35	Carpaccio, 66	Coconut Curry Cauliflower Soup, 128	Chicken Supreme Pizza, 96	Cinnamon Rolls, 153
23	Turkey Hash, 35	Keto Croque Monsieur, 66	Parmesan Asparagus, 128	Baked Jerked Chicken, 96	Chocolate Ice cream, 153
24	Crustless Veggie Quiche, 36	Keto wraps with Cream Cheese & Salmon, 67	Cream Cheese Pancakes, 128	Chicken Schnitzel, 96	Strawberry ice cream, 154
25	Keto Zucchini Bread, 36	Savory Keto Broccoli Cheese Muffins, 67	Sugar–free Mexican Spiced Dark Chocolate, 129	Broccoli & Chicken Casserole, 97	Lava Cake, 154
26	Blueberry Bavarian Cream 26	Keto Rusk, 67	Tuna in Cucumber Cups, 129	Baked Fish with Lemon Butter, 97	Lemon Mousse, 154
27	Quick Keto Toast, 36	Flaxseed hemp Flour Bun, 67	Parmesan Crisp, 129	Roasted Leg of Lamb 73	Chocolate Almond Butter Fat Bombs, 154
28	Keto Loaf of Bread, 37	Turkey Burgers and Tomato Butter 51	Onion Rings, 129	Grilled Cheesy Buffalo Chicken, 98	White chocolate, 155
29	Blueberry Loaf, 37	Keto Wrap, 68	Cold Crab Dip, 130	Middle Eastern Shawarma, 98	Coconut Peanut Butter

				Balls, 155
30	Simple Loaf of Bread, 38	Savory Keto Muffins, 68	Baked Coconut Shrimp, 130	Tex Mex Casserole, 98	Quick and Simple Brownie 137

RECIPES INDEX

CHICKEN BREAST

Broccoli and Chicken Casserole, 97
Buttery Garlic Chicken, 77
Cheesy Bacon and Broccoli Chicken, 77
Chicken Alfredo, 59
Chicken Casserole, 89
Chicken Schnitzel, 96
Creamy Chicken Bake, 89
Creamy Garlic Chicken, 69
Creamy Slow Cooker Chicken, 77
Creamy Tuscan Garlic Chicken, 95
Crunchy Chicken Milanese, 76
Green Chicken Curry, 89
Grilled Cheesy Buffalo Chicken, 98
Grilled Chicken Salad with Oranges, 81
Keto Butter Chicken, 94
Keto Sheet Pan Chicken and Rainbow Veggies, 64
Low Carbs Chicken Cheese, 59
Parmesan Baked Chicken, 76

CHICKEN DRUMSTICKS

Baked Garlic and Paprika Chicken Legs, 78
Buffalo Drumsticks and Chili Aioli, 49

Garlic Chicken, 49

CHICKEN THIGHS

Baked Jerked Chicken, 96
Braised Chicken Thighs with Kalamata Olives, 78
Chicken Curry with Masala, 78
Chicken Pan with Veggies and Pesto, 70
One Pan Pesto Chicken and Veggies, 93
Simple Keto Fried Chicken, 94

CHICKEN WINGS

Baked Garlic Parmesan Wings, 131
Chicken Wings and Blue Cheese, 52

CHIPS, CRISP, AND NACHOS

Chips, 109
Kale Chips, 118
Keto Tortilla Chips, 59

CHOCOLATE

Chocolate Almond Butter Fat Bombs, 154
Chocolate Chili, 108
Chocolate Fat Bomb, 120
Chocolate Ice Cream, 153
Chocolate Macadamia Nut Fat Bombs, 139
Chocolate Peanut Butter Cups, 119
Chocolate Pudding Delight, 148
Chocolate Sea Salt Smoothie, 25
Chocolate Spread with Hazelnuts, 136
Creamy Hot Chocolate, 135
Keto Hot Chocolate, 143
Keto Peanut Butter Chocolate Bars, 139
Sugar-Free Mexican Spiced Dark Chocolate, 129
Tropical Chocolate Mousse Bites, 142
White Chocolate Bark, 142 White Chocolate, 155

DESSERTS, SWEETS

Almond Mousse, 27
Apricot Pudding, 151
Blueberries and Cream, 151
Coconut Peanut Butter Balls, 155
Coconut Pear Cream, 149
Coconut Raspberry Slice, 142
Cottage Cheese Pudding, 134
Creme Brule, 120
Delicious Coffee Ice Cream, 135
Easy Peanut Butter Cups, 116
Egg Custard, 132
Fatty Bombs with Cinnamon and Cardamom, 136
Grapes Compote, 151
Keto and Dairy-Free Vanilla Custard, 138
Keto Coconut Flavored Ice Cream, 123
Keto Frosty, 47
Keto No-Churn Blueberry Maple Ice Cream, 121
Keto Peanut Butter Cup Style Fudge, 137
Keto Raspberry Ice Cream, 139
Lemon Mousse, 154
Lemon Soufflé, 133
Lemony Coconut Cream, 149
Matcha Skillet Souffle, 141
Mocha Ice Cream, 133
No-Churn Ice Cream, 119
Peach Jam, 150
Peanut Butter Fudge, 149
Rhubarb Compote, 150
Special Keto Pudding, 148
Strawberry Ice Cream, 47
Sugar-Free Blueberry Cottage Cheese Parfaits, 57
Sugar-Free Lemon Bars, 135
Truffle Balls, 146
Vanilla Crème Brûlée, 133
Vanilla Mousse, 26

EGGS

Bacon Egg Bites, 33
Cheddar Scramble, 31
Cream Cheese Eggs, 23
Deviled Eggs Keto Style, 112
Eggs in Avocado Cups, 31
Eggs with Watercress, 42
Keto Croque Monsieur, 66
Mexican Scrambled Eggs, 34
Parsley Soufflé, 41
Savory Keto Broccoli Cheese Muffins, 67
Savory Keto Muffins, 68
Scrambled Egg Bites, 32
Spicy Deviled Eggs, 130

FISH

Baked Coconut Haddock, 101
Baked Fish Fillets with Vegetables in Foil, 99
Baked Fish with Lemon Butter, 97
Baked Salmon, 46
Baked Salmon and Pesto, 48
Baked Salmon with Almonds and Cream Sauce, 99

Blackened Tilapia with Courgettes Noodles, 126
Buttered Cod, 46
Cherry Tomatoes Tilapia Salad, 76
Cold Crab Dip, 130
Fish & Chips, 99
Incredible Salmon Dish, 88
Lemon Baked Salmon, 46
Mustard Glazed Salmon, 86
Pan-Seared Halibut with Citrus Butter Sauce, 100
Pickle, 110
Salmon and Lemon Relish, 86
Salmon Bowls, 87
Salmon Burgers with Lemon Butter and Mash, 50
Salmon Cakes with Fried Pork Rind, 19
Salmon Keto Cutlets, 83
Salmon Pasta, 74
Salmon Scramble, 34
Salmon Stuffed with Shrimp, 88
Skillet Fried Cod, 74
Trout and Chili Nuts, 47
Tuna Casserole, 66
Tuna in Cucumber Cups, 129

FRUIT MEALS
Almond Papaya Mix, 152
Baked Apples, 22
Bavarian Strawberry Butter, 28
Blackberry Stew, 149
Blueberry Bavarian Cream, 26
Pineapple Stew, 150
Raspberry and Coconut, 148
Strawberry Bavarian, 26

GRAIN, BEANS, LEGUMES
Fried Green Beans Rosemary, 116
Low Carb Green Bean Casserole, 84

LAMB
Braised Lamb Shanks, 91
Garlic & Thyme Lamb Chops, 72
Lamb Chops and Herb Butter, 50
Middle Eastern Shawarma, 98
Roasted Leg of Lamb, 73

MEATBALLS
Bacon-Wrapped Meatloaf, 50
Keto Meatballs, 73
Keto Sloppy Joes, 92
Meatballs with Curry, 106
Meatballs in Cheese Sauce, 107

MORE BEEF MEALS
Ancho Macho Chili, 95
Barbacoa Beef Roast, 79
Beef & Broccoli Roast, 80
Beef & Cabbage Stew, 102
Beef & Mushroom Chili, 104
Beef & Veggie Casserole, 89
Beef and Kale Pan, 85
Beef and Squash Skillet, 43
Beef Stew, 101

Easy One-Pan Ground Beef and Green Beans, 61
Garlicky Prime Rib Roast, 105
Low Carb Beef Stir Fry, 93
Mexican Beef Salad, 75
Roasted Tenderloin, 105
Tex Mex Casserole, 98
Thai Beef Salad, 80

MORE CHICKEN MEALS
Asian Chicken Lettuce Wraps, 55
Buffalo Chicken Jalapeno Poppers, 131
Chicken Quesadilla, 79
Chicken Taco Avocados, 56
Chili Cheese Chicken with Crispy and Delicious Cabbage, 125
Keto Buffalo Chicken Empanadas, 65
Keto Buffalo Chicken Meatballs, 124
Keto Quesadillas, 56

MORE PORK MEALS
Coffee BBQ Pork Belly, 72
Crispy Cuban Pork Roast, 50
Jamaican Jerk Pork Roast, 73
Pork Casserole, 88
Pork Skillet, 44
Pork Stew, 108
Slow-Cooked Kalua Pork & Cabbage, 74
Slow Cooked Roasted Pork and Creamy Gravy, 49

MORE VEGETABLES
Bok Choy Samba, 42
Crustless Veggie Quiche, 36
Cucumber, 112
Cucumber Sushi, 110
Fennel Quiche, 35
Five Greens Smoothie, 48
Green Veggies Quiche, 32
Mixed Vegetable Patties - Instant Pot, 73
Red Curry with Vegetables, 82
Roasted Tri-Color Vegetables, 61
Spinach in Cheese Envelopes, 117
Spinach Rich Ballet, 41
Veggies & Walnut Loaf, 92
Zesty Olives, 112

MUFFIN, CUPCAKES, COOKIES
Bacon & Egg Breakfast Muffins, 21
Caramel Pecan Muffins, 144
Cheesecake Cupcakes, 119
Chocolate Mug Muffins, 137
Chocolate-Coconut Cookies, 123
Cinnamon Roll Cookies, 144
Coconut Crack Bars, 47
Crisp Meringue Cookies, 140
Homemade Graham Crackers, 114
Homemade Thin Mints, 114
Keto Chocolate Chip Cookies, 122
Keto Chocolate Greek Yoghurt Cookies, 123
Keto Coconut Flake Balls, 123
Keto Matcha Mint Bars, 121
Keto No-Bake Cookies, 114

Low-Carb Almond Coconut Sandies, 120
No-Bake Coconut Cookies, 115
Peanut Butter Chocolate Cupcakes, 147
Peanut Butter Cookies, 119

MUSHROOMS
Cheesy Mushroom Slices, 117
Mushroom and Salmon Sliders, 43
Mushroom Omelet, 25
 Risotto with Mushrooms, 84
Sausage Stuffed Mushrooms, 132
Stuffed Portobello Mushrooms, 60

NUTS
Bavarian Cream with Vanilla and Hazelnuts, 26
Bavarian Coffee with Hazelnuts, 28
Blueberry Nutty Oatmeal, 19
Cute Peanut Balls, 137
Hazelnut Bavarian with Hot Coffee, 29
Nougat, 27
Nutty Yoghurt, 113
Salted Toffee Nut Cups, 140

OMELET
Caprese Omelet, 34 Pepperoni Egg Omelet, 41

ONION
Onion Rings, 129

PANCAKES, TOASTS
Banana Pancakes, 22

Banana Waffles, 24
Cream Cheese Pancakes, 128
French Toast with Coffee Drink, 29
Keto Waffles with Blueberries, 24
Quick Keto Toast, 36
Ricotta Pancakes, 30
Yoghurt Waffles, 30

PASTA, NOODLE
Italian Keto Casserole, 83
Keto Lasagna, 95
Protein Gnocchi with Basil Pesto, 85
Skinny Bang-Bang Courgettes Noodles, 65

PEPPERS
Bell Pepper Nachos, 126
Bell Pepper Sandwich, 43
Low Carbs Mexican Stuffed Bell Peppers, 60

PIES, CAKES
Carrot Cake Chia Pudding, 143
Carrot Cake Energy Balls, 143
Cinnamon Rolls, 153
Cocoa Mug Cake, 120
Cream Cake, 134

Dark Chocolate Espresso Paleo and Keto Mug Cake, 121
Flourless Keto Brownies, 141
Instant Pot Matcha Cheesecake, 141
Keto Brownies, 148
Keto Cheesecakes, 147
Keto Cheesecake Stuffed Brownies, 138
Keto Raspberry Cake and White Chocolate Sauce, 122
Keto Triple Chocolate Mug Cake, 138
Lava Cake, 154
Mint Chocolate Pie, 145
Quick and Simple Brownie, 137

PIZZA
Chicken Supreme Pizza, 96
Keto Breakfast Pizza, 39
Keto-Friendly Skillet Pepperoni Pizza, 45

PORK RIBS
Creamy Pork Stew, 89
Keto Barbecued Ribs, 51
Pork & Chiles Stew, 109
Slow Cooker Barbecue Ribs, 79

PORRIDGE, CEREAL, GRANOLA
Banana Porridge, 42
Cinnamon Crunch Cereal, 153
Coconut Keto Porridge, 23
Nut Porridge, 41
Peanut Butter Power Granola, 113

PRAWNS, SCALLOPS, CRABS
Bacon-Wrapped Scallops, 131
Avocados Stuffed with Crab Salad, 20
Herb Butter Scallops, 100
Scallops and Fennel Sauce, 87
Spicy Crab Dip, 125

PROSCIUTTO
Prosciutto and Mozzarella Bomb, 63
Salmon Skewers Wrapped with Prosciutto, 49

PUMPKIN, BUTTERNUT SQUASH
Keto Pumpkin Pie Sweet and Spicy, 126
Lemon Chicken Spaghetti Squash Boats, 60
Maple Pumpkin Dessert, 152
Pumpkin Cream, 152

SALAD
Broccoli Bacon Salad, 53
Easy Spinach and Bacon Salad, 61
Egg Salad Recipe, 52
Fresh Broccoli and Dill Keto Salad, 62
Keto Broccoli Salad, 64
Keto Caesar Salad, 65
Keto Egg Salad, 54
Loaded Cauliflower Salad, 54
Mushrooms & Goat Cheese Salad, 63
Parmesan Brussels Sprouts Salad, 55
Radish, Carrot & Cilantro Salad, 127

Shrimp Avocado Salad, 127
Summer Tuna Avocado Salad, 63
Tuna Salad, 46

SANDWICHES, WRAPS
Almond Coconut Egg Wraps, 24
Basil Avocado Frail Salad Wraps & Sweet Potato Chips, 57
Brunch BLT Wrap, 23
Cole Slaw Keto Wrap, 64
Keto Chicken Club Lettuce Wrap, 64
Keto Wrap, 68
Keto Wraps with Cream Cheese and Salmon, 67
Mushroom Sandwich, 42
No-Bread Italian Subs, 56
Roasted Lemon Chicken Sandwich, 45

SAUSAGES
Creamy Basil Baked Sausage, 24
Keto Beef and Sausage Balls, 122
Sausage Omelet, 34

SHRIMP
Baked Coconut Shrimp, 130
Buffalo Shrimp Lettuce Wraps, 53
Keto Shrimp Scampi Recipe, 94
Salmon & Shrimp Stew, 89
Shrimp & Bell Pepper Stir-Fry, 91
Shrimp and Cauliflower Delight, 87
Shrimp and Sausage Bake, 100
Scampi with Garlic, 70
Stuffed Apples with Shrimp, 81 Tangy Shrimp, 75

SOUPS
Cabbage Soup with Beef, 71
Cauliflower Leek Soup, 57
Cauliflower Rice Soup with Chicken, 71
Coconut Curry Cauliflower Soup, 128
Fresh Avocado Soup, 69
Keto Chicken & Veggies Soup, 58
Low-Carb Broccoli Leek Soup, 58

Low-Carb Broccoli Lemon Parmesan Soup, 62
Low-Carb Chicken Taco Soup, 58
Low-Carb Seafood Soup with Mayo, 58
Quick Pumpkin Soup, 69

TOFU
Crispy Peanut Tofu and Cauliflower Rice Stir-Fry, 93
Onion Tofu, 40
Tofu Mushrooms, 40
Vegan Keto Scramble, 25

TURKEY
Baked Turkey Breast with Cranberry Sauce, 82
Turkey and Cream Cheese Sauce, 48
Turkey and Tomatoes, 86
Turkey and Veggies Mix, 44
Turkey Burgers and Tomato Butter, 51
Turkey Hash, 35

WHOLE CHICKEN
Keto Chicken with Butter and Lemon, 48

Printed in Great Britain
by Amazon

81606521R00102